'I wish I had been given this book when I first entered ministry. The biblical exegesis is extremely helpful, which should come as no surprise given Paul's academic rigour. His ability to communicate is second to none. I devoured this book like a hungry man presented with a hearty meal, and I would encourage anyone involved in the ministry to the bereaved to feast on its delights too. This is a great book, and it deserves to be widely read.'
Pastor Rob James, Baptist minister, writer, broadcaster and Executive Chair of Evangelical Alliance Wales

'This is a unique and treasure laden book that provides a rich resource for the preacher tasked with preaching into the important, but often difficult, occasion of a funeral. At the hands of a master exegete and honed pastor, the reader is led on a hope-filled journey that models how one can powerfully yet sensitively bring the good news of Jesus into the nuances of grief and loss in a multitude of contexts. This is an excellent book, and it ought to be on the shelves of every preacher in the land.'
Rev Jitesh Patel, Assistant Director of St Mellitus College East Midlands, convener of the New Wine Preaching Conferences

'With characteristic comprehensive clarity, Paul Beasley-Murray gives us practical and theological examples of different angles to preach at funerals. Using real life sermons, from real funerals, he weaves different themes and situations to give the preacher different tools to employ. In a society where funerals increasingly focus on the eulogy, here is a timely reminder that the Christian faith offers what secular celebrants never can – real hope based on the fact of the person of Jesus Christ. While it is true that what most people will remember is how they feel at a funeral, Beasley-Murray shares a lifetime of pastoral ministry that gives hope when the feelings fade. As always with Paul, you may not always agree with him but you will be made to think. I commend this book to the person asked to take a family funeral because, 'unlike the rest of the family, you're religious' and the experienced preacher alike. The contexts may vary but the truth does not change – we have a hope in a world where that is an increasingly rare commodity.'
The Rev Canon David Richards, St Paul's and St George's Church, Edinburgh

T0326772

'Paul Beasley-Murray has done it again! The minister's minister has mined his decades of pastoral experience, theological reflection and effective communication to bring us an exceptionally useful guide to a particularly challenging subject – preaching at funeral services.

Avoiding tired generalities, Beasley-Murray combines scholarship with accessibility and profundity with practicality. He skilfully expounds twenty passages – followed by twenty sermons – to help us, whatever our age or stage, not merely with the 'what' and 'how' of this exacting preaching challenge, but most importantly, the 'why'. Here is a truly hope-filled book to inform and inspire, packed with practical wisdom, grounded in rich experience and deep theology, enlivened by gentle scholarship and brilliant quotation. This is a book to savour – and to plunder – as we sharpen our message of gospel hope!'

His Honour Judge David Turner QC, Circuit Judge and Chancellor of the Diocese of Chester, Deputy President of the Clergy Discipline Commission and a Reader in the Diocese of London

THERE IS HOPE

Paul Beasley-Murray was born on 14 March 1944. He read Modern Languages (French and German) and Theology at Jesus College, Cambridge. While completing a PhD in New Testament studies under F. F. Bruce at Manchester University, he trained for the ministry at the Northern Baptist College, Manchester, and at the International Baptist Theological Seminary in Rüschlikon-Zurich. Ordained on 10 October 1970, he served with the Baptist Missionary Society in the Democratic Republic of the Congo/Zaire, where he taught New Testament and Greek in the Protestant Theological Faculty of the National University from 1970 to 1972. Paul pastored two churches: Altrincham Baptist Church, Cheshire, from 1973 to 1986 and Central Baptist Church, Chelmsford, Essex, from 1993 to 2014. He was also Principal of Spurgeon's College, London, from 1986 to 1992.

His wife, Caroline Beasley-Murray OBE, was for over twenty years HM Senior Coroner for Essex. Paul and Caroline have four married children and eight grandchildren.

Throughout his ministry Paul has been a prolific author. IVP have published several of his books: *The Message of the Resurrection* (2000); *Joy to the World: Preaching at Christmas* (2005) and *Transform Your Church: 50 Very Practical Steps* (2005). Other books include *Power for God's Sake? Power and Abuse in the Local Church* (Paternoster, 1998; Wipf & Stock, 2005); *Living out the Call Book 1: Living to God's Glory*; *2: Leading God's Church*; *3: Reaching God's World*; *4: Serving God's People* (Feed-a-Read, 2015, revised); *This is My Story: A Story of Life, Faith and Ministry* (Wipf & Stock, 2018); *Make the Most of Retirement: A Guide for Ministers* (Bible Reading Fellowship, 2020) and *Fifty Lessons on Ministry: Reflections after Fifty Years in Ministry* (Darton, Longman & Todd, 2020).

THERE IS HOPE

Preaching at funerals

Paul Beasley-Murray

INTER-VARSITY PRESS
36 Causton Street, London SW1P 4ST, England
Email: ivp@ivpbooks.com
Website: www.ivpbooks.com

British Library Cataloguing-in-Publication Data
A catalogue record for this book is available from the British Library.

ISBN: 978-1-78974-362-3
eBook ISBN: 978-1-78974-363-0

Set in Minion Pro 11/14pt
Typeset in Great Britain by CRB Associates, Potterhanworth, Lincolnshire
Printed and bound in Great Britain by Clays Ltd, Elcograf S.p.A.

Produced on paper from sustainable sources

Dedicated to the memory of my mother,
Ruth Beasley-Murray,
3 June 1922–1 December 2020

Contents

Contents

Part 4
HOPE IN THE REST OF THE NEW TESTAMENT

Part 5
HOPE IN THE OLD TESTAMENT

Part 6
HOPE FOR ALL?

APPENDICES

Foreword

Rather than joining in the popular sport of 'What they didn't teach you at theological college', I want to say how grateful I was for the instruction I received in how to conduct and speak at funeral services. Nothing, however, quite prepares you, as a young minister, for having to speak on a reasonably frequent basis at funerals and for the variety of circumstances you are addressing. I remember, in my early years in ministry, searching around for help, to find only one brief guide published by Grove Books. There were books galore on the liturgy, but virtually nothing on preaching.

If only Paul Beasley-Murray's book had been available then! Paul, a veteran pastor and theologian, has provided us with a wonderful resource that will enrich the ministry of many. The introduction alone is helpful. It succinctly, but not simplistically, covers a number of areas, including contemporary attitudes to death, the unique Christian hope of the resurrection and, most helpful of all, discusses what is the purpose and nature of a sermon at a funeral, and even its length. Even if readers come to different conclusions than Paul's on some issues, his book sets out the issues we all have to settle about our role in preaching at funerals.

The introduction is followed by twenty sermons actually preached at funerals. As real-life (sorry, about that!) sermons, they encompass a variety of situations and people whose lives are being commended to God: believers and unbelievers, young and old; those who died after a long life and those who died, from our viewpoint, all too soon; the ones very personal to us and ones for people we did not know at all. The appendices offer further help for the difficult funerals that we all have to take from time to time.

The addresses have all the hallmarks of Paul's ministry. They are thoughtful, appropriate, well-researched, theologically literate, communicated in an interesting way and have a fitting evangelistic edge. There is substance here without the content being overly heavy. The variety of Scripture passages on which they are based shows something of the multiple relevant voices found in the Bible, which will help any pastor to avoid predictability and repetition.

No doubt, many readers may seek to simply reproduce these sermons. That would be a mistake. If preaching is 'truth through personality', as Phillips Brooks famously claimed, we need to preach our own sermons, not Paul's (Beasley-Murray, that is, not the apostle!) But Paul's may provide a model and guide. They will also prove a wonderful resource, as they are full of quotable quotes, illustrations and insights that few will be able, or should try, to resist.

Even today, when there are fifty-seven varieties of funerals and celebrants who have no religious faith are becoming common, the conduct of funerals in our churches remains one of the most significant ministries we can undertake, reaching many of no faith or fringe faith, as well as pastoring the people of God. My wife and I can both bear witness to the impact funerals can have, providing people with an opportunity to take their first steps towards joining the community of faith. I remember asking Romanian Christian friends during Ceausescu's day how they made an impact for Christ, given the restrictions they suffered. 'Funerals' was the surprising answer! I also remember Professor Tony Walter, an expert in death studies, saying in a lecture some years ago that conducting funerals was one of the church in the UK's most missed opportunities.

To make them meaningful, we need all the help we can get. Books on this field are very rare indeed. We should be thankful to Paul Beasley-Murray for giving us many examples of how to minister effectively to people at a sensitive point in their lives. It is to be hoped that this book will not only prove a great resource but also stimulate creativity on our own part, to speak of our central hope at a time when many face only darkness and despair.

The Reverend Dr Derek Tidball
*Baptist minister and author, formerly pastor
and principal of London School of Theology*

Preface

As I said in my initial submission to IVP, there are plenty of books on preaching and plenty of books on funerals, but – within a British context at least – I am not aware of any guide to preaching at funerals.[1] This, I dare to believe, is one of the great strengths of *There Is Hope: Preaching at Funerals*. Another strength is that it reflects my experience of taking hundreds of funerals: although I have been involved in theological education (for two years in an African university and for six years as principal of Spurgeon's College), for almost thirty-five years I was a pastor.

My experience of ministry is reflected in the way in which the book is constructed. Each section is in two parts: first, I have expounded the passage in question and in so doing have drawn upon the insights of others; then I have reproduced a sermon I preached on the passage. As readers will notice, I have also ensured that the sermons reflect a wide variety of pastoral situations, ranging from a baby who died in the womb to a twenty-one-year-old student who took his own life; from an eighteen-year-old who died from a genetic disorder to a ninety-eight-year-old who longed to see her Saviour; from a woman cut down in her prime by cancer to a dementia sufferer who had become a shadow of his former self. The twenty sermons reflect not only a wide variety of Scripture passages but also a wide variety of settings.

Some readers might be surprised to see that I have chosen the New Revised Standard Version (NRSV) over against the New International Version (NIV) as my preferred English text and might be tempted to question my evangelical credentials. However, my choice reflects my background: as a member of the Society of New Testament Studies, I was influenced by the fact that that the NRSV is the preferred version of almost all British university theological faculties. Nonetheless, recognizing that the preferred version of many of my readers will be the NIV, I have quoted from the NIV whenever this deviates from the NRSV. I have also quoted from three other versions. In the first place, there is the Good News Bible (GNB), which for many years has been my preferred version for preaching, on the grounds that with its limited vocabulary – it was produced with non-English-speaking readers in mind – it is the most easily understood translation for the average person. In the second place, I use the Revised English Bible (REB), a revision of the New English Bible, which was presented to me on the occasion of my ordination in 1970 and happens to be not just a good translation but also the only truly British translation. Third, I quote from the Revised New Jerusalem Bible (RNJB), which, in spite of its Roman Catholic origin, is unbiased 'confessionally' and is often exceedingly fresh. In addition, I have quoted from the English Standard Version (ESV), perhaps the most literal translation of English translations of the Bible, which has gained favour with many evangelical Christians. Finally, from time to time I have quoted from Eugene Peterson's paraphrase *The Message*, which sometimes really hits the spot.

To save misunderstanding, I need to make it clear that when I have quoted somebody with approval, this does not necessarily mean that I agree with every aspect of that person's theological position. Needless to say, this applies not just to Pope Francis and Pope John XXIII (both of whom I have quoted) but also to Anglicans, Methodists, Pentecostals, Presbyterians and even to some fellow Baptists! My experience over the years is that I have been enriched by many of those with whom I have not appeared to have much in common. Not to be prepared to learn from other traditions is a bit like singing hymns written only by fellow evangelicals – how constricting that would be, not least at Christmas.

Finally, I have tended to use people's real names unless I felt there was a good pastoral reason for anonymity, in which case I have made one up. Nowhere, however, have I indicated whether I am using a real name or a fictional name.

Part 1
INTRODUCTION

The gospel is a message of hope

May the God of all hope fill you with all joy and peace in believing, so that you may abound in hope by the power of the Holy Spirit.
(Rom. 15:13)

Christian hope is resurrection hope

The good news is that there is hope – God raised Jesus from the dead! 'God', wrote the apostle Peter, 'has given us a new birth into a living hope through the resurrection of Jesus Christ from the dead' (1 Pet. 1:3). It was 'concerning the hope of the resurrection of the dead' that the apostle Paul was on trial (Acts 23:6; see also 26:6).

'Christian hope is resurrection hope' declared brilliant German theologian Jürgen Moltmann in his groundbreaking book devoted to the 'Last Things'.[1] This hope is at the heart of Christian believing, and what a difference this hope makes. When Cardinal Hume, a former Roman Catholic Archbishop of Westminster, was diagnosed with terminal cancer, he rang to tell his friend Timothy Wright, the Abbott of Ampleforth, who replied 'Congratulations! That's brilliant news. I wish I was coming with you!'[2] Dietrich Bonhoeffer, the great German Christian who was put to death by Hitler's henchmen, evinced a similar confidence in life after death when he declared, 'Death is the supreme festival on the road to freedom.' As he was taken away to be hanged, he said to a British fellowprisoner, 'This is the end – for me, the beginning of life.'[3]

Christian hope is not a whistling in the dark but is sure and certain. In the Church of England's committal service, the dead are committed to be buried or cremated

3

in sure and certain hope of the resurrection to eternal life
through our Lord Jesus Christ,
who will transform our frail bodies
that they may be conformed to his glorious body,
who died, was buried, and rose again for us.[4]

Christian hope is not a form of optimism. Indeed, according to the American theologian Stanley Hauerwas, optimism is a form of 'hope without truth'.[5] Rather, Christian hope is based upon a past reality, for the Bible teaches that in rising from the dead Jesus blazed a trail through the valley of the shadow down which those who have put their trust in him may follow too. In the words of Jesus, with which I begin every funeral, 'I am the resurrection and the life. Those who believe in me, even though they die, will live' (John 11:25).

Yes, there is hope. Over the years I have had many occasions to study the New Testament documents. As a PhD student I devoted three years of my life to examining the implications of the resurrection of Jesus for the early church. Later, after using a sabbatical to study the resurrection further, I wrote a book for preachers, *The Message of the Resurrection*.[6] Today I am more convinced than ever that God raised Jesus from the dead, and that in doing so he broke down death's defences for all who believe.

Our hope for the future is secure

We boast in our hope of sharing the glory of God.
(Rom. 5:2)

'Christian hope', said Pope Francis, 'is not a ghost and it does not deceive. It is a theological virtue and therefore, ultimately, a gift from God that cannot be reduced to optimism, which is only human. God does not mislead hope; God cannot deny himself. God is all promise.'[7]

What a contrast there is between Christian hope and hope as understood by the ancient Greeks. My attention was drawn recently to the story of Pandora. According to a Greek myth found in one of Hesiod's poems, Prometheus stole the secret of fire from the gods and shared it with humankind. As an act of revenge, Zeus ordered Hephaestus to create the first woman, which he did out of earth and water, and ordered each of the other gods to endow her with a 'seductive gift'. Zeus named this 'beautiful evil' Pandora ('all-gifted') and sent her off to Prometheus' brother Epimetheus. Pandora had been warned not to open the jar (today known as a 'box' because of a sixteenth-century mistranslation), but her natural curiosity got the better of her. As she lifted the lid, she released every evil on to the earth, bringing the world's golden age to its close. Aghast, she hastened to replace the lid, but the contents of the jar had already escaped – all except hope. 'This', wrote Hesiod, 'was the will of aegis-bearing Zeus the Cloudgatherer.'[8]

Down through the centuries there has been much debate about the significance of hope in Pandora's box. Does it imply that hope is preserved to make the sufferings of this life more bearable? Or, in what is a story of revenge, does it mean that hope is denied to us, making life all the more miserable? Or, like the other contents of the jar, is hope an evil, bringing torment to us? It is this third interpretation that Friedrich Nietzsche adopted: 'Man', he wrote, 'believes the ill which remains within [the jar] to be the greatest blessing . . . Hope, in reality, is the worst of all evils, because it prolongs the torments of Man.'[9]

Whereas for Christians hope is a positive virtue, in the ancient world hope was viewed as a delusion. In a famous speech recorded by Thucydides in his *History of the Peloponnesian War* the Athenians declare somewhat cynically:

Hope, danger's comforter, may be indulged in by those who have abundant resources, if not without loss at all events without ruin; but its nature is to be extravagant, and those who go so far as to put their all upon the venture see it in its true colours only when they are ruined; but so long as the discovery would enable them to guard against it, it is never found wanting.[10]

Hope, as far as Thucydides was concerned, deceives and misleads. Or, as the agnostic American politician Robert Ingersoll said in a speech in 1892, 'Hope is the only universal liar who never loses his reputation for veracity.'[11]

By contrast, Christian hope in God does not mislead. In the words of Stephen Travis, a Methodist theologian:

> To hope means to look forward expectantly for God's future activity. The ground of hope is God's past activity in Jesus Christ . . . Thus the believer looks forward to the resurrection of God's people and the arrival of God's kingdom, confident because Jesus has inaugurated the kingdom and has been raised from death.[12]

Christian hope is an expression of faith in God. To quote the apostle Paul, 'In hope we were saved. Now hope that is seen is not hope. For who hopes for what is seen?' (Rom. 8:24). This relationship between hope and faith is helpfully defined by Jürgen Moltmann, who wrote:

> In the Christian life faith has the priority but hope the primacy. Without faith's knowledge of Christ, hope becomes a utopia and remains hanging in the air. But without hope, faith falls to pieces, becomes a faint-hearted and ultimately a dead faith. It is through faith that man [sic] finds the path of true life, but it is only hope that keeps him on that path.[13]

Anglican minister Sam Allberry has made the point that whereas we normally speak of hope as something we do, in the Bible hope is something we have:

> It [hope] is about looking forward to something that is certain. I have the hope of eternity with Christ. We still don't control the thing for which we have hope, but God does and has promised eternity to us. There is no degree of risk or disappointment. This hope cannot be frustrated by anyone. Unlike all our other expressions of hope, this is hope that won't disappoint us.[14]

The God and Father of our Lord Jesus Christ is not in the business of misleading his creatures. He is to be trusted. Our hope for the future is secure.

Hope for a world without hope

Without hope and without God in the world.
(Eph. 2:12, NIV)

'But there's got to be hope!' cries Mary in the film *On the Beach*.[15] A nuclear war has wiped out civilization in the northern hemisphere and radioactive dust is drifting southwards, inexorably spreading radiation sickness, death and oblivion. The film tells how Mary, her husband Peter and other Australians on the coast of Victoria live out their last doom-filled months before the End.

We live in a world where hope is in short supply. In the years of the Cold War, nuclear threat was ever present. Since then, the population crisis has raised questions of whether the Earth can sustain the ever-increasing number of people living on her. More recently, we have become aware of the challenge of climate change: the world is getting warmer and warmer, but will its nations really be able to reduce their emissions of carbon dioxide? As I write, humankind is in the grip of the coronavirus pandemic and, at this time, already over five million have died. Thank God, with the development and production of new vaccines, there is now light at the end of the tunnel. But how many more millions will yet die before the vaccines have been distributed around the world?

Underlying all these fears is the ultimate crisis, one which has always been with us: death. Although there have been remarkable advances in medical science, no one has discovered a cure for death: the mortality rate is still 100%. Death for most people is still 'the most fearful thing of all'.[16] Death, said Paul Ramsey, a Christian ethicist, 'is an irreparable loss, an unquenchable grief, the threat of all threats, a dread that is more than all fears aggregated'.[17]

The apostle Paul described his contemporaries as 'having no hope and without God' (Eph. 2:12). Little has changed. We live in a world which is largely without hope and without God. For most people today, death is the end. When, at the end of the service at the crematorium, the coffin makes its final journey, it is quite literally 'curtains'. As a result, many try not to think of death. Josh Glancy, a regular columnist in the *Sunday Times Magazine*, reflecting on the theme of mortality in the context of the coronavirus pandemic, wrote:

> Over recent decades we have become increasingly allergic to death. We shy away from contemplating it and hide ourselves from seeing it: at 33, I've yet to see a dead body. I suspect I am not alone.
>
> Instead we chase wellness and tech-enhanced immortality ... But the pandemic has shown us that this is one fight we cannot win ... As we prepare to exit lockdown, it's time we looked death in the face; time as Shakespeare's Richard II put it, to 'talk of graves, of worms, of epitaphs'. Of course, we should fight the virus with all our might and protect every life we can, but we should do it calmly and humbly, accepting that nature's rules still apply to us.[18]

In a 2008 poll of over 1,000 adults in the UK, 20% admitted to fearing both the way they will die and death itself. Significantly, the highest proportion of people fearing both the way they will die and death itself were aged from eighteen to twenty-four; 30% said that they fear the way they will die, but not death itself; a further 25% couldn't or wouldn't answer questions about death because they found the subject too emotive and too personal. Death makes most people feel uncomfortable.[19]

This modern ambivalence towards death is reflected in the way loved ones are remembered on tombstones. This became clear to me the spring of 2007 when visiting the graveyard of St Brelade's Church in Jersey. As I wandered around, I discovered that most of the recent tombstones lacked any Christian hope, even although they were to be found in a church cemetery. I jotted down the following inscriptions. 'Love, laughter and compassion' is a wonderful tribute to a wife, but was that all her husband could say? 'Peace, perfect peace' read another inscription. Similarly, 'Rest in peace darling' marked the grave of a 'devoted husband'. A not-too-dissimilar gravestone for a husband and wife read 'They lie resting here together'. Although better than the plain 'RIP',[20] do these do justice to the new life that will be ours? What about the joy of heaven?

The inscription 'May you peacefully walk with the wind at your backs and the sunshine on your face' for the parents and their baby son is part of a lovely Celtic blessing, but it seems a self-centred view of life after death. 'He raged against the dying of the light' marked the grave of a son who had died at the age of twenty-two. Understandable, but should this be the last word? Equally, I was not convinced that 'Thy will be done' on the tomb of a child, who died at the age of three in 1875, was much better. Was it God's will that this child should be taken?

Then there were stones with inscriptions such as 'Always remembered', 'We do not die for ever. We live on in the lives of those we love' and 'To live in hearts of those we leave behind is not to die.' Yes, I hope that my loved ones will remember me, but there is nothing here about the life that awaits those who love God.

'Good night and God bless, dear' was the message one husband had chosen for his wife. Presumably, this is what he had said every night to his beloved. But where is the hope of the glorious awakening? More positive were the words 'Until we meet again: in memory of a dear husband.' Yes, in heaven we shall be reunited with our loved ones who have died in Christ, but with so many others too!

Epitaphs relating to Christian hope were, on the whole, restricted to graves a century or more old, although I did spot two exceptions: one, from 1987, read 'Revelation 21:3–4' (but this presumes that people know their Bible!); the other, from 1997, read 'In God's keeping.' 'Until the day dawns and the shadows flee away' (1894) was quite nice, but left a lot to be said. The tombstone I most appreciated dated from 1876: 'In memory of Captain John Hamon, buried at sea, and of his widow and their five children: Rest in the Lord with a joyful hope of a glorious resurrection through Jesus Christ our Lord.'

Hope for a church uncertain of its hope

Christ [is] in you, the hope of glory.
(Col. 1:27)

It is not only non-Christians who lack hope. Increasingly, many Christians are not sure what they believe about life after death.

A survey in the mid-1990s conducted by Durham professor Douglas Davies showed that up to a third of Anglicans and a similar number of Methodists said they believed personal life simply came to an end at death, and only a third professed specific belief in a definite spiritual survival. Only 4% believed in a resurrection of the whole person.[21]

A 2017 survey of 2,010 British adults commissioned by the BBC revealed that 25% of those who described themselves as Christians did not believe in the resurrection of Jesus and that 31% did not believe in life after death.[22]

According to a 2018 survey of attitudes to death in the UK, some 34% of Christians felt unable even to talk about death with their family or with friends.[23] As I later commented:

> It may well be that some, even though they know that 'the sting' of death can be removed through faith in the crucified and risen Lord Jesus (1 Cor. 15:56–57), have yet to learn to truly put their trust in Jesus. For them death is still 'the king of terrors' (Job 18:14: see also Psalm 55:4). They have perhaps yet to discover that Jesus, by destroying the one who has the power of death 'has freed those who all their lives were held in slavery by the fear of death' (Heb. 2:15).[24]

These are remarkable statistics, bearing in mind that Christianity is a religion of hope. As has often been said, the church is 'the community of the resurrection', and yet it would appear that many are uncertain about the difference the resurrection of Jesus makes to those who put their trust in him. All the more reason for preachers to help Christians and non-Christians alike to overcome their fear of death. As I wrote in one of my blogs:

In a recent article in *The Observer*, under the heading of 'We can't be squeamish about death. We need to confront our worst fears', Dr Rachel Clarke, a palliative care specialist, wrote: 'As the coronavirus spreads through the British population, there is one fact we can all agree on. Whether we like it or not, society's greatest taboo – death and dying – has been thrust unequivocally centre stage' . . .

Fear of death (*thanataphobia*) is, of course, nothing new. It is what distinguishes humans from animals. Ernest Becker in his Pulitzer Prize-winning *The Denial of Death* argued that human beings cannot accept that all we are – our conscious self, our loves, our profound aspirations for beauty, goodness, truth – is going to cease to exist for ever, in a literal blink of an eye.[25]

The idea of death, the fear of it, haunts the human animal like nothing else; it is the mainspring of human activity – activity designed largely to avoid the fatality of death, to overcome it by denying . . . that is the final destiny.

Even today, death remains 'the great human repression', 'the universal complex'. Dying, it has been said is 'the reality man [sic] dares not face and to escape which he summons all his resources'.[26] Death is still the last thing we talk about. Doctors hate telling people they are terminally ill. The families of the terminally ill hate telling their loved ones they are going to die. Instead, we pretend that they are going to get better.

However, the good news of Easter Day is that coronavirus need no longer have the last word. Jesus has conquered death – death is a power that no longer needs to be feared. To quote the unknown writer of the letter to the Hebrews, Jesus shared our flesh and blood 'so that through death he might destroy the one who has the power of death, that is the devil, and free those who all their lives were held in slavery by the fear of death' (Heb. 2:14, 15). Or to quote from what J. B. Phillips described as the greatest chapter in the Bible, 'God gives us the victory through our Lord Jesus Christ' (1 Cor. 15:7), for, in the quaint words of the eighteenth-century preacher William Romaine, 'Death stung himself to death when he stung Christ.'

Yes, Jesus has risen from the dead, and in rising has brought life and immortality to light. The atheist Bertrand Russell, who sought to give a philosophical undergirding to the permissive society of the 1960s, as he came to the end of his life wrote in his autobiography: 'No dungeon was ever constructed so dark and narrow as that in which the shadow physics of our time imprisons us; for every prisoner has believed that outside his walls a free world existed; but now the prison has become the whole universe. There is darkness without and when I die there will be darkness within. There is no splendour, no vastness, anywhere; only triviality for a moment, and then nothing.'[27] But Russell was wrong. There is purpose, there is hope, there is life for men and women of faith.

Here is good news for a dying world. Jesus has broken through death's defences. Jesus, in rising from the dead, has carved a trail through the valley of the shadow of death, and we through faith may follow him. Or in the words of C. S. Lewis:

> He is the 'first fruits', the 'pioneer of life'. He has forced open a door that has been locked since the death of the first man. He has met, fought and beaten the King of Death. Everything is different because He has done so. This is the beginning of the New Creation: a new chapter in cosmic history has begun.[28]

This is a time to heed the cry of the Italian philosopher Tomaso Campanella to the late Renaissance painters of his day:

> Paint Christ not dead but risen! Paint Christ, with his foot set in scorn on the split rock with which they sought to hold him down! Paint him the conqueror of death! Paint him the Lord of life! Paint him as what he is, the irresistible

Victor who, tested to the uttermost, has proved himself in very deed mighty to save.[29]

Hope for those who mourn

Christ Jesus our hope . . . abolished death and brought life and immortality to light.
(1 Tim. 1:1; 2 Tim. 1:10)

'Blessed are those who mourn', said Jesus, 'for they will be comforted' (Matt. 5:4). Clearly the blessing of which Jesus spoke is not in the mourning but in the comfort that is received! However, there will be little comfort if at funerals preachers do not speak of the hope that God offers us in Jesus. I have been a Christian minister for more than fifty years. In that time I have taken literally hundreds of funerals – and at every one of those funerals I have sought to point to the difference that Jesus makes to living and to dying. Through the writing of *There Is Hope*, I want to encourage other preachers to do the same. For, sensitively handled, funerals provide a wonderful opportunity to share the good news of Jesus.

Some years ago I was asked to write an article on the extent to which I saw funerals as part of our church's vision and outreach. What, for instance, was my motivation in holding funerals for non-churchgoers? I gave the following response.

I sense that I may disappoint the editor. For first and foremost I see a funeral as an opportunity to exercise pastoral care as distinct from engaging in evangelism. At all funerals I see my role as first and foremost that of ministering the grace of God to the mourners. Yes, I am there to help the congregation celebrate the life of a friend and loved one – but primarily I am there to assure the congregation that there is nothing which can ever separate them from the love of God.

At every funeral service, and not just at the service of a non-churchgoer, there is an evangelistic edge to my address. I always speak about the difference Jesus makes to living and to dying. I always speak about God wanting to draw near us in our need and encourage people to put their faith in God. For I am conscious that at every funeral service I take, whether it be a funeral of a Christian or not, non-Christians are present. Yet although the Gospel is clearly presented, I do not feel it right to present a direct Gospel challenge. This would be an abuse of my position: I am there to bring God's comfort into the situation. Even then, I sometimes wonder how much the mourners take in – they are often too upset or too numb to hear.

What difference has all this made to those whom I have sought to help? God alone knows! People tell me that they are grateful for my help. However, if it be asked, has anybody come to faith as a result of the funerals I have taken, the answer is probably 'No'. In church growth terms, only two people have become regular churchgoers as a result of my ministry at funerals. But, dare I say it, there is more to Christian ministry than making disciples. When it comes to funerals, whether they be of Christians or not, I am content to speak of God's love and his grace, and to leave the outcome to God.[30]

I would like to believe that my approach to funerals is shared by ministers in general. However, I fear that the emphasis in many funeral services is on the eulogy rather than the sermon – and indeed, if there is a sermon, then this is to a large extent an opportunity for a further eulogy. Of course, there is a place for tributes, but the task of the preacher is, above all, to speak of the hope that is ours in Jesus.[31] In that regard, I find it significant that in the Roman Catholic Church, eulogies are banned.

Some months ago I attended the funeral of a good man who had filled his long life with many worthwhile activities. The church was crowded with old men in black suits, most of whom were wearing black ties. There were a few women present. The lady next to whom I sat told me that she believed in God, but didn't know where Jesus fitted in. She thought that all religions had the same 'head office', with Christianity, Hinduism and Judaism being 'branches' of the 'head office'. For her, what counted in life was a moral system to live by.

After a lifetime of taking funerals, attending a funeral in which I had no part was an interesting experience. It is always instructive to see how other ministers handle a service, although on this occasion I had the impression that it had, in fact, been largely drawn up by the family.

I enjoyed the music. Music does indeed uplift the soul. Having said that, I found the choice of 'All things bright and beautiful' a little strange. Was this a sign, I wondered, that the deceased's churchgoing was limited to childhood's days?

The two Scripture readings were a little unusual. The first was from the Sermon on the Mount and included the Beatitudes, together with Jesus' teaching on our calling to be salt and light in the world (Matt. 5:1–16) – in the context of a funeral, some of these words of Jesus' gained new significance. The second reading was from 1 Corinthians 12:4–7, 27–13:1 and focused on the gifts of the Spirit, in particular the gift of teaching. In the context of the funeral of an educationalist, this was perhaps apposite, even though Paul's focus was on teaching in church rather than in a school or college.

The dominating feature of the service were six thoughtful tributes from former colleagues and friends. I had not realized how distinguished the deceased had been. Without exception, the tributes were interesting – but not one revealed whether the man we were honouring had been a person of faith.

In fact, apart from the opening and closing prayers, there was no reference to Jesus, and the difference that Jesus makes to living and to dying. Instead, the sermon was about how churches need to be places which encourage learning, which express love to the needy and which create a legacy in the lives of future generations. All that is true, but this is not the gospel. At the end of the service the bereaved family were assured that the church would continue to pray for the deceased in the hope that he might be received at the last by God and his angels!

I wondered, however, what all those black-suited men made of the service. I wondered what the lady sitting next to me made of it. Indeed, I wondered what the family of the deceased made of it. Would they have been surprised to discover that without the resurrection of Jesus there would be no church – indeed, that there would be no Christianity?

As Baptist minister Paul Sheppy has rightly said, at a funeral it is not enough for the story of the dead person to be told honestly; rather, the narrative needs to be framed in the story of Jesus, whose death and resurrection assure us that our death is not God's last word. Sheppy went on to say:

> What we say here addresses the central questions of the funeral and offers a Christian answer. 'Where is Daddy now?' and 'What will God do to our friend?' are questions that will be asked whether we wish it or not. We need to be ready to speak of God's love in Christ from which not even death can separate us (Rom 8.38–39). If we do not offer Christ's answer to the question, in what sense has the funeral been a Christian one? If we do not lead people to the love of God, where is that hope of which the Scripture speaks?[32]

Indeed, Thomas Long, an American Presbyterian professor of preaching, in his guide to the Christian funeral entitled *Accompany Them with Singing*, would go much further. For him, the heart of a funeral service is not a sermon by a preacher but, rather, the hymns and psalms of the church, in which the church bids farewell to their fellow brother or sister in Christ. In this regard he quoted from the fourth-century *Apostolic Constitutions of the Apostles* (6:30): 'In the funerals of the departed, accompany them with singing, if they were faithful in Christ, for precious in the sight of the Lord is the death of his saints.'

It is in this context that Long argued:

> A Christian funeral is a continuation and elaboration of the baptismal service. If baptism is a form of worshipful drama performed at the beginning of the Christian life, a funeral is – or should be – an equally dramatic, and symmetrical, performance of worship performed at the end of life . . . In baptism, new Christians are 'buried with Christ by baptism into death'

and they come up from the waters raised to 'walk in newness of life'. In funerals, these same Christians, having travelled the pilgrim way, are once again buried with Christ in death in the sure confidence that they will be raised to new life.[33]

I confess that this thought had never occurred to me before reading Thomas Long's book. However, more recently I was fascinated to discover that at the moment of Eugene Peterson's death, his son Erik placed his hands upon his father's head and said:

> Together, we are witnesses to this glad fact: that in sure and certain hope of the resurrection to eternal life, through Christ Jesus our Lord, I declare that the baptism of Eugene Hoiland [sic] Peterson is now complete.[34]

Long continued:

> In baptism, the faithful sang them into this new way of life; now they gather around to sing them to God in death . . . The funeral is not just a collection of inspiring words said on the occasion of someone's death. It is rather a dramatic event in which the church acts out what it believes to be happening from the perspective of faith . . . As the church has been travelling with the baptized saint along the road of faith, the church now walks with the deceased on 'the last mile of the way' to the place of farewell.[35]

For Long, funeral sermons are 'proclamations of what the gospel has to say about *these* people walking along *this* path carrying the body of *this* brother or sister in sorrow over *this* loss and in joyful hope of the resurrection'.[36] It is this need to proclaim the gospel which, for him, constitutes the only genuine *sine qua non* for a funeral. In striking fashion, he declared:

> The indispensability of shouting out the good news of Easter at a funeral gets highlighted when we realize that there are

actually two preachers at every funeral. Death – capital-D Death – loves to preach and never misses a funeral. Death's sermon is powerful and always the same: 'Damn you! Damn all of you! I win every time. I destroy all loving relationships. I shatter all community. I dash all hope. I have claimed another victim. Look at the corpse; look at the open grave there is your evidence. I always win! . . .'

It is the great privilege of the funeral preacher to shake a fist in the face of Death, to proclaim again the vow of baptism and the cry of Easter triumph: 'O Death, we reject all your lies! O Death, where is your sting? Thanks be to God, who gives us the victory in Jesus Christ!'[37]

Preaching hope

But how are they to call on one whom they have not believed? And how are they to believe in one of whom they have never heard? And how are they to hear without someone to proclaim him? . . . faith comes from what is heard, and what is heard comes through the word of Christ.
(Rom. 10:14–15, 17)

The underlying assumption in this book is that a funeral service will always include a sermon. However, to my surprise, I discovered that this has not always been the case. In the Church of England, for instance, The Book of Common Prayer contains no provision for a sermon; The Alternative Service Book 1980 simply says that 'a sermon may be preached'.[38] In contrast, Common Worship states 'a sermon is preached'.[39] Even Baptists, for whom the sermon is sometimes said to be 'the primary sacrament', used to regard the sermon at a funeral as optional,[40] whereas the latest British Baptist worship manual states that 'a sermon follows' after the reading of Scripture.[41] Although clearly God can speak through the Scriptures alone, nonetheless I am convinced that there is a place at a funeral for the minister to declare the good news of Jesus, and in this way 'confront the reality of death with the hope of resurrection'.[42] In that regard I find it significant that a survey of ministers and bereaved people in Sheffield in 1989/1990 found that 'for many bereaved people the address is the part of the funeral which is remembered most clearly and which represents the greatest source of comfort'.[43]

I believe that, as with all preaching, the funeral address needs to be rooted in God's Word. The Bible is the source of the preacher's authority. The task of the preacher is to enable people to hear God speak to them. In practical terms this means that preachers will normally need to have a passage of Scripture to expound. My impression is that this is more the exception than the rule and that there is probably more topical preaching at funerals (and weddings) than at almost any other occasion. In that regard, I checked out a collection of sermon outlines, and of the thirteen outlines for a funeral, only two had a suggested Scripture reading.[44] The danger of this approach is that funeral sermons easily become a repetition of tired generalities.

As with all preaching, the address needs to be relevant to the congregation. Inevitably at a funeral the preacher will want to relate the sermon to the loved one who has died. However, the primary task of the preacher is not to give a eulogy, but to speak of the hope that Jesus offers us all.

As a result, *There Is Hope: Preaching at funerals* is essentially a series of sermons on the Christian hope preceded by a study of the Scripture passage in question, where I have dealt in greater depth with some of the issues involved. I am conscious that there is a very real difference in style between the study and the sermon. I believe that preachers, for the sake of their own integrity, must wrestle with the text of Scripture, ensuring they have really understood what the writer was seeking to say in the first instance. However, accuracy in exegesis is not enough: what counts is understanding on the part of the hearers. This is why my sermons tend to be 'simple' rather than 'learned', for communication is the preacher's ultimate challenge.[45]

As will become immediately apparent, I am not seeking to offer a series of ready-made sermons. That is an impossibility, for every one of these sermons was written with a person in mind. However, what these sermons do offer is a series of approaches which readers are welcome to use and develop within their own context.

I recognize that it is a risky business reproducing a sermon in print. For instance, I am told that my direct and personal style of preaching ensures that I engage well with a congregation, but sometimes in print a more laid-back and nuanced approach works better. Related to this is that what 'works' well in the immediacy of the preached word on the 'cold' page may seem simplistic. Furthermore, there is the danger that I could be seen to be bombastic, as if I were setting up my sermons as a benchmark against which all others might be measured. As I have discovered over the years, writing a book can be akin to putting one's head on the block. The truth is that what makes a great sermon is when the words of the preacher are empowered by God himself. 'Preaching at its best', wrote Michael Quicke, 'is a God-happening, empowered by Father, Son and Holy Spirit'.[46]

The sermons I have included are, for the most part, relatively short. I believe that at most funerals ten minutes is probably quite long enough and almost certainly fifteen minutes the maximum.[47] On the occasion of the death of a baby, five minutes might be quite sufficient. It is amazing what a well-crafted, succinct message can achieve. The Queen's Christmas Day Message, for instance, is less than five minutes in length, but always contains something to talk about. Preachers need to bear in mind that the mourners are often still too numb with grief to absorb a lengthy sermon. As for friends and colleagues who may be present, few will ask themselves, 'I wonder what the minister will preach about' – at a funeral (as at a wedding) the sermon is not the centre point of the service.

I have thoroughly enjoyed the challenge of writing this guide to preaching at funerals. In particular, I have gained great delight from studying and then expounding some of the great passages of Scripture relating to the hope that is ours in Christ. I trust that those of my readers who are preachers will, in turn, enjoy sharing this hope with others.

Finally, as will be seen, the twenty expositions are grouped in four main categories: Hope in the Gospels; Hope in the letters of Paul;

Hope in the rest of the New Testament; and Hope in the Old Testament. My reason for placing those of 'Hope in the Old Testament' last is that, ultimately, their message of hope has to be interpreted through the lens of the cross and resurrection of Jesus. The passages I have chosen are not the only Scriptures dealing with the hope that is ours in Christ; they are, however, among the most important.

Embodying hope

One final and important thing needs to be said before we look at the Scriptures themselves. Preaching has its limitations, not least at a funeral. However eloquent the preacher, however inspirational or comforting the sermon, if the preaching is not an expression of ongoing pastoral care, then it is likely to have little more effect than 'a noisy gong or a clanging cymbal' (1 Cor. 13:1). First and foremost, the bereaved need a pastor, not a preacher.

Why, then, have I not written a guide to the pastoral care of the dying and the bereaved, as distinct from a guide to preaching at funerals? For the simple reason that there are already plenty of good books available on the pastoral care of the dying and the bereaved, but nothing quite like this guide to preaching.

I have assumed that, in most cases, ministers taking a funeral will already have been journeying with the deceased and their family, often for months, if not a year or so. The exceptions will be sudden deaths or families without any previous contact with the church who request the funeral director to find a minister to take the funeral. Certainly, in my thirty-four years of pastoring two churches, the care of the dying was always a priority. Although, as a senior minister of two relatively large churches, I had to delegate much of the routine pastoral care, I always felt it right to be alongside families as they went through the lifecycle of birth, marriage and death. Visiting the dying, whether at home, in hospital or in the hospice, was important for me.

Similarly, I have assumed that, in almost every case, ministers taking a funeral will want to journey with the bereaved, not just in the immediate days after the death but also in the months and sometimes years ahead. It did not matter if it was my 'day off' – whenever I was notified of a death, I immediately went to see the family. In the days between the death and the funeral, I would normally see them at least twice, and sometimes three times. After the funeral I felt it important to continue to be there for the bereaved as they worked through their grief.

Sadly, in spite of these assumptions, I know that not every minister sees the pastoral care of the dying and the bereaved as a priority. Indeed, I vividly remember attending a conference for ministers of 'larger churches' where I was accused of having a 'small church' mentality. Leadership is what counts. Much as I appreciate the importance of leadership, for me pastoral care is at the heart of ministry, whatever the size of the church. Yes, I delegated much, and from very early on in my ministry was keen on ministry teams (made up of 'lay' people) taking responsibility for such areas of church life as social action, evangelism, nurture and pastoral care, but I was always there for the crises of life.[48]

It was first and foremost within this context of pastoral care that I would seek to 'excite fresh hope and faith in God'. Yes, I would also seek to do the same from the pulpit, but it began in the home. So in the context of preaching at a funeral, pointing to the hope that is ours in Christ was just an extension of my pastoral care.

Preaching has been variously defined as 'God at work', 'Logic on fire' or 'Truth through personality'.[49] It is this last definition, coined by the nineteenth-century American Episcopalian minister Phillips Brooks in 1871, which seems particularly appropriate for a funeral, where the preacher is normally not a 'guest' preacher but, rather, a known and, hopefully, loved minister who, through his or her ongoing pastoral care, embodies the sure and certain hope of resurrection through our Lord Jesus Christ. For, as I said at the beginning of this section, what is needed on such an occasion is not a preacher but a pastor.

Of course, preaching is important at a funeral. I would not have written this guide to preaching if I did not believe in preaching. However, in the context of a funeral, preaching is, first and foremost, an exercise in pastoral care, as we encourage the mourners to put their faith and hope in God, who raised his Son from the dead. True, with non-church people often present, there is an opportunity to share the good news of the hope that Jesus offers but, on this occasion, evangelism is secondary to pastoral care.

Part 2

HOPE IN THE GOSPELS

1

Mark 10:13–16

Jesus has a special love for children

[13]People were bringing little children to him in order that he might touch them; and the disciples spoke sternly to them. [14]But when Jesus saw this, he was indignant and said to them, 'Let the little children come to me; do not stop them; for it is to such as these that the kingdom of God belongs. [15]Truly I tell you, whoever does not receive the kingdom of God as a little child will never enter it.' [16]And he took them up in his arms, laid his hands on them, and blessed them.

Jesus cares for children

Children had an unusually special place in the affections of Jesus. 'Let the little children come to me,' he said, 'do not stop them; for it is to such as these that the kingdom of God belongs' (Mark 10:14; see also Matt. 19:14 and Luke 18:16). Jesus cared deeply for children. In the words of the American commentator James Edwards, 'One will search ancient literature in vain for sympathy toward the young comparable to that shown by Jesus.'[1]

In Jesus' day children did not count. Children had no rights. There was no organization such as the NSPCC.[2] In the ancient world, children – along with women, slaves and animals – belonged on 'the margins of society'.[3]

It was not until comparatively recently that society began to pay any real attention to children and their needs. According to the English historian Lawrence Stone, 'The cruel truth ... may be that most parents in history have not been much involved with their children and have not cared much about them.' Stone tells of how the writers of antiquity treated infanticide as a normal and sensible way to dispose of unwanted children; of how seventeenth-century nurses played catch-ball with tightly swaddled infants and sometimes dropped them in the process, with lethal results; and of how children were blinded and otherwise mutilated to attract alms.[4] As Rodney Clapp, a long-time editor of the influential American magazine *Christianity Today*, pointed out, the assumption of some Christians nowadays is that 'biology dictates affection and tenderness for children' is simply not true.[5]

Jesus, by contrast, valued children. We see this when people bring children for him to 'touch' (Mark 10:13) – that is, to bless. His disciples, however, 'spoke sternly' to the parents – or, as other versions translate, they 'rebuked them' (NIV and ESV), or 'scolded' them (GNB). Presumably, they did so for what they thought was the best of reasons. Perhaps they felt that it was more important for Jesus to be teaching and preaching, healing and casting out demons rather than bothering about children. Significantly, Jesus was of a decidedly different opinion. 'When Jesus saw this, he was indignant', says Mark 10:14. The Greek translated as indignant, *aganaktein*, is stronger in meaning: he was furious; he was seething; he exploded with anger. He said (or did he shout?) 'Let the children come to me; do not stop them.' In doing so, said Anne Richards, 'He insists that those with the least case for his attention get all of it . . . Everyone looking on could not help but understand that the Teacher was giving children his attention, welcome and love. Every child is welcomed and proclaimed to be good in God's sight. God finds in children a community of grace.'[6] The children did not have to prove their worth. In the words of James Edwards:

> The emphasis in this brief story falls on the children themselves rather than on their virtues, real or imagined. In this story children are not blessed for their virtues but for what they lack; they come only as they are – small, powerless, without sophistication, as the overlooked and dispossessed of society. To receive the kingdom of God as a child is to receive it as one who has no credits, no clout, no claims. A little child has

absolutely nothing to bring, and whatever a child receives, he or she receives by grace on the basis of sheer neediness rather than by any merit inherent in him- or herself.[7]

On another occasion we hear Jesus saying, 'Take care that you do not despise one of the little ones; for, I tell you, in heaven their angels continually see the face of my Father in heaven' (Matt. 18:10). Whatever else this means, we see here that 'children are close to God's heart'.[8] Or in the words of Dick France, a former Principal of Wycliffe Hall, Oxford, 'Every "little one" matters to God.'[9]

In the context of a tragic death of a child, we can therefore draw great comfort from this. As David Saville said in his guide to funerals:

A child is completely safe with God. What Jesus Christ has done by his death and resurrection to bring the world back to God and to belong to him for ever most certainly applies to children. They are covered by God's plan and purpose of love for his people, even if they never had a chance to hear, understand, or personally respond.[10]

For this reason, when I came to take the funeral of a baby who had died in the womb, I decided to preach on Jesus' words 'Let the little children come to me.'[11] The sermon was very short – on that occasion, I felt the 'liturgy' was more important.[12]

Sermon: Jesus welcomes children

A sermon preached on the occasion of the death of a baby in the womb. There had been a private service of committal in the local crematorium chapel; later in the day we held an evening service in our church's 'meeting place'. Many came to support the grieving parents and their two young children, who were far from their home in Uganda.

It has been said, 'Few things in life leave us more helpless, hopeless and faithless than the death of a child.' This certainly is true of baby

Philip. Paul and Fiona had been looking forward so much to his coming, but now your hopes have been dashed; only the week before he died you had shared the news with Martin that he would be having a baby brother to play with, but now there is no brother. Not surprisingly, you are stunned, shattered. This is the context in which we meet this evening. And I ask myself, what on earth can I say to you?

Perhaps the first thing to say is that we, too, share in your bewilderment. We, too, share something of your pain. Furthermore, at this time of loss, we want to assure you that we are here for you. We want you to know that we care for you, as we also do for Martin and Paula.

But as a minister, I want to say something more. Tonight, I want to remind you of the special place children had for our Lord. 'Let the children come to me,' Jesus said, 'and do not stop them, because the kingdom of God belongs to such as these.' On that occasion, the disciples discovered, to their amazement, children had a special place in the affections of Jesus. I dare to believe that Philip too has a special place in the affections of Jesus. For as Jesus welcomed those children of old, so Jesus now welcomes Philip, too, into his kingdom. We can, in faith, entrust Philip to his loving care, knowing that the strong love of Jesus encompasses all those who die in tender years. Philip's life that was all too short in this world is now complete in Jesus. We can indeed praise God for his love.

2

Luke 20:27–40

In the new world everything will be different

27Some Sadducees, those who say there is no resurrection, came to him 28and asked him a question, 'Teacher, Moses wrote for us that if a man's brother dies, leaving a wife but no children, the man shall marry the widow and raise up children for his brother. 29Now there were seven brothers; the first married, and died childless; 30then the second 31and the third married her, and so in the same way all seven died childless. 32Finally the woman also died. 33In the resurrection, therefore, whose wife will the woman be? For the seven had married her.'

34Jesus said to them, 'Those who belong to this age marry and are given in marriage; 35but those who are considered worthy of a place in that age and in the resurrection from the dead neither marry nor are given in marriage. 36Indeed they cannot die any more, because they are like angels and are children of God, being children of the resurrection. 37And the fact that the dead are raised Moses himself showed, in the story about the bush, where he speaks of the Lord as the God of Abraham, the God of Isaac, and the God of Jacob. 38Now he is God not of the dead, but of the living; for to him all of them are alive.' 39Then some of the scribes answered, 'Teacher, you have spoken well.' 40For they no longer dared to ask him another question.

Seven weddings and a funeral

According to the distinguished British New Testament scholar N. T. Wright, 'Far and away the most important passage about resurrection in the gospel tradition is the answer Jesus gives to the Sadducees' question.'[1] However, at first sight, it is also one of the most difficult passages to preach on, for the question that is posed reflects a culture that is not our own.

> Teacher, Moses wrote for us that if a man's brother dies, leaving a wife but no children, the man shall marry the widow and raise up children for his brother. Now there were seven brothers; the first married and died childless; then the second and the third married her, and so in the same way all seven died childless. Finally the woman also died. In the resurrection, therefore, whose wife will the woman be? For the seven had married her.
> (Luke 20:28–33)

What a ridiculous question! But it was also a hypocritical question, because it was put by a group of people who didn't believe in any form of resurrection (20:27). Dawn Ottoni-Wilhelm, a professor of preaching and worship at Princeton Theological Seminary, also pointed out how demeaning to women the Sadducees were: 'They not only mock resurrection from the dead but also accept without question the notion of patriarchal authority to preserve a man's name and perpetuate inheritance among male family members. The Sadducees show no concern for the woman, who is passed along from brother to brother. With no rights or privileges of her own she also experiences the shame of barrenness. They further objectify the widow by wondering who she will "belong to" in the resurrection to come.'[2]

The framing of the question reflects the Mosaic institution of 'levirate marriage', which was designed to prevent a man's name and family dying out (see Deut. 25:5–10); it also ensured that there would be provision for the destitute widow. To what extent this policy was put into practice is debatable. There are only two instances of a similar principle being invoked in the Old Testament, and in both cases the surviving relative was reluctant to play his part (Gen. 38:6–11; Ruth 4:5–10). The truth is that what we have here is a trick question. It is not based on a real situation. We are not dealing with just two brothers, but seven brothers for one bride!

The Sadducees were a rich and powerful elite who dominated the Jewish politics of the time. They accepted only the first five books of Moses (the Torah) and did not believe in resurrection of any kind. They were the 'rationalists' of their day. Dead people do not rise from the dead. Death is final. They did their best to rubbish the notion of resurrection. They remind me of cynics who glibly equate resurrection with 'resuscitation', and then ask what happens to people whose ashes are scattered to the winds after cremation!

Over against the Sadducees were the 6,000 Pharisees, who we might describe as the 'Bible believers' of their day. For them, the resurrection was a central tenet of their faith. 'Whoever denies the resurrection of the dead has no share in the world to come', declared the Mishnah (Sanh. 10:1). However, their idea of resurrection was an indefinite prolongation of this life. True, there would be some modifications and improvements: all enemies would be overthrown, and delights would be multiplied. But essentially it would be the same kind of life as this one. So they would discuss such matters as would a man rise clothed or unclothed? If clothed, then would he rise with the clothes he had on or other clothes? It was all very literal and all very crude. To emphasize the delights of the kingdom, they would talk of men begetting thousands of children, and of women having no pain in childbirth. Had there been any Pharisees listening in, they would have found it exceedingly challenging to answer the question about whose wife the woman would be. This is a question that had no easy answers for the literalist. How on earth would Jesus answer it?

In Mark and Matthew, where we also have an account of this story, Jesus begins by bluntly telling them they are wrong, and accuses them of knowing 'neither the scriptures nor the power of God' (Mark 12:24; Matt. 22:29). As the American Methodist Ben Witherington commented, 'Jesus in essence accuses the Sadducees not just of bad exegesis, but of a failure of nerve, a failure to believe in a God whose yes to life is louder than Death's no and whose power is great enough to create something out of nothing.'[3] Significantly, power is so much a characteristic of God that, in Mark 14:62, the word 'power' is used as a synonym for God. God by definition is 'the Almighty' (Mark 14:62, GNB). Or in the words of James Edwards, 'God's power to create and restore life bursts the limits of both logic and imagination. Heavenly realities are no more predicated on earthly experience than postpartum life is predicated on life in utero.'[4]

In Luke's account, Jesus begins by negating the assumption of a continuity between earthly and heavenly life. 'Those who belong to this age marry and are given in marriage; but those who are considered worthy of a place in that age and in the resurrection from the dead neither marry nor are given in marriage' (20:34, 35). As Frederick Dale Bruner pointed out, Jesus 'as much attacks Pharisees who knew too much about the resurrection as he does Sadducees who believe too little of it'.[5] Resurrection is not the same as 'resuscitation', as though life in the world to come were a starting all over again, with perhaps life slightly or considerably improved.

The question arises: although Jesus clearly says that 'no new marriages will be initiated',[6] will those of us who are married in this world still be with our earthly spouse (or spouses) in the world to come? Dick France mused, 'Perhaps heavenly relationships are not something *less* than marriage, but something *more*. He [Jesus] does not say that the love between those who have been married on earth will vanish, but rather implies that it will be broadened so that no one is excluded.'[7] Indeed, the American preacher Timothy Keller argued that spouses will definitely be together, and added, 'And who better than your spouse of many years to be able to rejoice in your new resurrected self? When all your sins and flaws are removed from your soul and body your spouse will be able to say with infinite joy, "I always knew you could be like this. I saw it in you. But now look at you!"'[8] The fact is that, as France acknowledged, we do not know: 'Our problem is that we . . . have only this life's experience to measure what is to come.'[9] By contrast, Michael Green, a prominent British evangelical leader, went even further and suggested that, 'In the future life, marriage is a thing of the past ... The intimacy that a human being shares with one other person in marriage is universalized in the joy and love of heaven.'[10] Certainly, on the basis of Jesus' reply to the Sadducees, all we can say for certain is that, in the words of Ian Paul, an Anglican scholar, 'Yes, we will be "sexed" in "heaven" – but it will not have the significance that it does in the present age.'[11]

Jesus went on, 'Indeed, they cannot die any more, because they are like angels and are children of God, being children of the resurrection' (Luke 20:36). In what regard will we be 'like' angels? N. T. Wright pointed out Luke's explanatory phrase about the angels is subtly different from that of Mark and Matthew: 'Instead of saying that the resurrected are *like* angels, he has Jesus say that they are *equal* to angels, using the rare word *isangeloi*.'[12] Indeed, 'equal to angels' is the translation adopted by the ESV. Do note, Jesus does not say that we will *become* angels. It is in respect of the fact that we will not die that we are like or equal to angels.

Significantly, Jesus grounds his belief in resurrection in the Scriptures and, in particular, on Exodus 3:5, part of the Torah accepted by the Sadducees: 'The fact that the dead are raised Moses himself showed, in the story about the bush, where he speaks of the Lord as the God of Abraham, the God of Isaac, and the God of Jacob. Now he is God not of the dead, but of the living; for to him all of them are alive' (20:37, 38).

As France makes clear, 'The argument is based on the nature of God's relationship with his human followers: the covenant by which he binds himself to them is too strong to be terminated by their death. To be associated with the living God is to be taken beyond the temporary life of earth into a relationship which lasts as long as God lasts.'[13] God does not break his covenant: he did not break it with Abraham, Isaac and Jacob; nor will he break it with us.[14] 'For Jesus,' said James Edwards, 'the call of God establishes a relationship with God, and once a relationship with God is established, it bears the promise of God that cannot be ended. Indeed, God's promise and power conquer the last enemy – death itself.'[15] Or, as John records Jesus saying in his Gospel, 'Anyone who comes to me, I will never drive away . . . And this is the will of him who sent me that I should lose nothing of all that he has given me, but raise it up on the last day' (John 6:37, 39; see also 10:28).

The Sadducees tried to make the resurrection of the dead seem ridiculous, but they failed. Jesus well and truly rebutted their argument. God is 'the God of the living' – he is the God of Abraham, Isaac and Jacob, and of all who put their trust in him. In the words of Ben Witherington, 'The Sadducees believed in a resurrection of a sort – raising up an heir for a brother. Jesus believed in a very different and more powerful sort of immortality – raising up the dead.'[16]

Sermon: heaven is beyond description

This sermon was prepared in the first instance for an All Saints' Day service to which we invited the relatives and friends of all those whose funerals I and my team had taken in the previous twelve months. Clearly, church people were present, but so too were many others.

'The Gospel without the Resurrection,' said Michael Ramsey, former Archbishop of Canterbury, 'is not merely a Gospel without its final chapter; it is not a Gospel at all.'[17] Later, as he came towards the end of his life, a publisher friend wanted to put together an anthology of some of his sermons and other writings and asked what he would most like to be included: 'Tell them about heaven! That's where we are going; that is what we were created for. Heaven is the meaning of our life here. Tell them about heaven.'[18]

Heaven is beyond all description. The life to come will be a new order beyond all the conventions of our time – thank God! This is the thrust of an encounter Jesus had with a group of Sadducees who asked a silly question designed to expose what they deemed to be the stupidity of belief in an afterlife. The question revolved around a woman who had seven husbands, one after the other.

> Teacher, Moses wrote for us that if a man's brother dies, leaving a wife but no children, the man shall marry the widow and

raise up children for his brother. Now there were seven brothers; the first married and died childless; then the second and the third married her, and so in the same way all seven died childless. Finally the woman also died. In the resurrection, therefore, whose wife will the woman be? For the seven had married her.

(Luke 20:28–33)

Ho ho ho. Yes, as the question was put, you can imagine some of the Sadducees just creasing up with laughter.

To understand the story, we have to realize that, in the book of Deuteronomy, the custom of so-called 'levirate' marriage is found. This was a device to prevent a man's name and family dying out, something which was especially important at a time when there was no belief in an afterlife. When a man died childless, his brother was to take his widow and raise up children for the deceased. By the time of Jesus, this custom had fallen into disuse. The question therefore raised by the Sadducees was purely hypothetical. They were simply putting forward a bizarre situation to show how absurd the doctrine of resurrection was. Why, the law of Moses, by its provision of levirate marriage, shows – by implication at least – that the doctrine of resurrection is a non-starter.

So how did Jesus respond?

In the first place, Jesus affirmed the doctrine of resurrection. He did so not by going back to some obscure passage in the Bible that the Sadducees had never noticed before but, rather, to one of the central passages of the Old Testament Scriptures, the appearance of God to Moses at the burning bush, when he revealed his name (Exod. 3).

The fact that the dead are raised Moses himself showed, in the story about the bush, where he speaks of the Lord as the God of Abraham, the God of Isaac, and the God of Jacob. Now he is God not of the dead, but of the living; for to him all of them are alive.

(20:37, 38)

37

The argument is as follows. Each of the so-called patriarchs – Abraham, Isaac and Jacob – had been long dead when God said to Moses, 'I am the God of Abraham, the God of Isaac, and the God of Jacob.' Now, reasoned Jesus, these words could only be true if these men were in some sense alive beyond the grave, for God cannot be the God of mouldering corpses: 'He is not the God of the dead, but of the living.' All three men, by their faith in God, had been friends of God. The good news is that although we may lose our friends by death, God does not – he holds on to them. Once we have committed ourselves to God, he commits himself to us, for ever.

Jesus believed in the resurrection. Indeed, living the other side of the cross, we can go on to affirm that Jesus did not simply teach the resurrection – he is the resurrection. His life verified his teaching, for the tomb was empty. In the words of the angel to the women that first Easter Day, 'He has been raised; he is not here' (Mark 16:6). Yes, Jesus lives, and, as he said to his disciples, 'Because I live, you also will live' (John 14:19). But, of course, in his argument with the Sadducees, Jesus could not point to his own resurrection – that had yet to take place. Instead, he pointed to the faithfulness of God. God is faithful to those who acknowledge him and seek to go his way.

Second, Jesus went on to affirm that God is a God of transformation: 'In the resurrection from the dead [they] neither marry nor are given in marriage. Indeed, they cannot die any more, because they are like angels.' My mind goes to the words of the Lord at the end of Revelation (21:5): 'See, I am making all things new.' In heaven, everything will be radically different.

Jesus said two things about heaven. First, marriage, though a necessary feature in this world, will not be a feature in the world to come: 'they neither marry nor are given in marriage' (Luke 20:35). Here, those who marry are the men, while those who are given in marriage are the women. Second, 'they cannot die any more, because they are like angels' (20:36). By that, Jesus means death will not be a feature in the world to come. If death is no more, then there is no need for procreation – and so for people at the time of Jesus, a major reason for marriage is removed.

For those of us who are happily married – or have been happily married – this picture of heaven might at first sight appear rather depressing. Heaven might appear to be a bit of a comedown if marriage is out. But wait a minute: the absence of marriage doesn't mean a levelling down of relationships, so that life is then lived on a lower level; rather, our present relationships are transformed and taken up into the fullness of life in the family of God. In heaven, our present relationships with one another will be transcended into something more glorious. Physical sexuality will cease – exclusive relationships will cease – but not love. In the words of the apostle Paul's great hymn to love, 'love never ends' (1 Cor. 13:8); 'love is eternal' (GNB) and, therefore, 'love never fails' (NIV).

Fair enough, you may say, but on this Sunday, when we remember loved ones who have died, there is a more basic question: 'Will we know one another?' Will we, in a way perhaps beyond our understanding, be 're-united' with our loved ones who we miss so much? Will we be able to see one another again? Will we be able to recognize one another?

Although there is much that we do not know about the life to come, I see no reason why we shall not be able to know one another. The Bible talks of us having a 'spiritual body' (1 Cor. 15:44) when God takes us to himself: we will not be vague shades, but personalities in our own right.[19] I believe we can affirm that relationships will be restored, but they will be transcended too. The great Swiss theologian Karl Barth once put it this way. When asked at a conference of pastors' wives, 'Will we see our loved ones on the other side?' he replied, 'Yes, but with others too!'[20] Or as John Bunyan once put it: 'There you shall enjoy your friends again that have gone thither before you; and there you shall with joy receive even every one that follows into the holy place after you.'[21] Indeed, Justin Thacker suggested that:

In the new earth we will interact with one another primarily in terms of our oneness in Christ, that is, as brothers and sisters in him. This does not mean that other concepts – strangers, friends, wife, husband, children, colleague – will no longer apply. I do think we will be able to say, 'Oh yes, we used to work together', or 'we once were married'. However, our shared identity in Christ will be so dominant that these other means of relating will simply be irrelevant.[22]

Heaven will be a place of transformation. Present relationships will be transcended – and extended. In the words of Isaiah, quoted by the apostle Paul, 'What no eye has seen, nor ear heard, nor the human heart conceived . . . God has prepared for those who love him' (1 Cor. 2:9; see also Isa. 64:4).

We can with confidence affirm that our loved ones who have died in Christ are indeed safe in the Father's hand. This is not wishful thinking – this is truth. This truth is to be seen in the Scriptures and is based, above all, on the power of God displayed in Jesus, his Son.

3

John 3:16; 10:10

Eternal life

3:16 For God so loved the world that he gave his only Son, so that everyone who believes in him may not perish but may have eternal life.

10:10 The thief comes only to steal and kill and destroy. I came that they may have life, and have it abundantly.

Jesus is salvation

Many preachers today talk about the salvation that Jesus offers us all. However, the reality is that the Gospels only record two occasions when the word 'salvation' crossed his lips: in Luke 19:9 ('Today salvation has come to this house') and John 4:22 ('Salvation is from the Jews'). Instead, in the first three Gospels, the expression most frequently on the lips of Jesus was 'the kingdom of God', whereas in the fourth Gospel, it is the term 'life' or 'eternal life'. However, there is no contradiction between the Synoptic Gospels and the Gospel of John. In the words of one New Testament scholar who wrote extensively both about the kingdom of God and about the Gospel of John:

> In the teaching of Jesus, as in Jewish writings contemporary with the New Testament, the supreme blessing of the kingdom of God is 'life'. For that reason it is often spoken of as 'eternal life', since it is life in the eternal kingdom, or as the Jews often put it, the life of the age to come.[1]

It is this concept of 'life' or 'eternal' life' which formed the purpose for the writing of the Gospel of John: it was 'so that you may come to believe that Jesus is the Messiah, the Son of God, and that through believing you may have life in his name' (20:31).

The expressions 'life' and 'eternal life', used interchangeably in John, are found a total of thirty-six times. For John, 'this is eternal life, that they may know you, the only true God and Jesus Christ whom you have sent' (17:3). 'As in the Old Testament', commented the Australian Colin Kruse, 'this knowledge is not simply having information about God; it is having a relationship with him, involving response, obedience and fellowship.'[2] What is distinctive about John's portrayal of the 'life' Jesus offers us is that this life of God mediated through his Son is both present and future. On the one hand, this life may be experienced in the present: 'Very truly, I tell you, anyone who hears my word and believes him who sent me has eternal life, and does not come under judgment, but has passed from death to life' (5:24). On the other hand, we will only fully experience this life in the future: 'Do not work for the food that perishes, but for the food that endures for eternal life, which the Son of Man will give you' (6:27).

This is the context in which we need to interpret John 10:10. When Jesus declared, 'I came that they may have life, and have it abundantly' (10:10), he was speaking, on the one hand, of life in the here and now, that already we can experience the joy and peace, the purpose and the fulfilment which come from knowing God as our Father; but, on the other hand, he was speaking of the even fuller and more abundant life that we may know beyond death. In the words of the NIV, Jesus came that we might have life 'to the full', or, as the GNB puts it, that we might experience 'life in all its fullness'. 'It means,' wrote Don Carson, 'that the life Jesus' true disciples enjoy is not construed as more time to fill (merely "everlasting life") but life at its scarcely imagined best, life to be lived.'[3] It is 'Life with a capital L!'

This is also the context in which we need to interpret John 3:16: when Jesus (or have we here a summary statement by John?) declared 'God so loved the world that he gave his only Son, so that everyone who believes in him may not perish but may have eternal life', he had both the present and future in mind. Already, those who believe may experience something of the life that belongs to the life of 'the age to come'. As Craig Koester notes, 'Physical death remains a reality for people of faith, yet the life that faith brings is called "eternal" because it is a life lived in relationship to the God who is eternal.'[4]

The translation of the Authorized Version is misleading: 'everlasting life' can give the impression that the life Jesus has to offer is simply 'unending life'. However, the underlying Greek word (*aionios*) literally means 'of the [new] age' and is better translated as 'eternal life'.[5] 'Eternal life' refers to life in terms of its 'quality' and also of its 'quantity'.

One American preacher sought to express the difference in terms of music:

> Everlasting music simply goes on and on, until it seems it will drive you out of your mind. Eternal music has something of the essence of life to it. Such music moves one deeply. And when Jesus spoke of eternal life, he meant an essential quality of life that continues to expand in its liveliness in every conceivable human dimension in and beyond time.[6]

The American New Testament scholar Dale Allison noted that cynics have urged heaven conceived in terms of 'eternal life' entails unbroken monotony: 'The argument is this: Given an infinite amount of time, everything would repeat itself again and again, with the inevitable result that a world without end would be tedium without end ... Infinite time means eternal recurrence, and eternal recurrence would be unbearable!'[7] Allison, however, was not convinced:

> Although some non-terminating sequences involve repetition – the inverse of 11 is .09090909 – other infinites don't: the irrational number pi has no reiterating pattern. Beyond the mathematical point, maybe the conundrum won't apply to heavenly subjects oriented to something other than self-fulfilment. Or maybe it won't hold for transformed individuals

who, as some theologians have supposed, will transcend time. Or maybe, as Gregory of Nyssa believed, eternal life will mean always moving from one beginning to the next, so that one will never arrive at any limit of perfection: fresh possibilities will always come into view. If God is truly an infinite mystery, how could such a mystery ever be exhausted?[8]

Sermon: God's amazing love

This sermon is included as a tribute to my maternal grandfather who, in his earlier days, had been a street preacher. He had a passion for evangelism and so, not surprisingly, this was the text of the sermon at his funeral. I have adapted the sermon to a wide variety of contexts, including a funeral. Although rooted in Scripture, the truth is that it is less 'expository' than most of my sermons.

John 3:16 is probably the most well-known verse in the Bible: 'For God so loved the world that he gave his only Son, so that everyone who believes in him may not perish but have eternal life.' There are, said Martin Luther, in the Bible a number of 'little Bibles', verses or passages of scripture which express in a summary fashion the good news of Jesus. John 3:16 is such a little Bible. It is the gospel in a nutshell.

Whenever I hear John 3:16 I am reminded of my maternal grandfather. As one entered his house, there was a large hall. On one side there was a sideboard adorned with art deco statuettes; on the other side, between two doors, there was a huge stag's head. At the far end, over the door that led to his library, was a framed scripture text – John 3:16 – printed out in black type. My grandfather was a preacher, and John 3:16 was at the heart of his preaching. So, when he died, the theme of the sermon was John 3:16 with its message of God's amazing love.

It is this message of God's amazing love which I want to focus on in today's funeral of our friend and loved one, John, in the hope that it will bring great comfort to you all. For, like my grandfather, he made the message of John 3:16 his own.

God's love is amazing, so amazing that it reminds me of the book *Guinness World Records* and its collection of improbable but true facts. Did you know that the longest bout of hiccups has lasted fifty-five years? Indeed, according to my edition, the man is still hiccupping, his wife has left him (she could not stand the hiccups) and the poor man is unable to keep his false teeth in. Did you know that the heaviest woman on record is the late Mrs Percy Pearl Washington? She weighed 62 stone and 12 pounds, or almost 400 kilos. Did you also know that the greatest number of children produced by one mother was sixty-nine? In twenty-seven confinements, a poor Russian peasant gave birth to sixteen pairs of twins, seven sets of triplets and four sets of quads!

Thank God none of us is likely to endure such a fit of hiccups. None of us is ever likely to weigh so much. None of us is ever likely to give birth to so many children. However, for a few minutes, I want us to consider a further four amazing facts which are equally improbable, but true. But, unlike the hiccups, they are not just odd, irrelevant facts but facts which can bring us great comfort.

First, amazing fact number one: God loves the world. That is amazing! It is almost beyond belief that the God who made the heavens and the earth, who set in motion the evolutionary process, who sustains our everyday life, should love you and me! It's mind-boggling! Can you imagine God taking an interest in our world, let alone in people like you and me? The nearest parallel to God's love for us would be if you were to have a crush on an ant. Such a crush would be ludicrous. But God does love you and me.

What is more, God loves not just the best of us but also the worst of us! In fact, he loves the whole world. God loves not just good people like my grandfather or our friend and loved one, John – he loves too the terrorist and sexual pervert. Amazingly, God loves you and me. Let's be honest: we are not always the most loveable of creatures, whatever your girlfriend might say about you. There is so much in each of us which is selfish and greedy, unloving and unkind. But God loves us. He loves the world – he loves everybody.

How do we know it is true? This leads us on to our second amazing fact: God gave his only Son. That too is almost incredible. How could anybody love us so much? What parent would be willing to sacrifice their son or daughter? However much you may admire somebody, would you be willing to offer your child's life in their stead? Some years ago, my eldest son, together with the rest of his class, were asked in a philosophy lesson, 'What would you do if you saw two people drowning in a river: one was your father, and the other a scientist on the verge of discovering the final cure for cancer? If you could save only one, which one would you save?' To my surprise, all the boys said 'My father!'

The fact is that whatever anybody else may think about our children or our parents, we value our families far too highly to put somebody else before them. However awkward the children can get, however difficult our parents can get, there is nothing more precious than our family. 'Blood is thicker than water,' we say. But John 3:16 declares that 'God gave his only Son.' God's love is almost beyond belief.

That leads me to my third amazing fact: God's gift is eternal life. That too is almost beyond belief. For nothing in this life is eternal – nothing lasts. The carpet we were told would last a lifetime ultimately wears out. The car in which we invested a small fortune rusts away. We live in a consumer society, where everything is built to fail. What is true of consumer 'durables' is also true of you and me. Neither drugs nor surgery can prolong life indefinitely. Nobody lives for ever. Along with income tax, death is the great certainty of life. We may smile, but it's true, so true, that many of us do our best to stick our heads in the sand and forget about it all.

Against this background, John 3:16 declares that God offers eternal life – life that goes beyond the grave. This is not mere prolongation of life. Who would want that? That would be hell itself. No, it's a new quality of life, life lived with God himself, a life which can begin in the here and now and goes on to eternity. If this all sounds highly improbable to you, then dare I suggest that this is only because you have never experienced it. As one preacher said, 'People who tell me there is no God are like a six-year-old saying there is no such thing as passionate love. They just haven't experienced him yet.'

Finally, the fourth amazing fact: eternal life is for those who believe. Reason says that God would scarcely offer such a fantastic gift without conditions: it would be like throwing pearls before swine. We surely must have something to *do* to deserve this gift of eternal life. This is the attitude of many people, even 'religious' people. If God is going to do something for us, then we have to work for it. God surely only gives eternal life to those who have lived a good life, who have been good parents, who have done a good turn for a neighbour.

But the good news is that eternal life is for those who believe. If eternal life were for those who deserved it, then none of us would ever experience it – not even the most respectable of us would get a look in, for the Bible tells us very clearly that our best is not good enough. There is no way of getting into God's 'heaven' through our own efforts. Thank God, we don't have to try to do the impossible. Jesus has done all that is necessary. He died on the cross that we might be forgiven. He has dealt with your sin and mine. All we have to do is to believe. For me, the great comfort of today is that, like my grandfather, John was a believer. As a young man, he put his trust in the God and Father of our Lord Jesus Christ, and that gives me great comfort. He is safe in God's eternal care.

4

John 11:1–44

Jesus offers life to all

[1]Now a certain man was ill, Lazarus of Bethany, the village of Mary and her sister Martha. [2]Mary was the one who anointed the Lord with perfume and wiped his feet with her hair; her brother Lazarus was ill. [3]So the sisters sent a message to Jesus, 'Lord, he whom you love is ill.' [4]But when Jesus heard it, he said, 'This illness does not lead to death; rather it is for God's glory, so that the Son of God may be glorified through it.' [5]Accordingly, though Jesus loved Martha and her sister and Lazarus, [6]after having heard that Lazarus was ill, he stayed two days longer in the place where he was.

[7]Then after this he said to the disciples, 'Let us go to Judea again.' [8]The disciples said to him, 'Rabbi, the Jews were just now trying to stone you, and are you going there again?' [9]Jesus answered, 'Are there not twelve hours of daylight? Those who walk during the day do not stumble, because they see the light of this world. [10]But those who walk at night stumble, because the light is not in them.' [11]After saying this, he told them, 'Our friend Lazarus has fallen asleep, but I am going there to awaken him.' [12]The disciples said to him, 'Lord, if he has fallen asleep, he will be all right.' [13]Jesus, however, had been speaking about his death, but they thought that he was referring merely to sleep. [14]Then Jesus told them plainly, 'Lazarus is dead. [15]For your sake I am glad I was not there, so that you may believe. But let us go to him.' [16]Thomas, who was called the Twin, said to his fellow disciples, 'Let us also go, that we may die with him.'

¹⁷When Jesus arrived, he found that Lazarus had already been in the tomb four days. ¹⁸Now Bethany was near Jerusalem, some two miles away, ¹⁹and many of the Jews had come to Martha and Mary to console them about their brother. ²⁰When Martha heard that Jesus was coming, she went and met him, while Mary stayed at home. ²¹Martha said to Jesus, 'Lord, if you had been here, my brother would not have died. ²²But even now I know that God will give you whatever you ask of him.' ²³Jesus said to her, 'Your brother will rise again.' ²⁴Martha said to him, 'I know that he will rise again in the resurrection on the last day.' ²⁵Jesus said to her, 'I am the resurrection and the life. Those who believe in me, even though they die, will live, ²⁶and everyone who lives and believes in me will never die. Do you believe this?' ²⁷She said to him, 'Yes, Lord, I believe that you are the Messiah, the Son of God, the one coming into the world.'

²⁸When she had said this, she went back and called her sister Mary, and told her privately, 'The Teacher is here and is calling for you.' ²⁹And when she heard it, she got up quickly and went to him. ³⁰Now Jesus had not yet come to the village, but was still at the place where Martha had met him. ³¹The Jews who were with her in the house, consoling her, saw Mary get up quickly and go out. They followed her because they thought that she was going to the tomb to weep there. ³²When Mary came where Jesus was and saw him, she knelt at his feet and said to him, 'Lord, if you had been here, my brother would not have died.' ³³When Jesus saw her weeping, and the Jews who came with her also weeping, he was greatly disturbed in spirit and deeply moved. ³⁴He said, 'Where have you laid him?' They said to him, 'Lord, come and see.' ³⁵Jesus began to weep. ³⁶So the Jews said, 'See how he loved him!' ³⁷But some of them said, 'Could not he who opened the eyes of the blind man have kept this man from dying?'

³⁸Then Jesus, again greatly disturbed, came to the tomb. It was a cave, and a stone was lying against it. ³⁹Jesus said, 'Take away the stone.' Martha, the sister of the dead man, said to

him, 'Lord, already there is a stench because he has been dead four days.' [40]Jesus said to her, 'Did I not tell you that if you believed, you would see the glory of God?' [41]So they took away the stone. And Jesus looked upward and said, 'Father, I thank you for having heard me. [42]I knew that you always hear me, but I have said this for the sake of the crowd standing here, so that they may believe that you sent me.' [43]When he had said this, he cried with a loud voice, 'Lazarus, come out!' [44]The dead man came out, his hands and feet bound with strips of cloth, and his face wrapped in a cloth. Jesus said to them, 'Unbind him, and let him go.'

An encounter with death and life

The raising of Lazarus from the dead has been called 'the most spectacular miracle in all of the four Gospels'.[1] Although we read of Jesus giving life to Jairus' daughter (Mark 5:21–24, 35–43) and of raising the son of the widow of Nain (Luke 10:11–15), in both these cases the deceased had only just died. In the case of Lazarus, he 'had already been in the tomb for four days' (11:17).

Lazarus was the brother of Mary and Martha (11:1–2). We hear about Mary and Martha in Luke's Gospel, where Martha complained to Jesus that her sister was not helping her with preparing the meal (Luke 10:38–41), but there is no reference to Lazarus. Lazarus only appears in John's Gospel. Who was he? There has been much speculation. I am attracted to the suggestion that Lazarus suffered from a disability. Sister Margaret Magdalen, a former British Baptist who joined the Anglican community of St Mary the Virgin, wrote:

It was an unusual *ménage à trois*. Why was Lazarus not married – given that marriage was obligatory for Jewish men with few exceptions? Why, too, were Martha and Mary unmarried since normally they would have been engaged, betrothed and married whilst still fairly young ... Was Lazarus perhaps handicapped – physically, mentally, or both? If so, it would help to explain the unusual composition of the household, the unmarried state of (it would seem) all three, and the intense grief of the sisters which was later to be shared by Jesus. A source of quite unique love would have been taken from them, for any of us who have lived amongst handicapped people will know all that is captured in that word 'unique'.[2]

All we really know about Lazarus is what we find here in John's Gospel. Lazarus means 'He whom God helps', a very appropriate meaning in light of John 11. Attention has been drawn to the fact that the names of all three family members – Mary, Martha and Lazarus – were found in 1973 ossuary inscriptions near Bethany. But in so far as all three names were common, 'this discovery cannot be labelled anything more than an interesting coincidence'.[3]

Mary, Martha and Lazarus lived in Bethany, which was 'near Jerusalem, some two miles away' (11:18) and is not to be confused with the Bethany 'across the Jordan', where John the Baptist was baptizing (1:28). It is the same village where, according to the other Gospels, Jesus stayed when he was visiting Jerusalem (see, for instance, Mark 11:11–12; 14:4). It seems to have become a bolthole for Jesus, being 'very convenient when Jesus went up to the feasts, and yet far enough away to offer peace, quiet and freedom from the pressure of being constantly surrounded by crowds'.[4]

'Jesus loved Martha and her sister and Lazarus' (11:5). Clearly, they meant a great deal to him. He could perhaps relax in their company. Their home was a haven of rest in the midst of unrelenting turbulence outside. Yet even this special family was hit by trouble. I find this significant: the people whom the Lord really loved had to go through a terrible crisis in their lives. True, there was a happy ending but, at the time, Mary and Martha did not know that. All they could see was that their brother became ill and died. God didn't seem to care for the one whose name meant 'the person God takes care of'. The first words of both of them to Jesus were 'Lord, if you had been here, my brother would not have died!' (11:21, 32). This was no mere statement of fact, but an expression of resentment. In that regard they were no different from us. In our anguish we begin to cry out against God, if not actually curse him. In Richard Llewellyn's story *How Green Was My Valley*, Gwilym Morgan lies crushed by a fall in the coal mine. When the news of his death is brought home to his wife, her first reaction is one of rage: 'God could have had him in a hundred ways; but he had to have him like that. A beetle under the feet. If ever I set foot in chapel again, it will be in my box, and knowing nothing about it.'[5] God's actions – if God's they are – are sometimes baffling. However, Jesus said, 'This illness does not lead to death [of Lazarus] . . . it is for God's glory, so that the Son of God may be glorified through it' (11:4). My experience is that where the inevitable questioning takes place within the context of trust rather than of bitterness, God is able to bring about something good (see Rom. 8:28). However, Mary and Martha had not that perspective. They were deeply upset (11:19) – they had lost their brother.

Jesus also was upset, for when 'Jesus saw Mary weeping, and the Jews who came with her also weeping, he was greatly disturbed in spirit and deeply moved' (11:33). Or was another emotion present? The word translated as 'greatly disturbed' (NRSV) or as 'deeply moved' (NIV and ESV) (*embrimaomai*) is an expression of anger[6] and was correctly recognized by Luther in his translation as the growl of a dog that has its hackles raised. Jesus snarls at death, which binds his friend.

'Jesus began to weep,' says John 11:35 – the shortest verse in the Bible. There has been much discussion as to why Jesus wept. Was it because of grief for Lazarus? 'Certainly not,' said one commentator:

> His illness and death had been stated to be for the glory of God (v. 4), and Jesus was now advancing to his tomb to call him from it, not to weep beside it. It is possible that the tears were motivated by the unbelief that caused him anger . . . It is, however, perhaps more likely that they were brought about by the sight of the havoc wrought among people through sin and death in this world.[7]

Gordon Bridger added that if his tears were 'in sorrow at the sense of desolation and loss that death brought to those who were still in the dark about the future life', then 'this story assures us that Jesus understands and cares about human sorrow'.[8]

This is the context in which Jesus came to the tomb and ordered that the stone blocking the entrance be removed (11:38, 39). Martha, as practical as ever, objected: 'Lord, already there is a stench because he has been dead for four days' (11:39). According to popular Jewish belief of the day, the body burst on the fourth day, and the soul, which had hovered over the body until then, finally departed. One thing is for certain: Lazarus was well and truly dead (see 11:14). Strange as it may seem, some sceptics have suggested that Lazarus simply went into a deep coma; Jesus then brought him round. Others have suggested that Lazarus only died 'spiritually', whereas physically he remained very much alive. For instance, William Barclay, a popular Scottish commentator and also a New Testament professor at the University of Glasgow, speculated that 'Lazarus had committed some terrible sin which shattered the home in Bethany, had done something which made his name stink like a corpse, so that he was dead to shame and honour.'[9] I am not convinced.

But for Lazarus, death was not the end. Jesus insisted that the stone to the entrance to his tomb be removed. He then 'looked upward' to heaven (11:41) and prayed. This is the only prayer by Jesus recorded in the Gospels prior to his working a miracle. Here we have a reminder that Jesus did not operate in his own strength – he was dependent on his Father. In his brief prayer, he affirmed his faith in his Father God: 'Father, I thank you for having heard me' (11:41). I find it significant that it was a prayer 'uttered in the midst of activity'.[10]

After praying, Jesus 'cried out with a loud voice, 'Lazarus, come out' (11:43). 'The dead man came out, his hands and feet bound with strips of cloth, and his face wrapped in a cloth' (11:44). Lazarus was 'a cadaver wrapped from head to toe' (Eugene Peterson, *The Message*). With all his wrappings, Lazarus could only have shuffled out of the tomb!

It is an incredible story – the mind boggles! But the one who commanded Lazarus to come out of the tomb was no ordinary man. This was Jesus, the Son of God, and with Jesus nothing is impossible.[11] True, eventually Lazarus died. In fact, we should not use the term 'resurrection' for Lazarus's coming back to life – he was simply resuscitated. But for John, the story of Lazarus's return to life is a 'sign' of the resurrection hope that is ours in Jesus. The life that Jesus gave Lazarus points to the new life that Jesus will give those who trust him today.

Indeed, the key statement in this story is where Jesus presents Martha with the reality of this life he offers when he declares 'I *am* the resurrection and the life' (11:25). Jesus not only gives life – he is life! Here we have not 'a rejection of Martha's faith, but an extension of it and a setting of it on a sure foundation'.[12] Jesus then draws out the meaning of this statement in the two parallel clauses that follow: 'Those who believe, even though they die; will live; and everyone who lives and believes in me will never die' (11:26). Those who believe are promised a share in a resurrection yet to come; and those who have a share in the life of the kingdom of God will never die. In this world, said American Presbyterian Marianne Meye Thompson, death is 'the most threatening of realities, and the life-giving God overcomes it – through resurrection to life'.[13]

What wonderful words these are! I begin almost every funeral service I take with them. But notice to whom these words of hope are addressed: to those who are prepared to believe. To Martha, Jesus said, 'Do you believe this?' (11:26). In one sense Martha already believed in life after death. For when Jesus said, 'Your brother will rise again', she had replied, somewhat mechanically, 'I know that he will rise again in the resurrection on the last day' (11:24): 'Sure, he'll rise – I've heard that one before.' But at that moment she is just mouthing a platitude – this thought brought no comfort to her heart. But then, all of a sudden, an intellectual creed translates itself into true faith: 'Do you believe this?' asks Jesus. 'Do you believe that I am the resurrection and the life?' 'Yes, Lord, I believe that you are the Messiah, the Son of God' (11:27). Martha believed in a way she had never believed before. I am reminded of a comment by C. S. Lewis, written in the context of his wife's death:

You never know how much you really believe anything until its truth and falsehood becomes a matter of life and death to you.

It is easy to say you believe a rope to be strong and sound as long as you are merely using it to cord a book. But suppose you had to hang by that rope over a precipice. Wouldn't you then discover how much you really trusted it?[14]

That is the nature of true Christian believing: truly trusting Jesus. There is a place for tears when a loved one dies, but there is also a place for tears of joy – for those who die believing in Jesus have entered into the very life of heaven itself.

Sermon: Jesus is the resurrection and the life

I prepared the following sermon for the funeral of a great friend of ours and, indeed, of many others. Her death came as a great shock, not just to her family but also to everybody else. Her death seemed so 'unfair'. The church was packed on the occasion of her funeral.

Elinor's death was, and is, a tragedy. She was only in her early sixties. By rights she should have had many more years to live. But she didn't. She died on the afternoon of Friday 1 September. Let's not faff around with all this sentimental nonsense that Elinor has simply slipped into another room. Death has taken her forcibly from our presence. I remember on the night of her death saying to her husband Paul that the Bible is quite realistic in its view of death. It describes death as 'the last enemy' (1 Cor. 15:26), as 'the king of terrors' (Job 18:14: see also Ps. 55:4). Death is a nasty business. In the words of the great Swiss psychiatrist Carl Jung, 'Death is indeed a piece of brutality. There is no sense in pretending otherwise. It is brutal not only as a physical event but far more so psychically: a human being is torn away from us, and what remains is the icy stillness of death.'[15] And so we grieve. We grieve the loss of a loved one. We grieve the loss of a good friend. We grieve the loss of one who was special to so many people.

But there is one key aspect to Elinor's life which makes all the difference to our grief today. Elinor was a woman of real Christian faith. Brought up in a Brethren home, from an early age, in the words of the poem read to us by Robert, she 'put her hand into the hand of God' and, over the years, she continued to hold on to God's hand. Yes, she had a strong faith in the Lord Jesus. And it is this strong faith in Jesus which makes all the difference. For, in the words of Jesus we quoted at the beginning of the service and which appear on our church banners, 'I am the resurrection and the life. Those who believe in me, even though they die, will live' (John 11:25).

For the unbeliever, death is the end. As the coffin makes its final journey at the crematorium, it is literally 'curtains'. There is nothing to hope for. John Diamond, the agnostic Jewish journalist and *Times* columnist, shortly before he died, wrote a book entitled *C: Because Cowards get Cancer Too*.[16] Although a witty account of his encounter with terminal cancer, it is pervaded by a sense of deep sadness. The final sentence of his account is about the purchase of a dog: 'A dog is a happy thing, and it will be happy for me for whatever time I've got left and as happy as things can be for the family when I am gone.' For him there was no hope of life beyond the grave.

How different John Diamond's funeral must have been from that of the British entertainer Roy Castle,[17] for Roy Castle was a Christian. When he died, his wife Fiona was able to say to her friends, 'No flowers, no fuss . . . just lots of joy.'[18] For the believer, death is but the gateway to a new and fuller life. In the words of the apostle Paul read earlier in the service, 'Christ has been raised from death, as the guarantee that those who sleep in death will also be raised' (1 Cor. 15:20, GNB). Jesus, through his death and resurrection, has carved out a trail through the valley of the shadow of death, and we, by faith, may follow in his footsteps. This is why Paul and his sons in Elinor's death announcement in *The Times* went on to quote a later verse from 1 Corinthians 15: 'thanks be to God, who gives us the victory through our Lord Jesus Christ' (1 Cor. 15:57).

This is why Paul and his family asked us not to come dressed all in black, but for there to be colour too. To quote, in a slightly amended form, a poem by American author Gertrude Knevels:

Shall I wear mourning for my loved one dead,
I – a believer? Give me red.

56

Or give me purple for the King
At whose high court my love is visiting.
Dress me in green for growth, for Life made new,
For skies her dear feet walk, dress me in blue,
In white for her white soul; robe me in gold
For all the pride that her new rank shall hold.
In earth's dim gardens blooms no hue too bright
To dress me for my love who walks in light.[19]

This does not mean we do not miss our loved ones; it does not mean that we do not mourn the loss of our loved ones. In this respect I think Fiona Castle got it wrong, for when I quoted her earlier, I did not quote her in full. She actually said, 'No flowers, no fuss, no *mourning*, just lots of joy.' There is a place for mourning, even at a Christian funeral. I find it significant that on the very occasion when Jesus spoke of his being the resurrection and the life, Jesus wept for his friend Lazarus (John 11:35). If Jesus could weep, then so too may we. But though we may weep for our loss, we need not weep for Elinor. She is safe in the Father's house. Death for us is indeed 'gain' (Phil. 1:21).

One of the most moving books I have read is *23 Days: A Story of Love, Death and God* by Francis Bridger, an Anglican minister and principal of a theological college, who tells the story of how his wife Renée was diagnosed with terminal cancer; twenty-three days later, she was dead. He then goes on to recount the devastating grief he experienced.

Grief has only one goal: to usurp your love's place. It wants to become your new companion, your new best friend. This is what it lusts after. But – and here's the real cruelty – it doesn't even attempt to play the seductress, enticing you into its presence with promises of consolation. No, it waits in hiding until it can steal up, knock you to the ground and stamp all over you as you writhe in agony. Then it delights in kicking the living hell out of you until your guts are bursting and you can take no more, leaving you a sobbing wreck crying out in desperation for your loved one to hold you in her arms and make everything right. But, of course, she can't. How I hate that bloody cancer.[20]

Bridger experienced death in the raw. But his is not just a story of love and death: it is also a story of God. Bridger railed against God, and understandably so. It was all so unfair. Yet in the midst of his despair, he discovered that God had not abandoned him. Let me read the final paragraph of his account.

> In the midst of human emotions of the most overwhelming kind, it is possible to know God . . . He enfolds our emotions, however negative, in his love and deals gently with them. He does not leave us or forsake us, whatever our feelings might tell us. And he does not desert us because we express them honestly. As I have discovered, it is in the storm centre of confusion and pain that he meets us . . . He invites us to discover him there . . . It is an awesome and challenging thought.[21]

Paul, Robert and Geoffrey [Elinor's husband and sons], I would not blame you for railing against God. There are no easy answers as to why God let Elinor die when she did – why did he not allow her even just a few more months of life? In the words of Minnie Louise Haskins, 'God hideth his intention.'[22]

But one thing I do know is that God loves us, and that there is nothing which can ever separate us from his love (Rom. 8:38, 39). So keep on believing. Indeed, that is what Jesus said to his disciples: 'Do not be worried and upset . . . Believe in God and believe also in me' (John 14:1, GNB). Literally, 'keep on believing in God, and keep on believing in me'.

When we lose a loved one, we find ourselves treading a lengthy path of grief. You don't just get over your loss within a matter of days and weeks. It takes months, sometimes years. But to those who mourn, Jesus says, 'Stop letting your hearts be in a turmoil. Keep on believing in God; keep on believing in me.' And you will find, as Francis Bridger found, and many others have found, that God is there. He is there for you.

5
John 14:1–6

Jesus calls us to place our hope in him

¹'Do not let your hearts be troubled. Believe in God, believe also in me. ²In my Father's house there are many dwelling places. If it were not so, would I have told you that I go to prepare a place for you? ³And if I go and prepare a place for you, I will come again and will take you to myself, so that where I am, there you may be also. ⁴And you know the way to the place where I am going.' ⁵Thomas said to him, 'Lord, we do not know where you are going. How can we know the way?' ⁶Jesus said to him, 'I am the way, and the truth, and the life. No one comes to the Father except through me.'

Keep on believing

It was the night before he was to die. Judas Iscariot had left the table (John 13:27) and Jesus knew that it was a matter of an hour or two before he would be arrested and put on trial. It was then that Jesus began to say farewell to his disciples.

The disciples, however, had only thoughts for themselves. Jesus had just spoken of betrayal. He had just foretold Peter's denial (13:38). 'What next?' the disciples must have wondered. This is the context in which Jesus said, 'Do not let your hearts be troubled' (14:1); 'do not be worried and upset' (GNB). Telling a person not to be nervous and not to be anxious does not normally help those who are 'on the edge'. But as Gerard Sloyan, an American Roman Catholic scholar, said, 'Here, however, the speaker is Jesus and he provides a means to the end.'¹

Jesus' remedy for fear is to 'believe in God' and to 'believe also in me'. To all intents and purposes Jesus was putting himself on the same level with God. 'Belief in Jesus,' wrote American Methodist bishop William Willimon, 'is not something added on to a belief in God, but rather belief in Jesus is our belief in God'.[2]

The grammar is significant. The underlying Greek contains a series of present imperatives: 'Stop letting your hearts be troubled'; instead, 'Keep on believing in God, and keep on believing in me.' The disciples already were believers, but now Jesus calls them to continue to believe in God and to continue to believe in him. It is tough enough to believe in God when 'the world may appear to have gone mad',[3] but it would have been even tougher to believe in Jesus as the Messiah and the Son of God when he was nailed to a cross.

Jesus went on to present his disciples with a reason for believing: 'In my Father's house there are many dwelling places. If it were not so, would I have told you that I go to prepare a place for you?' (14:2). The Authorized Version speaks of 'mansions', a term which then denoted 'a dwelling place', whereas today it suggests a large house or even a stately pile. In contrast, Luther's rendering, *Wohnungen*, suggests in present-day German a flat or an apartment, which is perhaps reflected in the NIV and ESV translation of 'rooms'. However, the underlying Greek noun (*mone*) simply suggests a place to stay; the cognate verb (*menein*) is found in John 15, where it is used of 'abiding' in the vine.

N. T. Wright argued that, in the light of Luke 2:49 and John 1:26, where the expression 'my father's house' refers to the Jerusalem Temple, 'Jesus is using the image of the large Temple complex as a picture of the many "rooms" which will be provided in the heavenly world, for which the Temple is both the early counterpart and the point of intersection.'[4] However, there is no compelling reason for this supposition. Nor is it true that the normal meaning of *mone* is 'of the temporary resting place, or way-station, where a traveller would be refreshed during a journey'. Indeed, as the use of the cognate verb (*menein*) in John 8:35 shows, *mone* suggests 'the permanence, indestructability, and continuation' of the union between God and those who have become children of God through God's

Spirit'.[5] This therefore undermines Wright's assertion that 'the "dwelling places" of this passage are thus best understood as safe places where those who have died may lodge and rest like pilgrims in the Temple, not so much in the course of an onward pilgrimage within the life of a disembodied "heaven", but while awaiting the resurrection which is still to come'.[6] The scholarly consensus is that Jesus was speaking about a permanent future life with God.

Jesus said he would 'go to prepare a place' for his disciples This preparation had nothing to do with making beds and ensuring that everything was in order for future guests. Rather, Jesus prepared a place for his disciples through his death, resurrection and ascension. Then, at God's good time, Jesus said, 'I will come again and will take you to myself, so that where I am, there you may be also' (14:3). Here we have a clear promise of the second coming of Christ, 'although in simpler and more "homey" language (literally so!) than the representations of the event such as those of Mark 13.24–27; 1 Thess. 4.15–18'.[7]

According to Craig Blomberg, an American scholar, Jesus almost 'baits' his disciples by adding 'You know the way to the place where I am going' (14:4).[8] Not surprisingly, Thomas, the loyal but undiscerning disciple (see 11:16), voices the incomprehension of the rest of the group: 'Lord, we do not know where you are going. How can we know the way?' (14:5).

Jesus replied, 'I am the way, the truth, and the life. No one comes to the Father except through me' (14:6). As Thomas's question reveals, here the emphasis is on Jesus being the way: he is 'the true and living way'. This is confirmed by Jesus speaking of coming to the Father through him alone. Within today's pluralistic world, this has proved to be one of Jesus' most controversial statements. How dare Jesus make such a claim? What about Muhammad, Confucius and the Buddha? Indeed, what about Moses? Are they not the way too? Are there not many paths to God? But Wright replied, 'They all provide *a* way towards the foothills of the mountain, not *the* way to the summit.'[9] Those who would like a more inclusive expression of the Christian faith would much prefer Jesus to have referred to himself as 'a way'. However, as Johannine specialist Craig Koester pointed out, 'The difficulty is that the word "the" stubbornly appears before each of the three terms "way", "truth" and "life" in Greek as well as English.'[10] The reality is that Jesus is indeed the one and only way to God. So what about those who have never heard of Jesus? In that regard, Whitacre wisely commented, 'This verse does not address the ways in which Jesus brings people to the Father, but what it does say is that no one who ends up sharing God's life will do so apart from Jesus, the unique Son of God who *is*, not just who conveys, truth and life.'[11]

Sermon: In heaven there is room for all

Over the years, John 14:1-6 has been the inspiration for many of my funeral sermons. On this occasion the deceased was a single lady who had died in her mid-seventies.

Today, as we remember our friend and loved one, Maureen, we can thank God not just for her past but also for her present. For Maureen was a lady possessed of a living faith, and precisely because of that faith, we know that for her death is not the end. On this day, when we are very conscious of our loss, let us focus our minds on the comfort that Jesus can bring. Let us hear again the words of Jesus: 'Do not let your hearts be troubled. Believe in God, believe also in me. In my Father's house there are many dwelling places. If it were not so, would I have told you that I go to prepare a place for you?' (John 14:1-2). On the basis of these words of Jesus, I want to say four things.

First, when Jesus said to his disciples 'In my Father's house are many dwelling places' (14:2), he was effectively saying that in God's house there is room for all. Space is never limited. God never has to put up a 'no vacancies' sign! Or, as an American preacher put it, 'The Father doesn't do downsize.'[12] As far as you and I are concerned, there is a limit to the number of people who can stay with us at any one time. We only have so many bedrooms. But not so in heaven. Heaven never becomes overcrowded. Heaven is as wide as the heart of God, and in heaven there is room for all. Therefore, Jesus said to his friends, 'Don't be afraid. People may shut their doors upon you, but in heaven you will never be shut out.' To us, too, Jesus says, 'Let not your hearts be troubled. Believe in God, believe also in me.' There is room for you; there is room for Maureen; there is room for all.

A second reason not to 'be worried or upset' (GNB) is that Jesus has gone on ahead 'to prepare a place for' us (14:2). How does Jesus prepare a place for us? Remember at what stage these words were said. The cross and resurrection had yet to take place. The preparation which Jesus had in mind was his dying and rising for us all. The letter to the Hebrews speaks of Jesus having gone 'before us (6:20, GNB) 'as a forerunner on our behalf' (NRSV). In the Roman army, the 'forerunners' were the reconnaissance troops. Their task was to go ahead of the main army and blaze the trail; they had to ensure that it was safe for the rest of the troops to follow. Jesus has gone on ahead and blazed a trail through the valley of the shadow of death, and we, through faith, are called to follow him. 'Let not your hearts be troubled,' said Jesus. 'Believe in God; believe also in me.' We can with certainty entrust Maureen to God's safe keeping, for Jesus has prepared a place for her and, indeed, for all those who love him.

A third reason for not being worried and upset is that Jesus will be there with us in the Father's house: 'Where I am, there you may be also' (14:3). People have often speculated on what heaven is going to be like. Some have envisaged themselves twanging on a harp alongside the angels. According to the Qur'an, 'For the god-fearing awaits a place of security, gardens and vineyards, and maidens with swelling breasts' (78:31–34). The fact is that our knowledge about heaven is limited. But there is one thing we do know: heaven is where Jesus is. It is this one thing we can say with certainty about Maureen: she is with Jesus, and she will be with him for ever. 'Let not your hearts be troubled. Believe in God, believe also in me.'

How do we know that all this is true and that Maureen is now with her Lord? Because Jesus assures us that he is the way – the only way – to the Father: 'You know the way . . . I am the way, and the truth, and the life. No one comes to the Father except through me'

(14:4, 6). Jesus doesn't simply show us the way – he is the way. He takes us by the hand and leads us along the way that leads to life eternal. Many years ago, Maureen first put her hand into the hand of Jesus. Today, we rejoice that this same Jesus has finally brought her over into the kingdom of life and light. It is this that makes a difference to our sadness. Maureen, our friend and loved one, is in the Father's house. 'Let not your hearts be troubled. Believe in God, believe also in me.'

Part 3

HOPE IN THE LETTERS OF PAUL

6

Romans 8:31–39

Nothing can separate us from the love of God

[31] What then are we to say about these things? If God is for us, who is against us? [32] He who did not withhold his own Son, but gave him up for us all, will he not with him also give us everything else? [33] Who will bring any charge against God's elect? It is God who justifies. [34] Who will condemn? It is Christ Jesus who died, yes, who was raised, who is at the hand of God, who indeed intercedes for us. [35] Who will separate us from the love of Christ? Will hardship, or distress, or persecution, or famine, or nakedness, or peril, or sword? [36] As it is written,

> 'For your sake we are being killed all day long;
> we are accounted as sheep to be slaughtered.'

[37] No, in all these things we are more than conquerors through him who loved us. [38] For I am convinced that neither death nor life, nor angels, nor rulers, nor things present, nor things to come, nor powers, [39] nor height, nor depth, nor anything else in all creation will be able to separate us from the love of God in Christ Jesus our Lord.

A hymn of victory

Romans 8:31–39 is a great 'hymn' of victory.[1] There is nothing in this world or the next which can separate us from God's love in Christ Jesus our Lord. Many years ago, I argued that there are four verse-like affirmations which in different ways spell out this victory theme.[2]

Affirmation 1 (8:31–32): God is for us

This very phrase is 'a concise summary of the gospel.'[3] 'If God is for us, who is against us?' asks Paul defiantly. 'The note of exuberance and joyous elation is unmistakable,' said the Church of Scotland theologian James Dunn.[4] The force of the question, Dunn went on, 'derives from Jewish monotheism. The confidence is rooted not simply in *some* god being for us, but the *one* God. This is why the answer to the question itself can be left open and does not depend on the answer "No one". There may be many "against us" (see vv. 38–39), but in relation to the one God, they are as nothing.'[5] 'The proof that God is for us is seen in the fact that "he did not withhold his only Son' (8:32). 'The adjective ["only"]', commented Charles Cranfield, a Presbyterian who, like Dunn, was a distinguished New Testament professor at the University of Durham, 'serves to heighten the poignancy of the clause, emphasizing the cost to the Father of delivering up His dearest and most precious.'[6] Almost certainly there is a reference to Abraham who, in turn, did not withhold his only son Isaac (Gen. 22:16). If so, then the 'all things' God will give us probably refers to the inheritance which belongs to those of the 'seed' of Abraham.[7] If not, then it is simply a way of speaking of 'the fulness of salvation' we experience in Christ.[8]

Affirmation 2 (8:33–34): God will vindicate or 'justify' us

Paul switches to the imagery of the law court, where the believers stand before God the judge, accused by Satan (see Job 1 – 2 and Zech. 3:1–2), but defended by the crucified, risen and ascended Christ. 'In that case,' said Paul Achtemeier, 'whatever happens to us that we might construe as showing God's rejection – tribulation or anxiety, persecution or famine, poverty or war – has lost its power to mean that, because God is on our side. Gone for ever the temptation to assume ill fortune is evidence of God's rejection of us!'[9]

Affirmation 3 (8:35–37): No human power can separate us from the love of Christ[10]

Paul mentions seven threatening experiences that Christians might experience: hardship, distress, persecution, famine, nakedness, peril or the sword. Of these seven, Paul had experienced all but the last, although that would finally be his fate under Nero. Paul goes on to quote Psalm 44:22, which shows, said Cranfield, 'that the tribulations which face Christians are nothing new or unexpected, but have all along been characteristic of the life of God's people'.[11] Or, in the words of James Dunn:

> Neither the final death throes of this age, nor the situations of distress where every exit seemed to be blocked, nor the fierce persecution to which Paul was no stranger, nor the cruelly recurring phases known to every community when food supplies and personal resources fail completely, nor the daily risks which lurked round every corner even under Pax Romana, nor the final sword thrust of bandit or enemy soldier or executioner. As Christ himself passed through such suffering to the bitterest end and beyond, so his love reaches back to those still enmeshed within these tribulations, able to sustain them and bring them through to where he is.[12]

'No,' declared Paul, 'in all these things we are more than conquerors through him who loved us' (NRSV, NIV and ESV). Notice how Paul uses a heightened form of the Greek word to conquer: literally, 'we are hyper-conquerors'; 'overwhelming victory is ours' (REB); 'we have complete victory' (GNB); or perhaps, in today's language, 'we are superheroes'! Notice, too, the qualification 'through him who loved us': it is not as a result of our bravery or our determination that the victory is won, but through Christ – and, added Cranfield, 'not even by our hold on Him but by His hold on us'.[13]

Affirmation 4 (8:38–39): No non-human power can separate us from the love of God in Christ Jesus

'I am convinced', said Paul, that nothing can separate us from God's love in Christ. The underlying word is highly instructive: it is a Greek perfect (*pepeismai*), a tense which refers to a past event that remains true in the present. What is more, it is in the passive mood: 'I have become convinced and remain convinced.'[14] Paul's statement here is not a piece of purple prose Paul wrote without thinking; rather, it was a rational, settled and unalterable conviction of his. When it came to the love of God in Christ, for Paul there was no room for doubt and uncertainty. Paul first lists ten non-human threats. Significantly, death heads the list. Perhaps this is because of the reference to death in the psalm Paul has just quoted ('For your sake we are being killed all day long'). However, we can make the more general point that, just as for Paul death was 'the last enemy' (1 Cor. 15:26), so for many today death is the 'great adulterer' who separates us from our loved ones and as such is to be feared.[15] 'Life' perhaps represents 'the trials and distresses, enticements and distractions' which come our way in this world. Paul then lists a series of malign 'cosmic' powers: angels and rulers, things present and things to come, powers, height and depth, and 'anything else'. Commentators often give a good deal of space to distinguishing between the various 'powers', but the truth is that Paul, neither here nor elsewhere, was concerned with their individual identity. As Dunn has said, Paul's concern is pastoral rather than speculative: 'whatever names his readers give to the nameless forces which threaten the Creator's work and purpose, they are in the end impotent before him who is God over all'.[16]

Sermon: God's love is certain

Lloyd belonged to the Windrush generation. He came over to England from Jamaica to find work. A man of solid Christian faith, he had served as a Sunday school teacher, deacon and lay preacher. He died in his mid-eighties.

In one respect, Lloyd and the apostle Paul had a good deal in common. They were both men of conviction. They were both convinced of God's love for them, and indeed for us all.

One of the readings Lloyd chose for today's funeral was from Paul's letter to the Romans, in which the apostle declared, 'I am convinced that neither death nor life, nor angels, nor rulers, nor things present, nor things to come, nor powers, nor height, nor depth, nor anything else in all creation, will be able to separate us from the love of God in Christ Jesus our Lord' (Rom. 8:38–39). Or in the words of Eugene Peterson's paraphrase, 'I'm absolutely convinced that nothing – nothing living or dead, angelic or demonic, today or tomorrow, high or low, thinkable or unthinkable – absolutely nothing can get between us and God's love because of the way that Jesus our Master has embraced us' (*The Message*).

The apostle Paul was absolutely convinced of God's overwhelming love in Christ. 'I am certain,' says the Good News Bible. 'It is my fixed and unshakeable conviction that nothing can separate us from God's love.' When it came to the love of God in Christ, for Paul – as indeed for Lloyd – there was no room for doubt or uncertainty. For both of them, this was the fundamental rock upon which they built their lives.

There are some things Christians do not know or understand. There are some aspects to Christian believing where honesty compels us to say that we are agnostic – we just do not know. As one theologian said, we have no idea of the furniture of heaven or the temperature of hell. Heaven and hell may be realities, but they are realities which are hard to define and where we shall be in for a lot of surprises. But when it comes to the love of God, there is no need for doubt and uncertainty. We only have to look to the cross to see that God loves us – that God is for us. 'God . . . did not withhold his own Son, but gave him up for us all' (Rom 8:32). Or, as Eugene Peterson put it, 'God didn't hesitate to put everything on the line for us, embracing our condition and exposing himself to the worst by sending his own Son' (*The Message*). Yes, the cross is the ultimate proof that the God of this universe is a God of love. 'God', said Paul at an earlier point in his letter, 'proves his love for us, in that while we still were sinners Christ died for us' (Rom. 5:6).

Over the years there have been occasions when, as a pastor, I have not known what to say. I think of the time when I had to comfort a young couple grieving over the death of their baby daughter – their first child. All their hopes had been dashed. They were exceedingly distraught and there seemed to be nothing that I could say. Or I think of the time when I was called out to a home where a mother was dying, leaving behind four children. As the father took his wife to hospital, I stayed to look after the sleeping children. At midnight he returned – his wife was dead. At his request, we knelt down and he asked me to pray. What actually came to mind at that point was to thank God that, in the midst of all life's uncertainties, we could be certain of his love for us.

There are times when we may not feel the love of God around us. There are times when life is a struggle – when a loved one suffers, when death strikes, when injustice has the upper hand – and we wonder where this God of love is. But just as clouds cannot extinguish the sun, neither can even the worst which life has to offer deny the reality of the love of God for us.

The apostle Paul knew this from his own experience. He had had more than his fair share of trouble. He had known hardship, persecution, hunger, poverty and danger (8:35, GNB), but far from these experiences causing him to question God's love, they had caused him to become even more certain of it.

The same was true for Lloyd. Lloyd did not have the easiest of lives. When he came to England from Jamaica, he did not exactly find the Promised Land. There were many times when he suffered prejudice, ridicule and hardship, but none of these difficulties caused him to doubt God's love. Instead, they caused him to throw himself even more upon God and his love. With Paul, he said, 'I am convinced that nothing can separate us from the love of God in Christ Jesus our Lord.'

In particular, Paul and Lloyd were convinced that not even death could separate them from God's love. I find it significant that in Paul's list of things which people of his day feared, death was placed first. Death was and remains the one thing most dreaded of all. The grimmest reality of life is that it must end in death. Or, to personalize it: the grimmest reality of your life and mine is that one day it will come to an end.

People's reactions to death vary enormously. Some do their utmost to banish it from their minds and try never to think of it. Some make light of it, as if it is of no account: everything comes to an end; why should it be otherwise for us? Some see it as the most depressing fact of the universe and, because of it, see no point in life itself.

For people without faith, death is the end. That is why death can be such a fearful prospect. Aristotle, the ancient Greek philosopher (384–322 BC), wrote 'death is the most dreadful of things; for it is the end'.[17] Similarly, Blaise Pascal, the seventeenth-century French philosopher, wrote: 'The last act is tragic, however happy all the rest of the play is; at the last a little earth is thrown upon our head, and that is the end.'[18] Or in the words of a gritty account by British novelist Graham Greene, 'She came out of the crematorium, and there from the twin towers above her head fumed the very last of Fred, a thin stream of grey smoke from the ovens. People passing up the flowering suburban road looked up and noted the smoke; it had been a busy day at the furnaces. Fred dropped in indistinguishable grey ash on the pink blossom; he became part of the smoke nuisance over London, and Ida wept.'[19]

But death need not be the end. Indeed, death is not the end for those who put their trust in Jesus, who died and rose for them. Listen to the apostle Paul: 'I am convinced that neither death, nor life . . . nor anything else in all creation will be able to separate us from the love of God in Christ Jesus our Lord.'

The final word in the sentence holds the clue to Paul's certainty: 'Lord'. For Paul, as for all the Christians of his day, the lordship of Jesus was rooted in the resurrection of Jesus. As Paul says two chapters along in his letter to the Romans, 'If you confess with your lips that Jesus is Lord and believe in your heart that God raised him from the dead, you will be saved' (Rom. 10:9). Jesus is Lord – Lord over death, and Lord of life.

The resurrection is not a one-off amazing feat involving just one man. It is not a Guinness world record – something to be wondered at but not to be emulated. Rather, it was and is a history-making breakthrough involving all who believe. 'Because I live, you will live,' said Jesus to his disciples (John 14:19). On another occasion, Jesus said, 'I am the resurrection and the life. Those who believe in me will live, even though they die' (John 11:25). Or as Paul wrote to the Corinthians, 'Christ has been raised from death, as the guarantee that those who sleep in death will also be raised' (1 Cor. 15:22, GNB). We can liken the resurrection of Christ to a breach in a North Sea dyke – just as, once a hole has been made in the sea defences, the sea comes rushing in, so, once a hole has been blown through death's defences, life comes flooding into the world's wide graveyard.

We know that God loves us because of the cross of Christ. We know that God will love us for ever because of the resurrection of Christ. There is therefore nothing which can separate us from the love of God in Christ. It is this which makes the difference to our mourning today. We may mourn our loss of Lloyd, but we do not mourn his loss. For death, the great separator, has simply taken Lloyd into the nearer presence of his Lord, whom he loved and served for many years.

So, as I bring this address to an end, I believe that Lloyd would have me urge you to listen to the words of Jesus: 'Let not your hearts be troubled. Believe in God, believe also in me' (John 14:1). The truth is that, for those who believe, there is nothing – absolutely nothing in *The Message* – that can separate us from the love of God in Christ Jesus our Lord.

7

1 Corinthians 15:3–5, 20, 24–28, 54–57

Jesus, not death, has the last word

[3]For I handed on to you as of first importance what I in turn had received: that Christ died for our sins in accordance with the scriptures, [4]and that he was buried, and that he was raised on the third day in accordance with the scriptures, [5]and that he appeared to Cephas, then to the twelve.

[20]Christ has been raised from the dead, the first fruits of those who have died.

[24]Then comes the end when he hands over the kingdom to God the Father, after he has destroyed every ruler and every authority and power. [25]For he must reign until he has put all his enemies under his feet. [26]The last enemy to be destroyed is death.

[27]For 'God has put all things in subjection under his feet.' But when it says, 'All things are put in subjection,' it is plain that this does not include the one who put all things in subjection under him. [28]When all things are subjected to him, then the Son himself will also be subjected to the one who put all things in subjection under him, so that God may be all in all.

[54]When this perishable body puts on imperishability, and this mortal body puts on immortality, then the saying that is written will be fulfilled:

'Death has been swallowed up in victory.'
[55]'Where, O death, is your victory?
Where, O death, is your sting?'

[56]The sting of death is sin, and the power of sin is the law. [57]But thanks be to God, who gives us the victory through our Lord Jesus Christ.

Death has been defeated

Here, we shall focus on the theme of death's defeat as seen within the above four passages within 1 Corinthians 15 (vv. 3–5, 20, 24–28, 54–57).

Paul begins his great chapter on the resurrection by reminding the church at Corinth that death has been defeated by God raising Jesus from the dead (15:3–5). He quotes from an early Christian creed which stated:

that Christ died for our sins in accordance with the
    scriptures,
and that he was buried,
and that he was raised on the third day in accordance
    with the scriptures,
and that he appeared to Cephas, then to the twelve.

On closer examination, these four affirmations can be reduced to two propositions: 'Christ died' and 'he was raised'. The 'was buried' and 'appeared to Cephas [Peter], then to the Twelve' simply strengthen these two basic propositions.

First, 'Christ died for our sins in accordance with the scriptures' (15:3). The underlying Greek preposition (*huper*), translated 'for', normally means 'on behalf of' and is usually used of persons, so, for example, 'God proves his love for us in that while we were still sinners, Christ died for us' (Rom. 5:8). What we have in 1 Corinthians 15:3 is probably a form of shorthand, viz. Christ died 'on our behalf to deal with' our sins.

Second, 'he was raised on the third day in accordance with the scriptures.' The passive mood, 'he was raised', indicates that God is the implied subject: Jesus did not so much rise as God raised him and, in doing so, vindicated his death on the cross. The resurrection is God at work. The tense is perhaps even more significant. In the other three lines of this creed, a simple Greek past (*aorist*) is used: he 'died', 'was buried' and 'appeared'. But in this line, the verb is in the Greek perfect (*egegertai*), a tense which expresses a past action with consequences in the present. Christ was raised to life and lives for evermore is the implication. Christ is alive! This Greek perfect is repeated throughout the chapter when Paul is referring to Christ (15:12, 13, 14, 16, 17, 20). The reference to 'the third day' is, in one sense, a simple fact of history. Jesus was crucified on a Friday. Yet, when the women went to the tomb early on the morning of the first day of the week (Sunday), he had risen. What happened was an event, not just an experience. This phrase may also underline the reality of Christ's death: his body lay in a tomb for more than two days and, no doubt, in that time began to decompose. By implication, this fact of decomposition offers hope, for if God could transform his decomposing body when he raised his Son from the dead, he can do the same for us!

Precisely because God raised Jesus from the dead, there is hope for us. Midway through the chapter, Paul declares, 'Christ has been raised from the dead, the first fruits of those who have died' (15:20). Literally, Paul says that Jesus is 'the first-fruits of those who have fallen asleep' (so NIV and ESV). The expression 'the first fruits' recalls the harvest offered daily in the Jerusalem Temple during the seven weeks between Passover and Shavuot (the Jewish Feast of Weeks), a token of a greater harvest to come (see Lev. 23:9–14). It has been suggested that, in using this metaphor, Paul may have been conscious that Jesus rose from the dead about the same time as the first offering of barley was being made – the day after the Sabbath following the Passover. Here, the resurrection of Jesus is a sign to all the world of a great harvest of life to come. To put it another way, 'Christ has been raised from death, as the guarantee that those who sleep in death will also be raised' (1 Cor. 15:22, GNB). Or, in the words of Eugene

Peterson's paraphrase, 'Christ has been raised up, the first in a long legacy of those who are going to leave the cemeteries' (*The Message*).

This leads Paul to look forward to the day when Jesus 'hands over the kingdom to God the Father, after he has destroyed every ruler and every authority and power' (1 Cor. 15:24–28). As Roy Ciampa and Brian Rosner said in their magisterial commentary, the underlying motif here is of a dominion gone astray and needing to be crushed so that the proper dominion might be restored:

> Just as a Roman emperor would send out his leading general to put down seditious movements and rebellious vassal states and restore the emperor's authority throughout the empire, God has sent Christ to subdue all rebellion and opposition, to destroy all the enemies of God's kingdom, and to restore all of creation to its proper submission to the Father for his glory and the good of all creation.[1]

The 'enemies' of which Paul speaks are, in the first instance, the rulers, authorities and powers (15:24), 'those forces of structural or corporate evil that threaten to oppose the reign of Christ or to overwhelm God's people[2] . . . For he must reign until he has put all his enemies under his feet' (15:25). However, the ultimate enemy is 'death', here personified and described as 'the last enemy' (15:26). Contrary to those who believed in the immortality of the soul and viewed death as a friend who freed people from their bodies, Paul refused to make light of death. As the world has yet again discovered through its experience of the coronavirus pandemic, death can be a ruthless enemy. However, death's days are numbered – through the resurrection of Jesus, death has already suffered a mortal blow. As a result, 'sin and death still bring damage and sorrow; but they are no longer decisive forces'.[3]

'The last enemy to be destroyed is death' (15:26).[4] Significantly, Paul uses a present tense: death is being 'destroyed' (*katargeitai*). This may indicate that death is already in the process of losing its power. Alternatively, we may have here a 'prophetic' present – after all, death is still the 'last' enemy!

On that day when death has been subdued and Christ has handed over the kingdom to God the Father, then God will be 'all in all' (15:28): God will be supreme 'in every quarter and in every way'.[5] Creation will have been restored. In the words of Gordon Fee, 'At the death of death the final rupture in the universe will be healed and God alone will rule over all beings, banishing those who have rejected the divine offer of life and lovingly governing all those who by grace have entered into God's "rest".'[6]

As Paul draws his great chapter on resurrection to a close, he looks forward to the day when God's victory over death will be complete (15:54–57): 'Death has been swallowed up in victory' (15:54). Paul is quoting an amended form of Isaiah 25:8, where the word 'victory' has replaced the original 'for ever', a change helped by the fact that, in the Septuagint, the former is a common idiom for the latter. Paul adopted this change because he wished to highlight the victory that is ours in Christ. Significantly, the word victory (*nikos*) is only found three times in all of Paul's letters, and these three occurrences are here in 1 Corinthians 15:54–57.

Paul pursues the theme of victory as 'he mocks the enemy, whose doom has been sealed through Christ's own death and resurrection'.[7] He loosely quotes from Hosea 13:14: 'Where, O death, is your victory? Where, O death, is your sting?' Again, the original Old Testament scripture has been modified to bring out the note of victory. For whereas the Septuagint refers to the 'penalty' of the 'grave', Paul speaks of the 'victory' over death. These slight changes, however, should not cause concern. Paul was not grounding his argument in the Old Testament; rather, his argument was grounded in the 'victory' Christ has already gained in the resurrection.

The 'sting of death' to which Paul refers (15:56) is not some mild irritant, but is like a scorpion's sting (see Rev. 9:10). Christ has drawn out the poison, absorbing it in his own person on the cross. To use the language of Hebrews, in 'tasting death', he has 'destroyed him who has the power of death' (Heb. 2:9, 14). The victory is indeed ours 'through our Lord Jesus Christ' (15:57).

This causes Paul to conclude with a doxology: 'Thanks be to God, who gives us the victory through our Lord Jesus Christ (15:56). The use of the present tense is significant: already the victory is ours. For us, death has already lost its power.

Sermon: We are not helpless!

Alan was a distinguished paediatrician who had just turned seventy when he died of prostate cancer. A man of strong Christian faith, he cared deeply for his patients.

Elisabeth Kübler-Ross, a world-renowned thanatologist, told of an eight-year-old boy who was dying from an inoperable brain tumour. The child expressed his feelings about dying in the pictures he drew. One picture in particular showed his feeling of helplessness. In the background of his picture were a house, sunshine, trees and grass. In the foreground, he drew an army tank. In the front of the barrel of the tank was a tiny figure with a stop sign in his hand. Just as the tiny figure had no hope of stopping the tank, so the boy knew that he had no hope of stopping death. True, sometimes, through pills and potions, through chemotherapy and radiotherapy, and other therapies, we can delay the onset of death but, ultimately, we are helpless – death must have its way.

The good news of Easter Day is that there is one who has come to our rescue. In the words of the early creed of the church, which Paul quotes in 1 Corinthians, 'I handed on to you as of first importance what I in turn had received: that Christ died for our sins in accordance with the scriptures, and that he was buried, and that he was raised on the third day in accordance with the scriptures, and that he appeared to Cephas and then to the twelve' (15:3–5). Like all others before him, Christ died but, unlike all others, he did not die because of his sin but for our sins. There on the cross he took upon himself your sin and mine and, in doing so, Jesus dealt with sin's power. 'Death gets its power from sin' (1 Cor. 15:56, GNB), wrote Paul – but if sin has been robbed of its power so, too, has death. Hence, declares the creed, 'he was raised [to life]'. Death could no longer hold him. Indeed, what is true then remains true today, because the Jesus who was raised to life is alive for evermore. 'He was raised': the Greek perfect tense employed here signifies not just an event in the past but also an event that spills over to the present. Christ was raised to life and remains the risen Saviour. As a result, he is able to offer life and immortality to us all. The 'truth is that Christ has been raised from death, as the guarantee that those who sleep in death will also be raised' (1 Cor. 15:20, GNB). We are no longer helpless. Through the death and resurrection of Jesus, death has lost its power to hurt.

Like Elisabeth Kübler-Ross, Alan was a distinguished medical consultant. However, his speciality was not death but children. As a paediatrician, Alan was familiar with death – many a night he would sit by the bedside of a child dying of leukaemia and, with the parents, wait until death came. But for Alan, death did not have the last word – Jesus did (and does). Because of Jesus, life and not death triumphs.

Alan was a man of faith. His journey of faith had its roots in his childhood. As a young teenager he went to a Christian camp where he had a vision of Christ on the cross, which caused him to give his life to Christ. He later confessed his faith as a fourteen-year-old boy in the waters of baptism. Over the years he sought to share his faith with generations of boys and girls in Crusader Bible classes. He also sought to live out his faith as a doctor. Today, all the hymns were chosen by Alan as an expression of his faith. The reading from 1 Corinthians 15 was also chosen by Alan, to remind us of the resurrection life that is now his. Alan did not believe in death: he believed in life.

Alas, far too much sentimental 'bosh' has been written about the life to come. On one occasion towards the end of his life, I took Alan to the hospital to see an oncologist. While I was waiting, I dipped into a book by Barry Albin Dyer, an undertaker featured in an old TV programme called *Don't Drop the Coffin*. There Dyer tells of an occasion when he once knocked a full cup of tea from his desk on to the floor.

> As I looked at the eight pieces of china it came to my mind that while the cup was no longer a cup. . . the tea was still tea. A mess, to be sure, but still tea. I thought to myself that that is

exactly what happens to us when we die: our bodies break and can no longer be used for their purpose, but our true selves . . . are no longer contained in one place. Instead we spread out, no longer restricted by physical containment, and in some way we go on, too free to be brought to an end, unlike the cup.[8]

If our hope in life after death is based on such kitchen philosophy, then 'we deserve more pity than anyone else in the world' (1 Cor. 15:19). True, Dyer's homespun philosophy does bear witness to the well-nigh universal conviction that there must be more to life than this life – and yet there is no solid basis for such a conviction.

By contrast, the basis of the Christian faith is that life is to be found in the resurrection of Jesus and, as the early Christian creed quoted by the apostle Paul shows, for that there is much evidence. Not only was the tomb empty but also he appeared to Peter and to the Twelve, and to many others too.

God raised Jesus from the dead and, in turn, he will raise all who put their trust in Jesus. In the words of another early Christian creed, 'If you confess with your lips that Jesus is Lord and believe in your heart that God raised him from the dead you will be saved' (Rom. 10:9). In a way that defies all understanding, the resurrection is the guarantee that those who have entrusted their lives to his care will also share in his resurrection. To go back to the story of the boy dying with an inoperable brain tumour, we are not helpless. Through the death and resurrection of Jesus, death has lost its power. Therefore, with the apostle Paul, we may mock death and shout out, 'Where O death is your victory? Where O death is your sting?'

Death will not have the last word – Jesus has the last word. Death, the last enemy, has been robbed of its power. The sting of death has been drawn. Death, therefore, is no longer to be feared, for death is but the gateway into the presence of God himself. It is in this faith which Alan lived and in this faith he died. It is this faith which Alan would have us celebrate today.

Of course, we miss Alan. We wouldn't have loved him if we didn't now grieve for him. Tears are in order. Yet the tears we shed are for ourselves, for Alan, now released from all his physical limitations, is now with the Lord whom he loved and served for so many years.

Let us therefore celebrate and say with the apostle Paul, 'Thanks be to God who gives us the victory through our Lord Jesus Christ' (1 Cor. 15:57).

8

1 Corinthians 15:35–48

We shall be changed

[35]But someone will ask, 'How are the dead raised? With what kind of body do they come?' [36]Fool! What you sow does not come to life unless it dies. [37]And as for what you sow, you do not sow the body that is to be, but a bare seed, perhaps of wheat or of some other grain. [38]But God gives it a body as he has chosen, and to each kind of seed its own body. [39]Not all flesh is alike, but there is one flesh for human beings, another for animals, another for birds, and another for fish. [40]There are both heavenly bodies and earthly bodies, but the glory of the heavenly is one thing, and that of the earthly is another. [41]There is one glory of the sun, and another glory of the moon, and another glory of the stars; indeed, star differs from star in glory.

[42]So it is with the resurrection of the dead. What is sown is perishable, what is raised is imperishable. [43]It is sown in dishonour, it is raised in glory. It is sown in weakness, it is raised in power. [44]It is sown a physical body, it is raised a spiritual body. If there is a physical body, there is also a spiritual body. [45]Thus it is written, 'The first man, Adam, became a living being'; the last Adam became a life-giving spirit. [46]But it is not the spiritual that is first, but the physical, and then the spiritual. [47]The first man was from the earth, a man of dust; the second man is from heaven. [48]As was the man of dust, so are those who are of the dust; and as is the man of heaven, so are those who are of heaven.

The resurrection of the body

'How are the dead raised?' (1 Cor. 15:35). Ultimately, the answer must be if God created the world *ex nihilo*, then in the light of that supreme miracle, everything is possible. To an all-powerful God, the resurrection of the body creates no difficulties. This is what Paul, to all intents and purposes, states right at the beginning of his argument when he writes 'Fool!' (15:36). A fool in the Bible is a person who fails to take God into account (see Ps. 14:1; 53:1; 92:6; Luke 12:16–21). The objection that is being raised is not a sign of ignorance but, rather, a sign of a godless attitude. In the words of Jesus, 'for God all things are possible' (Matt. 19:26; Mark 10:27).

However, here the question is not so much 'How is it possible?' but, rather, 'In what form?' 'With what kind of body do they come?' (15:35). Or in the paraphrase of Eugene Peterson, 'Show me how resurrection works. Give me a diagram: draw me a picture. What does the resurrection body look like?' (*The Message*). Paul answered the question by pointing out that creation itself provides multiple analogies or models of resurrection.

First, there is the analogy of the seed: 'What you sow does not come to life unless it dies. And as for what you sow, you do not sow the body that is to be . . .' (15:35–37). The analogy of the seed illustrates that one living thing, through death, can have two modes of existence. Unlike Jesus' use of the figure of a 'seed' in John 12:24, Paul is not concerned to bring out the necessity of death but, rather, the fact of transformation. Death is not the end; death simply means change. Furthermore, this process of change or transformation is a process which is in God's hands. The divine passive in 15:37 (literally 'what is sown') is clarified in 15:38: 'God gives it a body . . . to each kind of seed its own body.'

Two things here are worthy of comment. First, when Paul writes, 'What you sow does not come to life unless it dies', he implies that, contrary to the common Greco-Roman view, this life is but a shadow of the life to come. In the words of Roy Ciampa and Brian Rosner, 'The afterlife to which Christians ultimately look forward is not like the experience of a leaf after it has died and fallen from a tree only to rot away, but more like the experience of a seed that germinates and then enters into a flourishing life of colour and beauty to which its previous existence is hardly capable of being compared.'[1]

Second, 'it is', said Anthony Thiselton, a heavyweight Anglican theologian, 'the same self, but the same self will assume a different form, namely a glorified mode of existence appropriate to resurrection life'.[2] The Christian understanding of the resurrection of the body is that, along with change, there will also be a continuing sense of identity. The resurrection of the body involves continuity. The same self can pass through differing forms. We see this already in this life where a baby, an infant, a teenager, a middle-aged person and an elderly person can be 'the same self, but their vehicle of expression identity, and communication may differ radically at the same time'.[3]

Then, there is the analogy of different kinds of bodies, each of which is given by God to enable it to adapt to its particular existence: 'All flesh is not the same . . . There are also heavenly bodies and there are earthly bodies' (15:39–41). On the one hand there are different kinds of 'animal' life (humans, beasts, birds and fish); on the other hand, there are different kinds of 'heavenly' bodies (sun, moon, stars). God is not locked into giving his creatures one kind of body. God is a God of infinite creativity and variety.

On the basis of these analogies, Paul concludes, 'So it is with the resurrection of the dead' (15:42). The resurrection will involve transformation into a new kind of body suitable for its new form of existence.

Paul then proceeds to demonstrate that the resurrection of the body will be a superior form of existence. The limitations of this present life, with all its indignities and weaknesses, will be left behind. In four clauses, each repeating the verbs 'it is sown . . . it is raised', Paul contrasts the old with the new (15:42–44). The first three clauses go together and develop the theme that, in the resurrection, we will have new bodies, where all the limitations, frustrations and disabilities of our present bodies will be no more. The fourth clause explains how these changes have come into effect. In the following exposition, it will be seen that I have found the insights of Anthony Thiselton particularly helpful.

In the first place, 'what is sown is perishable, what is raised is imperishable'. 'In this context', wrote Thiselton, '[the Greek word] *phthora* denotes a *process* rather than a *quality*. It denotes *decreasing capacities, increasing weakness*, ready *exhaustion*, and that which finally closes upon itself as *stagnation*'.[4] Scientists tell us that from around the age of twenty-five, the ageing process begins, but becomes very evident as we move into old age. 'By contrast the Greek word *aphtharsia* denotes not simply *negation* of decay, but if decay is a process, the opposite of decay is reversal of decay: *increasing* vitality and strength.'[5] What a wonderful hope that is!

In the second place, 'it is sown with dishonour, it is raised in glory'. According to Thiselton, 'The "humiliation" or "dishonour" (NRSV) may in part allude to the lowly position of the pre-resurrection mode of being in contrast to resurrection splendour, but it may equally, indeed more probably, call to mind that, in the case of fallen humanity, the body has often become a vehicle for unworthy attitudes and actions (see 15:50)'.[6] I am attracted to the GNB translation: 'When buried it is ugly and weak; when raised it will be beautiful and strong', for like the previous couplet it is reminiscent of the ageing process.

In the third place, 'it is sown in weakness, it is raised in power'. Here, again, there could be a reference to old age. In the words of Thiselton:

> One reason why the old, everyday body is beset with 'weakness' is that it is subject to the ravages of time . . . The earthly body is subject to injuries, incapacities, and accidents that may befall it in the *past*. Sometimes this weakness is exacerbated by mistaken or sinful choices made in the past: the abuse of the body through addiction or overindulgence, or the burdens derived from bondage to sin that may produce psychosomatic effects.[7]

Paul then adds a fourth contrast, which is different in character: 'It is sown a physical body, it is raised a spiritual body' (15:44). As commentators point out, the distinction here has to do with 'the difference between ordinary human life and life empowered by God's Spirit'.[8] Or, in the words of N. T. Wright, the adjectives Paul uses describe 'not what something is composed of, but what it is animated by. It is the difference between speaking of a ship made of steel or wood on the one hand and a ship driven by steam or wind on the other'.[9] Or, to quote Thiselton, 'Paul uses the adjective in this epistle to denote that which reflects or instances the presence, power and transforming activity of the Holy Spirit.'[10]

It is precisely because of the transforming power of the Spirit that we cannot equate resurrection with resuscitation – it is transformation. As Paul said, 'flesh and blood cannot inherit the kingdom of God, nor does the perishable inherit the imperishable' (15:50). Some believe that Paul in the first instance refers to the living ('flesh and blood') and then to those who have died ('the perishable'). Alternatively, both expressions may be synonyms. One thing is certain – 'we will all be changed' (15:51), both the living and the dead.

The transformation will be instantaneous. It will take place 'in a moment', literally 'in a moment of time that cannot be divided', 'in the twinkling of an eye', before an eye can blink; the 'trumpet' of the end time will sound (see Isa. 27:13; Jer. 51:27; Zech. 9:14) and 'the dead will be raised imperishable'. For the Christian, here is music to the ears. No wonder this passage formed the basis for one of the most moving passages in Brahms's *German Requiem* (the only Protestant requiem!)

But Paul is not finished. He continues to underline the fact that 'we will be changed' (v. 52): 'This perishable must put on imperishability, and this mortal body must put on immortality' (v. 53). Was Paul just piling synonym upon synonym? Or does the first clause refer to the deceased whose bodies have long since perished, and the second clause to the living who have yet to exchange their 'mortal' bodies to share in the resurrection? Again, the details are unclear, but there is no doubt as to what Paul's overall point is: transformation will be the order of the day.

What will this change look like? Down through the centuries Christians have asked all kinds of questions. If heaven be paradise restored, then will we be like Adam and Eve, naked and without shame? Or will we be wearing the finest of clothes, as befits our new status as citizens of heaven? And how old will we appear? If someone dies in his nineties, will he appear in the streets of the New Jerusalem as an old person, somewhat bent and stiff with age? And if someone dies at the age of ten, will she appear as a child? By the end of the thirteenth century, theologians reached a consensus: as each person reaches their peak of perfection around the age of thirty, so they will be resurrected as they would have appeared at that time – even if they never lived to reach that age.

The fact is that, when it comes to life after death, there are many questions to which we do not know the answer. As Paul wrote in 1 Corinthians 2:9, drawing upon Isaiah 64:4 and 65:17, 'What no one ever saw or heard, what no one ever thought could happen, is the very thing God prepared for those who love him' (GNB). Heaven is beyond our imagining and far more glorious than we could ever dream of. We limit God the moment we begin to try to depict the new world that is coming.

Sermon: Remember – we will all be changed

My mother in her final years became increasingly blind and deaf and dependent on carers. She was a sad shadow of her former self. Then she fell and broke her hip and, in the midst of the COVID-19 crisis, was transferred into a nursing home, where she was bed-bound and eventually lost all cognition. At that point, she was no longer living, just existing. She had well and truly outlived her years. When she died at the age of ninety-eight, it was a 'blessed release'.

The following is the sermon I prepared for her funeral. I would not normally recommend a minister taking his own mother's funeral, but the new minister of her church did not know her, and so my siblings agreed that I should make an exception.

Some seven years ago, when I was visiting Mother, we talked about the hymn she wanted to be sung at her funeral: 'Some Day the Silver Cord Will Break'. It was written by Fanny Crosby (1820–1915), a blind American Methodist poet, who wrote 'Blessed Assurance, Jesus is Mine' and 'To God be the Glory, Great Things He Has Done'. However, most of her other eight thousand or so hymns have been forgotten, including the hymn my mother had chosen, the first verse and chorus of which declare:

Some day the silver cord will break,
And I no more as now shall sing;
But, O the joy when I shall wake
Within the presence of the King!

And I shall see Him face to face,
And tell the story, saved by grace:
And I shall see Him face to face,
And tell the story, saved by grace.

As Mother began to sing the hymn, I was deeply moved and understood why it resonated so strongly with her. Although it was only around 2010 that she began to lose her sight, by 2013 seeing was becoming increasingly difficult for her. The hymn looks forward to the day when we 'shall see Him face to face'. Or, as the last two lines of the final verse declare, on that day 'when my Saviour I will greet, my faith will then be changed to sight'. I am told that Fanny Crosby once said, 'When I get to heaven, the first face that shall ever gladden my sight will be that of my Saviour.'

Every verse of the hymn is full of biblical allusions. The very first line, for instance, is a quotation from Ecclesiastes 12:1–6, where the Teacher declares, 'Remember your creator in the days of your youth ... before the silver chord is snapped' (NRSV). The opening verses of Ecclesiastes 12 are exceedingly gloomy. They are all about the sadness of old age and the inevitability of death. Let me read them to you in the Good News Bible version, which gives clear expression to the complex allegory of death which is present.

So remember your Creator while you are still young, before those dismal days and years come when you will say 'I don't enjoy life' ... Then your arms, that have protected you, will tremble, and your legs, now strong, will grow weak. Your teeth will be too few to chew your food, and your eyes too dim to see clearly. Your ears will be deaf to the noise of the street ... Your hair will turn white; you will hardly be able to drag yourself along, and all desire will be gone.

Old age can be cruel! The Teacher concludes:

The silver chain will snap, and the golden lamp will fall and break; the rope at the well will break, and the water jar will be shattered.
(Eccl. 12:6)

The picture is of the beauty and fragility of the human frame. One day the chain or cord will snap and the rope will break – and that will be that. Here, there is no hope of life beyond the grave. Death is the end. As the Lord said to Adam and Eve after the fall, 'You are dust, and to dust you shall return' (Gen. 3:19; see Eccl. 12:7). The theme is *memento mori* – remember that we will all die! The Teacher is not revelling in the thought of old age and death; rather, he is encouraging his readers to make the most of life – *carpe diem* ('seize the day')!

Thank God that we who read these words today live on the other side of the resurrection of Jesus. The message to 'remember that we will all die' has been transformed for us into a new key: 'remember that we will all live'! In the stirring words of the apostle Paul, set to wonderful music by Handel in his *Messiah*, 'Behold, I tell you a mystery; we shall not all sleep, but we shall be changed in a moment, in the twinkling of an eye, at the last trumpet. The trumpet shall sound, and the dead shall be raised incorruptible' (1 Cor. 15:51, 52).

Death does not have the final word. The risen Lord Jesus has the final word. Then, for those who love the Lord Jesus, all the frustrations and limitations of the past will be over: 'When the body is buried, it is mortal; when raised it will be immortal. When buried, it is ugly and weak; when raised it will be beautiful and strong'

(15:42, 43, GNB). In the words of one commentator, our 'decreasing capacities, increasing weakness, ready exhaustion, and that which finally closes upon itself as stagnation' will be replaced by a new body marked by 'increasing vitality and strength'. Furthermore, our bodies, which 'have often become a vehicle for unworthy attitudes and actions', will then be marked by 'glory'. Our old everyday bodies, which have been 'subject to the ravages of time', will be transformed by the power of God's Spirit.[11]

What a future God has in store for us. We will be changed. Or, rather, Paul says, 'we will all be changed' (15:51), both the living and the dead. We will be together with all God's people. Then, said Jesus, people will come from the East and the West, from the North and the South, and sit down at the great feast in the kingdom of God (Luke 13:29, GNB).

My mother was a very sociable person. She had loads of friends. She was always in the business of entertaining. My memory of growing up is lots of food and lots of friends. But sadly, over the years, those friends died and her world shrank. But now all that has changed. The fact is that in the resurrection, we will be back with all our friends and together with many new friends too. What an amazing experience that will be.

But not only friends will be there: God will be there. God, said Paul, will then 'be all in all' (15:28). Or, as he says in 1 Corinthians 13:12, then we shall see God 'face to face' – and that will be glory. It is precisely because of this hope that, with Fanny Crosby, we can sing not just of the silver cord breaking but also of the waking within the presence of the King. Or, in the words of the chorus, 'And I shall see Him face to face, and tell the story, saved by grace.' It was in that hope that Mother lived, and it was in that hope she died.

9

1 Thessalonians 4:13–18

We will be together

[13]But we do not want you to be uninformed, brothers and sisters, about those who have died, so that you may not grieve as others do who have no hope. [14]For since we believe that Jesus died and rose again, even so, through Jesus, God will bring with him those who have died. [15]For this we declare to you by the word of the Lord, that we who are alive, who are left until the coming of the Lord, will by no means precede those who have died. [16]For the Lord himself, with a cry of command, with the archangel's call and with the sound of God's trumpet, will descend from heaven, and the dead in Christ will rise first. [17]Then we who are alive, who are left, will be caught up in the clouds together with them to meet the Lord in the air; and so we will be with the Lord for ever. [18]Therefore encourage one another with these words.

A royal reception awaits

It would appear that, during his brief stay at Thessalonica, Paul had led the new church there to believe that Jesus would soon return to usher in God's final kingdom and to welcome his people into his presence. But in the few months that had elapsed since Paul's visit, not only had Jesus not returned but also some of the new Christians at Thessalonica had died. These deaths had come as a great shock to many in the church and had caused them to wonder what the future held for their loved ones. In response to their doubts and concerns, Paul wrote to reassure his new converts. In 1 Thessalonians 4:13–18 he points out to them the tremendous future which awaits those who have put their faith in Christ.

Paul tackles the issue head-on. 'We do not want you to be uninformed about those who have died' (4:13), literally about those who 'have fallen asleep' – or, as the NIV puts it, those who 'sleep in death'. In talking about death, Paul uses a euphemism found elsewhere in the New Testament (see John 11:11–13; Acts 7:60; 13:36; 1 Cor. 7:39; 11:30; 15:20). It is tempting to assume that the very euphemism is a pointer to resurrection hope. Certainly, from a Christian perspective, death is as natural as sleeping. Just as sleep holds no terror for anyone, neither need death hold any terror for those who believe, for one day we shall wake up to a new life lived in God's nearer presence. This is a point which John Wyatt, a former English professor of neonatal paediatrics, has developed on more than one occasion.

> I have tried to imagine that feeling of being exhausted and drained after a long and gruelling day, and then, at long last, your head touches that soft pillow. And all you have to do is to give way to sleep, because you know that you are safe, secure and protected. Falling asleep is not something strange or terrifying, it is an experience that our heavenly Father gives us in advance so that we need not be fearful.[1]

Martin Luther is said to have commented, 'I shall go to sleep; and I shall know nothing more until an angel knocks on my tombstone and says, "Time to get up, Dr Luther! Judgment Day!"'[2]

However, it is unlikely that Paul was wanting to make such a theological point. The fact is that this euphemism was not peculiar to the Christian faith: it is found both in the Old Testament (such as Gen. 47:30; Deut. 31:16; 1 Kings 2:10; 22:40) and in the ancient world as a whole. Far from having a positive connotation, it could have a negative thrust. In contemporary paganism, death was viewed as a sleep from which there would be no awaking. The Greek playwright Aeschylus, for instance, referred to death as 'one unending night of sleep' (Eumenides 651). Similarly, the Roman poet Catullus wrote,

'The sun can set and rise again, but once our brief light sets, there is one unending night to be slept through' (Poem 5).

Although some Greek philosophers such as Plato taught a belief in the afterlife, a belief which could also be found in some of the mystery religions of Paul's day, these beliefs were lacking in substance and amounted to little more than viewing the life to come as a poor, second-best reflection of the present. Furthermore, these beliefs were not widespread. For unbelievers in general ('others'), the future held no 'hope' (see Eph. 2:12). According to Theocritus, 'hopes are for the living; the dead are without hope' (Idyll 4:42).

The hopelessness experienced by the pagan world in the face of death is well expressed in a letter of condolence from the second century AD, written to a couple whose son had just died, by an Egyptian lady named Irene, who had suffered a similar bereavement: 'I sorrowed and wept over your dear departed one as I wept over Didymas (her husband? her son?) . . . but really, there is nothing one can do in the face of such things. So, please comfort each other' (Oxyrhynchus Papyri 115). For Irene, as for non-Christians in general, death held within it no silver lining, for all hope of an afterlife was missing. This sense of hopelessness also comes to expression in a letter of Plutarch to a friend whose son has died: there he urges reason as the best cure of grief, in recognition of the fact that all people are mortal (Letter to Apollonius 103F–104A). Seneca in one of his letters, similarly, appeals to reason and scolds a friend for his unseemly display of excessive grief: 'You are like a woman in the way you take your son's death' (Epistle 99.2). In the ancient world there was little more that could be done in the face of death than maintaining, as it were, a stiff upper lip.

This is the background to Paul's exhortation to his readers not 'to grieve like others do who have no hope' (4.13). When Paul's pagan contemporaries grieved, they grieved the fact that death was the end – their loved ones had been cut off from the land of the living and from all the delights that life holds. Christians, who are inspired 'by hope in our Lord Jesus Christ' (see 1:3: 2:19), may mourn for themselves and their own sense of personal loss (see Rom. 12:15; 1 Cor. 12:26), but they do not need to mourn over those who have died in Christ. However, there is, as N. T. Wright has said, 'nothing unchristian about grief, and Paul can refer to grief, including his own, as a Christian phenomenon needing no apology' (see 1 Cor. 7:5–13; Phil. 2:27).[3] Or as G. K. Beale, an American biblical scholar, wrote, we 'should cry with tears of hope'.[4]

The basis of Christian hope is the resurrection of Jesus. Using a form of words which was probably derived from an earlier Christian creed, Paul states, 'We believe that Jesus died and rose again' (4:14). Significantly, Paul never speaks of Jesus as 'sleeping' in death. 'Jesus died' (see also 5:10). The stark truth of that statement underlines the dreadful reality of the death of Jesus, who, when he died, endured the full horror of the wages of sin (Rom. 6:23); it also underlines the mighty miracle of the resurrection.

The corollary of the death and resurrection of Jesus is 'that, even so, through Jesus God will bring with Jesus those who have died' (4:14). Two things call for comment. First of all, Jesus' resurrection will be the model, as is indicated by the expression 'even so' or 'in the same way' (houtos). Second, literally, as the ESV rightly translates, Paul writes of those who have died 'through' (dia) Jesus. The unusual preposition suggests that for those who have died trusting in Jesus, Jesus becomes the bridge between their death and eventual resurrection. Alternatively, it may be that Paul is speaking about dying 'in' Jesus (NIV) – that is, dying 'as Christians' (REB).[5] The implication is that 'in death, believers are not separated from Jesus'.[6]

At this point Paul launches into what is the fullest description of Christ's return in the New Testament, a description which Paul states is 'by the word of the Lord' (4:15). This statement, however, creates difficulties, for there is no known word of Jesus which corresponds exactly to what we have here in 1 Thessalonians 4. The nearest parallel is found in Matthew 24:31: 'He will send his angels with a loud trumpet call, and they will gather his elect from the four winds, from one end of the heavens to the other.' Because there is no closer parallel, some have wondered whether Paul is citing a saying of Jesus not preserved in the four canonical Gospels. Others have suggested that Paul is citing a Christian 'prophecy' uttered in the name of the risen Lord (see, for example, Rev. 16:15). alternatively, rather than alluding to a particular text, Paul may simply be summing up the teaching of Jesus found in the Gospels relating to the return of Christ (see especially Matthew 24:29–31, 40–41) and applying it to the present situation.

As Paul looks ahead to the Lord's return, he distinguishes between two groups: 'those who have died' (4:14) and those who 'are left' (4:15). The impression is that, at this stage, Paul anticipates at least the possibility of belonging to the latter group, for twice he writes of 'we who are alive' (4:15–17), whereas in his later writings he reckons with the possibility, if not the likelihood, of his own death (1 Cor. 6:14; 2 Cor. 4:14; Phil. 1:20). However, we should not make too much of this apparent change of emphasis. For, like Jesus himself, Paul refused to speculate about the timing of the End (5:1). His concern was with the fact of Christ's coming, not 'whether we are awake or asleep' (5:10).

When the Lord returns, 'we who are alive . . . will by no means [an emphatic double negative is used: *ou me*, which the NIV translates as 'certainly not'] precede those who have died' (4:15). It would appear that there were those at Thessalonica who feared that their loved ones who had died in Christ would be at a disadvantage. A similar idea was current in Judaism, that those who were alive at the end of the world would do better than those who were dead (see, for example, Dan. 12:12; also Ps. Sol. 17:50; 2 Esd. 1324). By contrast, as Gene Green, a former professor at Illinois' Wheaton College, rightly commented, Paul stresses that 'the dead in Christ will in no way be excluded from the grand celebration that will surround the Parousia of the Lord, but will enjoy a place of honour'.[7] The dead in Christ will not miss out on anything.

On the great day of resurrection, 'the Lord himself will come down from heaven, with a loud command, with the archangel's call and with the sound of God's trumpet' (4:16). Although there is no direct quotation from the Gospels, there are a number of echoes of the words of Jesus. For instance, the descent of the Lord recalls Jesus' description of the appearing of the Son of Man: 'They will see the Son of Man coming on the clouds of the sky with power and great glory' (see Matt. 24:30; Mark 13:26; Luke 17:24). Similarly, in

Matthew 24:31 (Mark 13; see also Mark 8:38) 'angels' – as distinct from an 'archangel' (of which Jude 9 is the only other reference in the Bible) – are associated with the coming of the Son of Man. There may well be a parallel to the 'loud command' in John 5:25, where Jesus declares 'The dead will hear the voice of the Son of God, and those who hear will live.' 'The sound of God's trumpet' is a frequent feature of Old Testament theophanies (for example, Exod. 19:16; Isa. 27:13; Joel 2:1; Zech. 9:14) and is found in Matthew 24:31: 'He will send out his angels with a loud trumpet call' (see also 1 Cor. 15:52; Rev. 11:15).

It is a moot point whether we should distinguish the loud command from the voice of the archangel and the trumpet call. Probably they are three different ways of expressing the same thought. The loud command is likened to the voice of an archangel (the indefinite article in the original Greek indicates that no particular archangel is in mind) and to the sound of a trumpet. The details are not to be pressed. Ultimately, these events defy description. What we have here is not so much a detailed programme as an artist's impression. Yet, underlying the pictures is essential truth. Christ is coming again in triumph. With an irresistible authority, the Lord will rouse those who are sleeping, 'and the dead in Christ will rise first'. Far from missing out, those who have died 'in Christ' will be the first to experience his glory. 'It will', says Ben Witherington, 'be the ultimate family reunion with the King.'[8]

Then 'we who are alive and are left will be caught up in the clouds together with them to meet the Lord in the air' (4:17). The coming of the Lord is reminiscent of the words of Jesus regarding the coming of the Son of Man, who comes 'in the clouds' (see Matt. 24:30; Mark 13:16; also Dan. 7:13). Clouds are a regular feature of biblical theophanies and are always a symbol of the divine glory (see Exod. 19:16; 24:15–18; 40:34; 1 Kings 8:10–11). The Lord comes in glory.

This coming of the Lord is marked by a 'reunion', when the dead and the living are reunited in Christ. 'We ... will be ... together' (4:17). What a wonderful thought this must have been for the Thessalonians. Heaven is a place of togetherness. Death may separate us from our loved ones, but in Christ we are brought together.

This coming of the Lord in glory is also marked by an event known as the 'rapture'. This word is derived from the Latin equivalent (*rapere*) of the underlying Greek verb (*harpazo*), which often implies violent action (see Acts 8:39; 23:10; Rev. 12:5). Here, the living are 'caught up in the clouds'; they are 'seized' or 'snatched away' by the irresistible power of God 'to meet the Lord in the air'.[9] They too share in the Lord's victory. 'The air' is no longer the place where the powers of evil hold sway (Eph. 2:2), but the place where Jesus is acknowledged as Lord of all.

Traditionally, this verse has been interpreted as the saints marching heavenwards. However, the opposite is the case. Paul is thinking of the Christians going out to meet King Jesus and then accompanying him back to earth. The underlying Greek phrase (*eis apantesin tou kuriou*) was used in Hellenistic times to describe the action of the leading citizens of a town, who would go out to meet a visiting dignitary with a view to then escorting him back to their city. The same phrase is found in Acts 28:15, where Luke describes how Paul was met by the Roman Christians some miles from the city. It is also found in Matthew 25:6, where the bridal party goes out to meet the bridegroom with a view to escorting him back to the wedding banquet. Although it is true that this interpretation is not demanded by the text, it accords with Paul's expectation of a 'creation set free from its bondage to decay' (Rom. 8:21). The fact is that Paul and the early church in general (see 2 Pet. 3:13; Rev. 21:1–10) looked forward to a new order of life in a new world of God's making.

'And so we will be with the Lord for ever' (4:17). This is the climax of Paul's vision of the future, and it contains the heart of the Christian hope. What matters, ultimately, is not the place of meeting, but the being 'with the Lord for ever' (see Phil. 1:23). As Paul makes clear towards the end of his letter, to be with the Lord is to experience salvation from the wrath of God (5:9–10). There, in the presence of the Lord, we are beyond the reach of evil, pain and suffering. It is this new quality of life – life with God – which makes the thought of it being 'for ever' desirable.

'Therefore encourage one another with these words' (4:18; also 5:13) – literally, 'keep on encouraging' one another, for a present imperative is used. Significantly, these words are not addressed to the church's leaders, but to the church in general. Paul encourages his converts to be involved in every aspect of pastoral care (see 1 Thess. 5:14; also 1 Cor. 12:25; Gal. 6:2).[10] Furthermore, as Paul makes clear, pastoral care is not just a matter of listening to others, important as listening may be. Pastoral care also involves the application of Christian truth to living. This truth centres on the resurrection of Jesus and its implications for those who believe.

Sermon: We grieve, but not without hope

This sermon is one that I preached at the funeral of a teenage boy who, at the age of three, had been diagnosed with a genetic disorder which causes the muscles to weaken and degenerate.

On a day like this, what is there to say? What do you say to parents when they have just lost their eighteen-year-old son? When you send a card of condolence, what do you write?

In the second century AD, an Egyptian lady named Irene was faced with this problem. In her letter of condolence to a bereaved couple whose son had died, she wrote that she was very sorry for them in their loss. She went on to say that she had wept over their lost son as she had recently wept over the loss of her own dear Didymas. We don't know who Didymas was. He may have been her husband or her son. She ended her letter, 'But against such things one can do nothing. Therefore comfort one another. Farewell.' What strange words! What possible comfort could they hold? For there was no silver lining Irene could discern in this couple's dark cloud of sorrow. Irene had nothing positive to say. All hope of an afterlife is totally missing.

Thank God, today we have something positive to say to Jonathan's family, for with Jesus there is hope. True, we do not want to minimize the grief that rightly surrounds the death of Jonathan. At any time, losing a loved one is hard, and harder still to lose a son (or daughter), let alone a son aged only eighteen. But, in the words of the apostle Paul, we do not 'grieve as others do who have no hope' (1 Thess. 4:13). It is this element of hope which enables us to call today's service a 'celebration'. For although the tributes have celebrated Jonathan's past, we can also celebrate Jonathan's present and the future. Jonathan was a believer – and where there is faith there is hope.

Sadly, for those who do not believe, there is no hope. Death is the end. Death, for the non-believer, can be a depressing, even dreadful thought. The only way to deal with death is either not to think about it or to laugh about it. But death is no laughing matter. It is a dreadful thing to lose a loved one for ever.

The good news is that our loved ones need not be lost. How do we know this is true? How do we know that this is not wishful thinking? Because of what God has already done in Jesus. In the words of the apostle Paul, 'We believe that Jesus died and rose again, *and so* we believe that God will take back with Jesus those who have died believing in him' (1 Thess. 4:14, GNB). The hope of our resurrection is based on the resurrection of Jesus. Because of what God has done in the past in Jesus, our future is certain – and so, too, is Jonathan's future. This is what we celebrate today. This is why there are colourful balloons everywhere in this church. This is why, instead of singing a funeral dirge, we sing songs of hope and of joy.

Of course, we are sad. In the words of Paul, we 'grieve'. Grieving is part of the cost of our loving. There would be something wrong in our relationship if we did not shed copious tears when a loved one dies. I confess that I too shed a tear when last Sunday week I stood around the hospital bed on which lay the lifeless form of Jonathan.[11]

Grief is the normal response to the loss of a significant person in our lives. What's more, if we don't express our grief, then all kinds of psychological complications can arise. In the words of a Turkish proverb, 'He that conceals his grief finds no remedy for it.' Even for Christians, grief is appropriate. To refuse to face up to the pain of death and to own our own loss is a nonsense. Life for our loved one, now free of his earthly limitations, may now be much better, but we are the poorer for our loss.

However, there is grieving and grieving. Paul says we do not have to grieve as 'others do who have no hope'. For the Christian, death is not the end. In the words of Jesus with which we began this service, 'I am the resurrection and the life. Those who believe in me, even though they die, will live' (John 11:25). For those who have put their trust in the Lord Jesus, there is hope.

The result is that, when we mourn, as mourn we do, we do not mourn so much for our loved ones as for ourselves. The grief we experience, the tears we shed, are over the loss that is ours. There is no need to grieve on Jonathan's account. To quote Paul again, 'We believe that God will take back with Jesus those who have died believing in him' (1 Thess. 4:14). With Jesus there is hope – hope that death is not the end but, rather, the beginning of a new life free from 'mourning or crying or pain' (Rev. 21:4). Jesus makes all the difference! He makes all the difference even on a day like today.

'Therefore', said Paul, 'encourage one another with these words' (1 Thess. 4:18). Unlike Irene of Egypt, we have reason to comfort one another. Yes, we grieve, but not without hope. Even amidst our sadness we have reason to celebrate.

10
2 Timothy 4:6–8

Homeward bound

⁶As for me, I am already being poured out as a libation, and the time of my departure has come. ⁷I have fought the good fight, I have finished the race, I have kept the faith. ⁸From now on there is reserved for me the crown of righteousness, which the Lord, the righteous judge, will give me on that day, and not only to me but also to all who have longed for his appearing.

Passing on the baton

Paul has just given Timothy the equivalent of an 'ordination charge' (4:1–5), culminating with the call to 'Carry out your ministry fully' (4:5); 'discharge all the duties of your ministry' (NIV). Timothy still would have many years of ministry ahead of him. By contrast, Paul knew that he was coming to the end of his time: 'As for me' (4:6 NRSV; also GNB; RNJB), says Paul. Literally, he says *ego*. Paul uses the emphatic first-person singular pronoun to draw a sharp contrast between himself and Timothy. Unfortunately, this contrast is not made clear in the NIV. As Ben Witherington noted, 'Here it appears the baton is actually being passed to Timothy.'[1] Paul's pastoral letters in many ways were an exercise in passing on the baton. He was passing on the lessons of ministry he had learnt to Timothy and to Titus.

'I am already being poured out as a libation' (4:6). Precisely because most people today do not know what a 'libation' or 'drink offering' (NIV; ESV) is, the GNB translates this as 'the hour has come for me to be sacrificed'. However, strictly speaking, a libation accompanied a sacrifice rather than being a sacrifice itself. Paul may be referring to the book of Numbers, where instructions were given on 'drink offerings' in place of blood offerings (Num. 13:5, 7); these drink offerings were the final ritual to the daily animal sacrifice and were poured out at the base of the altar (Num. 15:1–12). Similarly, in the Greco-Roman world of sacrifice, there was also a ritual involving libations. The key point that Paul is making is that the sacrificial process has begun. The verb that Paul uses is in a perfect past tense, which emphasizes the imminence of the end. 'Like a prisoner on death row, he knows that execution day awaits, but it is not immediately at hand.'[2] While he knew that he might still have another winter of imprisonment (hence his instruction to Timothy in 2 Tim. 4:13 to bring his cloak), Paul felt as if he was in the final process of offering his life as a sacrifice. In his letter to the church at Rome, he had described the Christian life as a whole as 'a living sacrifice, holy and acceptable to God' (Rom. 12:1); now the time had come to turn the metaphor into reality and for the sacrifice to be complete.

Today, ministry, in the Western world at least, is different. We do not face the threat of losing our lives in the cause of Christ. Yet, even so, for many ministers, 'sacrifice' is still a term with meaning. Sadly, God's people can behave in such a way that ministry can be a bruising and bloody affair.

'The time of my departure has come' declares Paul. The Greek word translated as 'departure' is *analusis*, from which we get our English word 'analysis'. It denotes a separation of one item from another and can be used to refer to the loosing of a ship from its mooring.[3] This word for 'casting off' was often used as a euphemism for death, which was seen as a journey to the underworld or afterlife. Death was viewed as a transition, not an end itself. Paul uses the cognate verb in Philippians 1:23 where, in the context of death (Phil. 1:21), he states: 'my desire is to depart [*analusai*] and be with Christ, for that is far better'. For Paul, death is the moment when the anchor is weighed, the ropes are slipped and the boat sets sail for another shore – which for Paul is the shore of eternity, where God is to be found.

Commentators have often remarked on Paul's calmness at this point. American Presbyterian Robert Yarborough noted that 'his demeanour is not frantic or fatalistic but composed'.[4] Similarly, American Methodist Thomas Oden wrote:

> Paul's valedictory is filled with quiet joy amid his afflictions. His living faith encourages others to face hazard and death as he did. He exhibited no fear of death in this letter, though he must have known that his approaching execution would be violent – the axeman would have his neck – yet he viewed his departure as release and victory.[5]

Sadly, some Christians find the thought of 'casting off' not easy to accept and, as a result, find it difficult to 'let go' of this life. In the words of a former palliative care specialist

> They continue to talk about getting better in spite of objective evidence of deterioration ... Sadly, often such people 'die badly'. They are like someone standing on a jetty with one foot in a boat and one on land. As the two drift apart, there comes a point where the tension will no longer hold, and in dying patients, this may be resolved by a retreat from reality into confusion and unreachable anxiety. Here the only useful answer could be appropriate sedation.[6]

Dying well involves letting go while holding on to God. The motto of Spurgeon's College, of which I was principal, comes to mind: '*teneo et teneor*'; 'I hold and I am held.'

Paul then makes three 'staccato-like' declarations, where each begins with a direct object and concludes with a perfect tense verb. The word order in Greek runs:

> the good fight I have fought
> the race I have finished
> the faith I have kept

The translation of the first declaration is disputed. The NRSV, along with the NIV, the ESV and the RNJB, has Paul say, 'I have fought the good fight.' However, the GNB and the REB believe that Paul was speaking not of a fight but of a race, which is then expanded into the second declaration. So the GNB reads, 'I have done my best in the race. I have run the full distance'; similarly, the REB translates it as, 'I have run the great race, I have finished the course.' The underlying Greek word (*agon*) is not clear, for it can be used both of a fight and of a race. The commentators are divided, although most appear to believe that Paul had an athletic context in mind.[7] I personally think that Paul was likening the Christian life to a long-distance race, like a marathon, which only ends when life ends.

Whatever the metaphor implies, Paul's overall meaning is clear: the struggle, the effort, the straining of every sinew with every muscle aching, will soon be over. In the meantime, the race still needs to be completed. In this regard the English translations are misleading. The NRSV translation ('I have fought the good fight; I have finished the good race') gives the impression that the struggle is over, whereas the actual tense used is a Greek perfect, which implies a past action that continues into the present. The bell has sounded and there is just one final bout or lap to endure!

As Paul looks back on the contest that has lasted almost three decades and that is now almost over, he is content with his performance: it has been a 'good' contest. Thomas Oden comments, 'He was in effect saying, "I have not dodged the responsibility given to me. I have not gone about it half-heartedly. I have been given a race to run. I gave it my all."'[8]

This leads Paul then to make his third declaration: 'I have kept the faith.' Again, here is a Greek past perfect: this is not a one-off event in the past, but a past action which continues into the present. Paul has kept and continues to keep the faith. He has been true to the faith which was entrusted to him and which, in turn, he then entrusted to Timothy.[9] What God had called him to do, he had done. He had been faithful to the last.

In declaring 'I have kept the faith', Paul was not boasting, but was saying, as it were, 'Thank God, I kept the faith.' According to Thomas Oden:

This was not self-adulation but thanksgiving for grace to finish the race, for the joy of having been enabled to ensure the whole contest. He was not boasting of his having won the race on his own, nor egocentrically pointing to his own courage or achievements. Rather he was pointing to the grace of God which had enabled the struggle.[10]

From looking backwards, Paul turns to look forwards: 'From now on there is reserved for me the crown of righteousness' (4:8). In athletic contests of ancient Greece, victors were awarded a laurel wreath. The prize here, however, is no laurel wreath, but eternal life – life lived in the presence of God, together with all those who have gone ahead of us. On the basis of this imagery, the English Puritans used to describe the day of their death as their 'Coronation Day'.

But in what respect is this a 'crown of righteousness'? There are two different ways of interpreting the Greek genitive, and scholars disagree as to what Paul meant. Is it a crown that consists in final righteousness? Paul, for instance, wrote in Galatians 5:5, 'For through the Spirit by faith we eagerly wait for the hope of righteousness.' This is what the GNB understands Paul to say and so it renders this phrase 'now there is waiting for me the victory prize of being put right with God'. Or is it the crown that is the reward for righteousness? James, for instance, wrote, 'Blessed is anyone who endures temptation. Such a one has stood the test and will receive the crown of life that the Lord has promised to those who love him' (Jas 1:12), and Peter wrote, 'When the chief shepherd appears, you will win the crown of glory that never fades away' (1 Pet. 5:4). The truth is that either interpretation is possible.

What is certain is that this crown will be given by 'the Lord, the righteous judge' (4:8). There is a degree of irony here, for Paul was about to stand before an unrighteous judge, who would condemn him to death. However, 'He was confident that the higher court would reverse the judgment of the lower court. Whereas the verdict of the lower court was to be death, the higher court's verdict was life, life with endless parole.'[11]

What's more, this crown of righteousness is not reserved for the great athletes of the faith like Paul, but is for 'all who have longed for his [the Lord's] appearing' (4:8). In a normal race, there can be only one winner, but here, all are champions – or, at least, all who persevere to the end!

Sermon: Free at last

This sermon was preached at the funeral of a close friend who had developed dementia in his late seventies.

Alan was one of the most thoughtful and challenging people I have ever met. A brilliant Oxford graduate, he had worked in the chemical industry before becoming the administrator of the Manchester Business School. Alan constantly challenged me and made me think. Alan was a wonderful man who proved to be a means of blessing to many. My task is not to give a eulogy, though, but to minister God's grace. When it came to choosing a passage of Scripture, my mind immediately went to 2 Timothy 4:6, where Paul says, 'The time of my departure [*analusis*] has come'. He uses the same metaphor in his letter to the church at Philippi: 'For me, living is Christ and dying is gain . . . I am hard pressed between the two: my desire is to depart [*analusai*] and be with Christ, for that is far better' (Phil. 1:21–23). In both passages Paul speaks of death as a time of departure.

As a chemist, Alan might have found it interesting that Paul uses the Greek word '*analusis*', from which we get our English word 'analysis', which involves a separating of items from each other. It is also a word which denotes the loosing of a ship from its moorings, but was often used, too, as a euphemism for death. In the ancient classical world, the passage into the afterlife was viewed as a voyage down the River Styx into the underworld. Coins were placed on the eyes of the deceased to pay the ferry pilot, who would give the dead person passage into the afterlife. Over against the pagans of his day, Paul had a much more positive view of the world to come. The journey Paul faced was a journey across the sea of death into the haven of eternity where, on his arrival, he would be 'with Christ'.

Charles Henry Brent (1862–1929), a former bishop in the American Episcopal Church, got to the heart of the seafaring metaphor when he wrote:

> What is dying? I am standing on the seashore. A ship sails into the morning breeze and starts for the ocean. She is an object of beauty and I stand watching her till at last she fades on the horizon and someone at my side says, 'She is gone.' Gone where? Gone from my sight, that is all. Just at the moment when someone at my side says 'She is gone,' there are others who are watching her coming, and other voices take up a glad shout, 'There she comes,' and that is dying.

But is there more to the metaphor? I believe there is. To unloose the moorings of a boat is to set it free to sail away. When Paul was writing to Timothy, his ship was still tied up. But, coming towards the end of his life, he longed to cast anchor – to unloose his moorings – and sail away. He wanted to be free of all life's restrictions and limitations. He wanted to leave this world for the next.

Surely the same must have been true for Alan. After years of increasing dementia, death for him was a 'blessed release'. Death for Alan marked the moment when the restrictions of this life were over. To paraphrase the words of Martin Luther King's epitaph, Alan is now 'Free at last, free at last. Thank God Almighty he is free at last.'

The fact is that our bodies do ultimately wear out; we are but mortal beings. I am told that from about the age of twenty-five, we are all wearing out. But, thank God, there is more to life than this life. For those who have put their trust in Jesus, there is another world to enjoy, a world free of physical restriction, a world lived in the very presence of God. Death is but a setting sail for a new and better world, and loved ones and friends, who have gone on ahead, are waiting to greet us.

Part 4

HOPE IN THE REST OF THE NEW TESTAMENT

11

Hebrews 6:17–19

Our hope is sure and certain

[17]When God desired to show even more clearly to the heirs of the promise the unchangeable character of his purpose, he guaranteed it by an oath, [18]so that through two unchangeable things, in which it is impossible that God would prove false, we who have taken refuge might be strongly encouraged to seize the hope set before us. [19]We have this hope, a sure and steadfast anchor of the soul, a hope that enters the inner shrine behind the curtain.

Our hope is sure

Hope, it has been said, runs as 'a scarlet thread' throughout Hebrews. There are five separate passages where the writer uses either the noun hope (*elpis*) or the cognate verb to hope (*elpizo*). Three of the references to hope are about the need to persevere.

- Hebrews 3:6: 'We are his [God's] house if we hold firm the confidence and the pride that belong to hope.' Or, as the NIV translates it, 'We are his house, if indeed we hold firmly to our confidence and the hope in which we glory.' In Hebrews, this hope relates to God's promises, which are centred on Jesus. The confidence derived from this hope enables Christians, wrote the Australian scholar David Peterson, 'to endure opposition and suffering with the certainty of a rich reward (10:35)'.[1]
- Hebrews 6:11: 'We want each one of you to show the same diligence so as to realize the full assurance of hope to the end.'

Here the recipients of the letter are encouraged to persevere in serving the saints (6:10) 'in order to make your hope sure' (NIV).

- Hebrews 7:19: 'There is . . . the introduction of a better hope, through which we approach God.' As Peterson noted, this hope is better because 'the outcome has already been achieved'.[2]

The need to persevere (see Heb. 12:1) also underlies Hebrews 11, with its great list of faith's heroes. These men and women of faith 'desire a better country – that is, a heavenly one. Therefore God is not ashamed to be called their God; indeed, he has prepared a city for them' (11:16). Here, something of the Christian hope is spelt out, even though the word 'hope' does not appear. Significantly, right at the beginning of this 'roll call' of faith, the relationship between hope and faith is defined.

- Hebrews 11:1: 'Now faith is the assurance [*hupostasis*] of things hoped for, the conviction [*elegchos*] of things not seen.' Or, as the NIV puts it, faith is 'confidence in what we hope for and assurance about what we do not see'. Through the use of these two terms, the author emphasizes the objective certainty of faith.

In other words, to say 'I believe' is the same as saying 'I am sure', 'I am certain.' In particular, we can be 'sure of the things we hope for' (GNB). In our use of the word today, 'hope' is often a synonym for uncertainty: for example, we hope that we will have good weather when we go away on holiday, but we can't be sure, especially if we holiday in Great Britain. But in the Bible, 'hope' is a synonym for certainty. To say that, as Christians, we have the hope that one day we shall spend eternity with Christ is not wishful thinking but a definite expectation.

How can we be so sure? It is precisely because of what God in the past has done for us in Christ that we can be certain of the present and of the future. This understanding of faith is found in Hebrews 6:18–20, which will form the rest of this study. God's promise to Abraham, confirmed by his oath:

strongly encouraged [us] to seize the hope set before us. We have this hope, a sure and steadfast anchor of the soul, a hope that enters the inner shrine, behind the curtain, where Jesus, a forerunner on our behalf, has entered . . .
(Heb. 6:18–20)

Here, the writer likens our hope in God to 'a sure and certain anchor of the soul' (6:19). Our hope is 'sure and steadfast' (ESV), 'firm and secure' (NIV) or, in the words of the REB, it is 'safe and secure'. Just as an anchor secures a ship to the ocean floor, so our faith links us securely with God. Faith is not just believing that God exists; it is also about anchoring ourselves to that God and knowing that we are secure in him, both for now and for eternity. Whatever storms life may bring, both in living and in dying, we know that the anchor of faith will hold us firm in God. In the context of one in four people experiencing mental ill health, Rob Merchant wrote:

> For a man [sic] who cannot see the half-full glass, knowing there is hope that despair can never overcome, never suck dry, is vital. Like the sun above us, hope in Jesus, our anchor of hope, is constant, vital, life-giving, warming to the very soul, and is always present regardless of whether we see it or not.[3]

Where did the Christians get the idea to use an anchor to symbolize their faith? The truth is that the anchor was a familiar literary metaphor in the classical world, used to depict the concept of security. The Roman poet Virgil, for instance, spoke of 'the firm grip of the anchor's teeth holding the ship fast' (*Aeneid* 6:3–5) – the anchor in question would have been an iron anchor with two wings rather than an ancient stone anchor. The Roman writer Heliodorus said that 'every hope is an anchor' (*Aethiopica* 8.6.9).

What is more, as Witherington has pointed out, this hope is not just an object: 'it becomes a person – Jesus – who has passed through the veil into the very presence of God'.[4] Significantly, the writer of Hebrews went on to describe Jesus as 'a forerunner on our behalf' (6:20 NRSV; similarly NIV and ESV). This is the only place in the New

Testament where the word 'forerunner' (*prodromos*) is used. In the Septuagint and other Greek literature, it refers to the herald who goes before a dignitary, an advance scout who goes before the army or the first fruits that foreshadowed or presaged the full crop. The term is frequently used for a person sent ahead by Caesar to find a camp for the rest of the army. Witherington noted, 'The sense is not just someone who arrives in advance to announce that others will follow, but it is someone who does something once he arrives to help accommodate or prepare for those who follow.'[5] In the context of Hebrews 6:20, this means that Jesus as 'a high priest for ever according to the order of Melchizedek' has prepared a place for us through his death and resurrection. More generally, we can say that Jesus has blazed a trail for us through the valley of death. It is his action as a forerunner that gives substance to our 'hope'.

Sermon: We have an anchor

The largest uniformed youth organization in the UK is the Boys' Brigade. Founded in 1893, it is similar to the Scouts but, unlike the Scouts, has to be church-based. George, whose funeral it was, and who had died in his nineties, had maintained a lifelong commitment to the Boys' Brigade.

Anchors come in all shapes and sizes. An anchor is a heavy weight, normally made of metal, used to connect a boat or ship to the bed of a body of water for the purpose of preventing the vessel from drifting due to wind or current. Used symbolically, an anchor reflects that which provides stability, confidence and certainty.

When I was young, I belonged to the Life Boys. Every Monday evening, I went down to our local Baptist church wearing a sailors' blue jersey and a round sailors' hat. On the jersey I wore a large brass badge featuring an anchor, the logo of the Boys' Brigade, of which we were the Junior Section. Although Life Boys are no longer, the Boys' Brigade continues, with its younger members now called Anchors.

Why do I mention this? Because, as a boy, George, whom we remember today with great affection, was a member of the Boys'

Brigade. He became a BB officer. Even when he was no longer a BB officer, he wore a small badge featuring an anchor in his buttonhole. Like any other member of the BB, he knew the motto 'Sure and steadfast', taken from the letter to the Hebrews, where the writer likens the Christian hope in Jesus as 'a sure and steadfast anchor of the soul' (Heb. 6:19, NRSV). Or, as the GNB translates it, 'We have this hope as an anchor for our lives. It is safe and sure.'

George, in his BB days, would have attended the monthly church parade services, where the Boys' Brigade hymn would have featured frequently. The hymn begins:

> Will your anchor hold in the storms of life,
> When the clouds unfold their wings of strife?

And ends:

> Will your eyes behold through the morning light
> the city of gold and the harbour bright?
> Will you anchor safe by the heavenly shore,
> When life's storms are past for evermore?

To this, the chorus replies:

> We have an anchor that keeps the soul
> steadfast and sure while the billows roll;
> fastened to the rock which cannot move,
> grounded firm and deep in the Saviour's love.

Today, anchor symbolism has largely fallen out of use – it all sounds very old-fashioned. However, up until around AD 300, the anchor was one of the primary Christian symbols. It was a secret sign of Christian believing. To quote American songwriter and singer Michael Card:

> If I'm a first- century Christian and I'm hiding in the catacombs and three of my best friends have just been thrown to the lions

or burned at the stake, or crucified and set ablaze as torches at one of Nero's garden parties, the symbol that most encourages me in my faith is the anchor. When I see it, I'm reminded that Jesus is my anchor.[6]

In the catacombs in Rome, where the early Christians were buried, anchors abound. In the cemetery of St Priscilla, for instance, some seventy examples of anchors are to be found.

It was as a young BB member that George became a follower of Jesus. He was a man of faith and a man of hope. His hope in Jesus crucified and risen served as 'a sure and steadfast anchor' to his soul. What a difference Jesus made to him – to his living and to his dying. It meant that he could face death with confidence, knowing that death would not be the end but, rather, the gateway into a new and fuller life. Thank God, the Christian hope is 'sure and steadfast'.

12

1 Peter 1:3-8

We have a living hope

³Blessed be the God and Father of our Lord Jesus Christ! By his great mercy he has given us a new birth into a living hope through the resurrection of Jesus Christ from the dead, ⁴and into an inheritance that is imperishable, undefiled, and unfading, kept in heaven for you, ⁵who are being protected by the power of God through faith for a salvation ready to be revealed in the last time. ⁶In this you rejoice, even if now for a little while you have had to suffer various trials, ⁷so that the genuineness of your faith – being more precious than gold that, though perishable, is tested by fire – may be found to result in praise and glory and honour when Jesus Christ is revealed. ⁸Although you have not seen him, you love him; and even though you do not see him now, you believe in him and rejoice with an indescribable and glorious joy.

A cascade of praise

'Blessed be the God and Father of our Lord Jesus Christ!' (1 Pet. 1:3). Peter begins his first letter on a wonderful note of praise. Praise just cascades from his lips, leaving him almost no time to breathe – or at least no time to put in a full stop. In the original Greek, the ten verses that run from 1:3 – 1:12 are but one sentence. Peter declares that God is to be 'praised' (NIV) because of what he has done for us in Jesus. God is the 'primary actor',[1] for he it is who gave us new life, raised Jesus from the dead and has reserved an extraordinary inheritance for us. No wonder he is worthy of praise!

If the apostle Peter indeed be the author of this letter – and certainly the very first verse of the letter would indicate that this was the case – then it is not surprising that these opening verses are dominated by the theme of resurrection, for, according to Luke, Peter's early preaching was dominated by the resurrection of Jesus (such as Acts 2:24, 31–32, 36; 3:15, 26; 4:2, 10).

It is significant that, in this opening hymn of praise, God is defined as 'the God and Father of our Lord Jesus Christ' (v. 3).[2] Jesus is not declared as the Son of God but, rather, God is described as the 'Father of our Lord Jesus Christ'. It is not that the Son has usurped the place of the Father but, rather, it is the Son who makes the Father known. All truly Christian preaching has therefore to begin with Jesus.

Jesus is described as 'our Lord Jesus Christ'. Is Peter here already anticipating the theme of resurrection? For, as Peter declared on the Day of Pentecost, it was through raising Jesus to life that God 'made this Jesus both Lord and Messiah [Christ]' (Acts 2:36). Jesus is Lord precisely because God raised him from the dead (see Rom. 10:6). Of interest is the possessive pronoun 'our'. Peter underlines the special bond not only between him and his Lord but also between the Lord and all those who 'love him' (1:8). The Christian religion is a personal religion. Christians do not, in the first place, believe in a set of doctrines. They believe in the Lord who 'loved them and gave himself for them' (see Gal. 2:20).

Perhaps because of his own personal experience of having let Jesus down, Peter was mindful of God's 'great mercy' extended to him (see also 2:10). However, the truth is that none of us deserves the new beginning that God has given us in Christ. Here in itself is cause for praise.

'He has given us a new birth into a living hope through the resurrection of Jesus Christ from the dead.' God, in raising Jesus from the dead, brought not only new life to his Son but also to all those who have 'faith' (1:5). Although the 'hope' of life beyond the grave remains only a hope, God has already transformed the lives of those who believe. Peter uses a simple past (aorist) participle to indicate that God 'has caused us to be born again' (*anagennesas*). Within the

New Testament, this Greek verb (*anagennan*) is only found here and in 1:23, but is closely related to the Greek expression found in John 3:3, 7 (*gennan anothen*), where Jesus talked to Nicodemus of the necessity of being 'born again' if he were to 'see the kingdom of God'. This 'new birth' is a dramatic metaphor to describe the transformation which takes place when we put our faith in Jesus. Peter, said American New Testament scholar Joel Green, announced 'a conversion of imagination', which involves 'personal reconstruction within a new web of relationships, resocialization within the new community and the embodiment of a new life-world evidenced in altered dispositions and attitudes'.[3]

In 1 Peter 1:3, the means God uses to bring about the new birth is 'the resurrection of Jesus Christ from the dead', whereas in 1 Peter 1:23, the means is 'the living and enduring word of God'. In reality, there is little difference between the two, for 'the living and enduring word of God' is the gospel message of resurrection. When the preaching of the message of the resurrection encounters faith in the heart of the hearers, then the radical process of new birth takes place.

It is important to note that faith, first and foremost, is centred on the risen Lord Jesus and on the life that he offers. Faith looks back to Easter Day and looks forward 'in hope' to the coming of the kingdom of God. This theme of hope finds repeated expression in 1 Peter, which has been described as 'a letter of hope in the midst of suffering, an affirmation of the resurrection under the terror of death'.[4] It is a 'living hope', in the sense that it has been engendered by the resurrection of Jesus and remains focused on the resurrection life that is in Jesus.[5] As for the other references to hope, in 1:13, Peter urges his readers to set their 'hope fully on the grace Jesus Christ will bring you when he is revealed' and when, in turn, the kingdom of God is to come in its resurrection fullness. A few sentences later, Peter specifically links together the twin concepts of faith and hope with the resurrection as he declares, 'God . . . raised him [Jesus] from the dead . . . and so your faith and hope are in him' (1:21). The theme of resurrection is absent when Peter mentions 'the holy women of the past' who 'put their hope in God' (3:5). However, undoubtedly the message of the resurrection was in his mind when he goes on to identify the Christian faith with 'hope': 'Always be ready to make your defence to anyone who demands from you an accounting for the hope that is in you' (3:15). The hope in question is our hope anchored in the resurrection of Jesus and is therefore 'the reason for the hope' (NIV) that we have.

It was this 'hope' in the resurrection which separated the Christians from their non-Christian neighbours. The non-Christian world at that time was a world 'without hope and without God' (Eph. 2:12). Death was a force to be dreaded. Sophocles, for instance, in 'Oedipus at Coronus', said, 'Not to be born at all – that is by far the best fortune; the second best is as soon as one is born with all speed to return thither one has come.' In the words of an epitaph found on a tomb just off the Appian Way that led to Rome, 'The sun will rise and set, but it is eternal darkness for me.'

By contrast, Christians were able to face death in the 'sure and certain hope' of resurrection. Peter describes the 'blessings' (GNB) to come as 'an inheritance that is imperishable, undefiled, and unfading' (1:4). It is 'imperishable' in the sense that it cannot decay with age: the life God has for us in Christ will never come to an end. It is 'undefiled' in the sense that it cannot be spoilt by sin: the life God has for us in Christ is perfection itself. It is 'unfading' in the sense that it cannot be debased with the passing of time: the life God offers in Christ will never lose its value.

These blessings are 'kept for you in heaven'. Peter employs a Greek perfect passive participle (*teteremenen*) to indicate a past action with results that continue into the present. The participle can have the sense that this life has been indefinitely reserved for the people of faith. Alternatively, it can have the sense that this life in heaven will remain immune from disaster (see Matt. 6:19–20; Luke 12:33).

Furthermore, this resurrection hope belongs to men and women of faith who 'are being protected by the power of God through faith for a salvation ready to be revealed in the last time' (1:5; see also 1:20; 4:7). Or in the words of the NIV, we are 'shielded' through our faith. Peter employs a military term to describe the security of Christian believers and, in so doing, uses a present participle (*phrouroumenos*).

The implication is that God's power remains in constant guard over those who put their trust in the God of resurrection. Indeed, it is the power that raised Jesus Christ from the dead which is the power that ensures the safety of those who have been born again.

'In this you rejoice' (1:6). It is the experience of God's resurrection power at work in the lives of those who have faith as also the hope of resurrection to come that is the cause ('in this') for great rejoicing, in spite of present 'trials' (1:6). Future joy outweighs the present grievous 'suffering'.[6] Joy was the mood of Easter (for example, John 20:20). Joy, too, was the hallmark of the early church, itself a community of resurrection (see Acts 2:46; also 4:16; 5:41; 16:34). Peter gives expression to an intensity of joy. The verb (*agalliao*) used here and in 1:8, is found in the opening lines of the Magnificat, where Mary cries out, 'My soul magnifies the Lord and my spirit rejoices in God my Saviour' (Luke 1:46–47). Although the underlying Greek (*agalliate*) could be an imperative ('Rejoice!'), almost certainly we have here the indicative. Those to whom Peter was writing did not have to be told to be joyful. They already 'greatly' rejoiced (NIV).

Peter was able to take a positive view even of present 'trials' (1:6). These have come 'so that your faith . . . tested by fire . . . may be found to result in praise and glory and honour when Jesus Christ is revealed' (1:7). For Peter, even the darkest of clouds can have a silver – or, rather, a golden – lining. The picture is of God refining faith as a goldsmith might refine gold: the end product is so much better; it is now free of impurity (see Ps. 66:10; Prov. 17:3; 27:21; Zech. 13:9; Mal. 3:3). Faith is 'more precious than gold' because one day even gold will perish (see also 1:18). No wonder Peter and his fellow believers rejoiced!

Peter elaborates on this joy, a joy which has its roots in a love for the risen Lord Jesus, unseen and yet present by his Spirit. 'Although you have not seen him, you love him; and even though you do not see him now, you believe in him and are filled with an indescribable and glorious joy' (1:8). Unlike Peter (see 2 Pet. 1:16), the Christians to whom he wrote had never had the privilege of physically seeing the Lord Jesus, yet they had come to 'love him'. Here is a reminder that the Christian faith is primarily a relationship and not a philosophy or a moral code. Until the day when they will indeed see him 'face to face' (1 Cor. 13:12), they 'now' are called to 'believe' in him. It is difficult to suppose that Peter was not alluding to the words of the risen Lord Jesus after Thomas's encounter with him: 'Have you believed because you have seen me? Blessed are those who have not seen and yet have come to believe' (John 20:29). As a result of their relationship with the risen Lord Jesus and the hope that is theirs in him, they 'exult with a joy which is beyond description and which is shot through with that glory which belongs to God himself' (1:8).[7] 'True joy', said American Presbyterian Lewis Donelson, 'comes from heaven.'[8] It is 'too great for words' (REB); it is 'inexpressible' (NIV, ESV).

This joy is deepened all the more because, as a result of their faith in the risen Lord Jesus, they are 'receiving . . . the salvation' of their 'souls' (1:9). Peter employs a present participle (*komizomenoi*): their future salvation is already in the process of being worked out in the present. Already they have been born again; however, their 'hope' of sharing in the resurrection of Jesus has yet to be realized. The 'salvation of your souls' is the nearest to which Peter comes to the Pauline doctrine of the resurrection of the body. The soul for Peter has the Semitic sense of the essential self and he refers to humans as 'living beings' (see Gen. 2:7). Or as N. T. Wright wrote:

> It denotes not . . . an 'immortal' element which all human beings automatically possess, a 'soul' which looks forward to the great day when it will be freed from physicality, but that aspect of the human being, renewed secretly and inwardly (rather like the 'inner human' in 2 Cor. 4:16), which carries the promise that is to be worked out in the entire human person.[9]

What a wonderful hope! No wonder Peter pours out a cascade of praise!

Sermon: The hope of glory

An African friend asked if I would take the funeral of her father. He had been a successful engineer in Uganda, but had died in the UK just after his eightieth birthday. Like many Africans, he had a strong Christian faith.

Today we have come to give thanks for the life of our friend and loved one, Michael. Alas, I never knew him. Yet, as I was preparing my address, I suddenly realized that we could have passed one another in the streets of Kampala. For, many years ago, when Idi Amin was still in power, my wife Caroline and I, together with our sons Jonathan and Timothy, drove through Uganda and stayed two nights in Kampala. I was twenty-six years of age, and Michael was probably thirty-five years old. At the time, Michael was a distinguished civil engineer in Kampala, engaged in the construction of many major public buildings in Uganda.

However, my task today is to speak not about Michael, but about the hope of glory that is ours. Today's service has been billed as 'a celebration of faith, hope and love'. Hope was central to Michael's faith. When, many years ago, he committed his life to the Lord Jesus, he was given 'a new birth into a living hope through the resurrection of Jesus Christ from the dead' (1:3).

But how confident can we be of this hope? What makes Christian hope any different from any other hope? It has been said that probably nothing in the world arouses more false hope than the first four hours of a diet!' How can we be sure that this hope of life beyond the grave is any more certain than the promises made by dieticians, politicians, second-hand car salesmen and the like?

Because God raised Jesus from the dead. Let me read again the words of the apostle Peter: 'Blessed be the God and Father of our Lord Jesus Christ! By his great mercy he gave us a new birth into a living hope through the resurrection of Jesus Christ from the dead' (1:3). Our hope of future life is based on the resurrection of Jesus.

Andrew Brown, a *Guardian* columnist, described 'the idea of resurrection into eternity' as 'nonsense in earthly terms'.[10] And, of course, in earthly terms it is nonsense! When we die, we die. Death is the law of life. But God, through raising Jesus from the dead, has brought in a new law of life beyond death. As one critic put it, 'What Brown hasn't allowed for is that pesky illogical Christian logic.'[11]

Peter expressed his certainty in the Christian hope by using three negative adjectives to describe the 'blessings God has in store for his people' (1:4). They are, first, 'imperishable': the blessings of the life to come cannot decay with age. My poor old teeth seem to be rotting away. However much I clean them, they cannot stand the ravages of time. But the life God has for us in Jesus will never decay, will never come to an end. The second is 'undefiled': the blessings of the life to come cannot be spoilt by sin. How this contrasts with your life and mine. Let's be honest, our lives have been spoilt, both by our own sinfulness and by the sinfulness of others. But the life God has for us in Jesus is perfection itself. Finally, 'unfading': the blessings of the life to come cannot be debased with the passing of time. What with inflation, any money we put on one side seems to have so little value. Years ago, a salary of £1,000 was regarded as a small fortune; today it would be a mere pittance. But the life God offers us in Jesus will never lose its value. In addition, Peter writes that these blessings are 'kept in heaven for you' by God himself, and because God keeps these blessings for us, they are thief proof – nobody can take them away. People can tie us to the stake, throw us to the lions, gas us in a concentration camp, exterminate us with a bomb or even gun us down from some safe house, but they cannot take away the life that God has for us. What a hope! Here, amid all life's uncertainties, is something which is certain. Death will not have dominion over us, for Jesus has destroyed the power of death.

We can be certain of the Christian hope. In the words of Peter, we shall 'see' Jesus (1:8). We shall see Jesus in all his glory, and share in his glory too. Precisely what that glory will be like, we do not know. In the words of the Swiss psychotherapist Carl Jung, 'What happens after death is so unspeakably glorious that our imagination and our feelings do not suffice to form even an approximate conception of it.' Or as the apostle Paul said, 'What we see now is like a dim image in a mirror; then we shall see face to face' (1 Cor. 13:12, GNB) – and on that day we shall see Jesus. No wonder Peter said that the thought of this salvation gives tremendous joy: 'You rejoice with an indescribable and glorious joy.'

Let me conclude by reading Eugene Peterson's paraphrase of Peter's opening words: 'Because Jesus was raised from the dead, we've been given a brand-new life and have everything to live for, including a future in heaven' (*The Message*). This is what makes Michael's funeral a celebration!

13

1 John 2:28 – 3:3

We shall see God

²⁸And now, little children, abide in him, so that when he is revealed we may have confidence and not be put to shame before him at his coming.

²⁹If you know that he is righteous, you may be sure that everyone who does right has been born of him.

³:¹See what love the Father has given us, that we should be called children of God; and that is what we are. The reason the world does not know us is that it did not know him. ²Beloved, we are God's children now; what we will be has not yet been revealed. What we do know is this: when he is revealed, we will be like him, for we will see him as he is. ³And all who have this hope in him purify themselves, just as he is pure.

Christ will come in glory

We 'have this hope in him [Jesus]' (1 John 3:3). This is the only time in the letters of John that the word 'hope' appears. Indeed, this is the only passage in the letters of John where the focus is on what N. T. Wright calls 'the ultimate future'.[1] And what a wonderful portrayal we are given of that 'ultimate future', when Christ will come in glory and we shall see God! Martyn Lloyd-Jones, a great preacher of the post-war period, declared of 1 John 3:2:

I suppose we must agree that nothing more sublime than this has ever been written, and any man [sic] who has to preach upon such a text or upon such a word must be unusually conscious of his own smallness and inadequacy and unworthiness. One's tendency with a statement like this always is just to stand in wonder and amazement at it.[2]

The verse just before, 1 John 3:1, is equally amazing. 'See', says John, 'what love the Father has given us' – or, in the words of the NIV, see 'what great love the Father has lavished on us'. The GNB, REB and RNJB, similarly, emphasize the greatness of God's love. However, this does not do justice to the underlying Greek adjective (*potapen*): although it could mean 'of what kind' (as in the ESV), originally it meant 'of what country'. Here we have a reminder that the Father's love belongs to another world; it is unearthly, unusual, inexplicable love. Some of the old hymns based on this passage speak of the Father's amazing or wondrous love. God's love is truly 'out of this world'. What is even more wonderful is that the love the Father gave he still gives. Here we have a Greek perfect (*dedoken*), which speaks of an action in the past that runs into the present. God still loves us. It is precisely because of this love that we have hope.

With this introduction in mind, let us now turn to the whole passage: 1 John 2:28 – 3:3. I wish to point you to four statements about the coming of Jesus, which, in turn, have four implications for the way in which we live our lives in the present.

First, in the words of the Scottish Methodist Howard Marshall, 'Although the timing of his coming is uncertain, the fact of his coming is certain.'[3] The writer declares 'when he is revealed' (2:28), or, perhaps better, 'whenever' he is revealed.[4] Although in 1 John the focus is the present connotations of eternal life,[5] this passage clearly refers to the future coming of Jesus. Although the expression 'the Second Coming' is not found in the New Testament,[6] Christ's promised return is very much part of the Christian hope. In the words of one of the eucharistic acclamations found in *Common Worship*, 'Christ has died: Christ is risen; Christ will come again.'[7] Sadly, today, this expectation of Christ's return has largely been lost. As Derek Tidball wrote:

Some greet the news with indifference, for they are so sucked into the here and now that they would regard his coming as an interruption to their plans and dreams. Others regard preparing for his coming rather as some young people view the dire warnings about smoking ... Still others are ignorant of this truth, even though it was central to the early Christian faith.[8]

Second, when Jesus 'appears' (2:28, ESV, GNB, NIV, REB, RNJB) he will 'be revealed' in all his glory. The word translated by most versions as 'appears' is actually the passive form of the verb 'reveal' (*phaneroo*), where the emphasis is on the invisible becoming visible. The hidden reality of who Jesus is will become public (see Col. 3:4; 1 Pet. 5:4). As Marshall commented, 'The first coming of Jesus was the revelation of the previously hidden Word of God in human form . . . Now he is again hidden from view, although he is spiritually present with his disciples, but one day he will again be revealed from heaven.'[9]

Third, 'at his coming' (2:28), Jesus will be seen to be the King and will be given a royal welcome. The Greek word underlying the English translation of the 'coming' is '*parousia*', and although in the letters of John it is only found here, in the New Testament as a whole, it is found twenty-four times and most frequently refers to the arrival of Jesus in glory (see Matt. 24:3; 1 Cor. 15:23; 1 Thess. 4:15; 2 Thess. 2:1; Jas 5:7–8; 2 Pet. 3:4). In the east of the Roman Empire it was the usual expression for the visit of a king or an emperor. Inevitably, such a visit was an occasion for celebration and rejoicing. As Marshall has commented, 'Even today, although we have become accustomed to seeing the face of the monarch or president on TV, people will still turn out in great numbers on state occasions to see and cheer the ruler; how much more must this have been the case in the ancient world where to see the emperor was possibly the event of a lifetime.'[10]

Fourth, when Jesus is 'revealed', his followers will be transformed: 'we will be like him, for we will see him as he is' (3:2). What an amazing experience that will be. This will be 'the ultimate revelation'.[11] 'Now we see in a mirror, dimly, but then we will see face to face' (1 Cor. 13:12). In the words of Oxford theologian Alister McGrath, 'To "see the face of God" is to have a privileged, intimate relationship with God – seeing God "as God actually is" (1 John 3:2), rather than having to know God indirectly, through images and shadows.'[12] For Augustine, the vision of God is 'the supreme good', the 'light by which truth is perceived, and the fountain from which all blessedness is drunk'.[13] The psalmist longed 'to behold the beauty of the Lord' (Ps. 27:4). The Christian vision of heaven is that one day it will be 'the common privilege of the entire people of God'.[14] In the words of John Donne, 'No man ever saw God and lived. And yet, I shall not live till I see God; and when I have seen him, I shall never die.'[15]

Not only will we see God but we will also 'be like him'. The sight of God will lead to our transformation. According to Colin Kruse, 'The sight of him will be enough to make us pure like him.'[16] The process of 'glorification' described by Paul in 2 Corinthians 3:18 ('All of us, with unveiled faces, seeing the glory of the Lord as though reflected in a mirror, are being transformed into the same image from one degree of glory to another') will be complete.

In the light of this hope, 'John' makes four more statements which are essentially a warning to his readers against any self-satisfaction and an encouragement to them to be ready for the return of Jesus.

First, he calls his readers to continue to 'abide' in Jesus (2:28) and so ensure that they will be 'confident' in Jesus' presence when he returns. The call to 'abide' in Jesus – which in the NIV is variously translated as 'continue' (1 John 2:28) or to 'remain' (John 15:5) or to 'live' (1 John 3:6) in Jesus – is a reminder of the call of Jesus in the Upper Room to 'abide' in him: 'Those who abide in me and I in them bear much fruit, because apart from me you can do nothing' (John 15:5). As Stephen Smalley noted, 'In 1 John this term appears twice to denote confidence before God in the context of prayer (3:21; 5:14), and twice to refer to the Christian's boldness in the face of God's judgment (here and at 4:17).'[17] Those who abide in Christ will 'not be put to shame'; instead, wrote Raymond E. Brown, they can 'have confidence' that Jesus will come 'as a loving friend and not as a judge'.[18]

Second, he urges his readers to confirm the reality of their faith by doing 'right': 'If you know that he is righteous, you may be sure that everyone who does right has been born of him' (2:29). Precisely what doing 'right' involves is uncertain: in the context of the verses immediately following; the emphasis would appear to be on holiness: 'No one who abides in him sins' (3:6). On the other hand, in the broader context of 1 John, the emphasis could be on loving one another: 'We know that we have passed from death to life because we love one another' (4:14).

Third, he reminds his readers of the wonder of their calling: they are 'called children of God' (3:1) and, by implication, they need to live up to their calling. They need to 'become' what by God's grace they already 'are'. Tom Wright wrote, 'It is not about trying to obey dusty rule books from long ago or far away. It is about practising, in the present, the tunes we shall sing in God's new world.'[19]

Fourth, John encourages his readers to ensure that they keep hold of the 'hope' by living lives marked by purity: 'All who have this hope in him purify themselves, just as he is pure' (3:3). Our future destination should determine our present behaviour. In the words of Colin Kruse, 'The hope of being like Christ in the future expresses itself in an effort to purify oneself to be like him in the present.'[20]

Sermon: Death is not nothing at all

I was with Mary when she died. She was in her mid-seventies and had been a true servant of God. She worked tirelessly for the church. So, when I was told that she wanted us to read Henry Scott Holland's 'Death Is Nothing at All' at her funeral, I felt we had no option but to do so, even though I had reservations about the poem.

'I've packed my bags and am ready to go.' So said Pope John XXIII (a reforming pope famous for calling the Second Vatican Council from 1962 to 1965) shortly before his death. Mary, too, was ready to go. As part of her preparation for dying, she had thought about what she wanted for her funeral service. In particular, she wanted us to read Henry Scott Holland's poem.

I was unhappy with Mary's choice. The poem seemed to me to go against the biblical description of death: there, death is described as the 'king of terrors' (Job 18:14) and the 'last enemy' (1 Cor. 15:26). However, I discovered that Scott Holland, a former Regius Professor of Divinity at Oxford, was not describing how death actually is but, rather, as we wish it to be.

The passage I shall read comes from a sermon Scott Holland preached at St Paul's Cathedral on Sunday 15 May 1910, shortly after the death of Edward VII. His text was 1 John 3:2–3: 'Beloved, we are God's children now: what we will be has not yet been revealed. What we do know is this: when he is revealed, we will be like him, for we shall see him as he is.' The sermon, entitled 'King of Terrors', began:

I suppose all of us hover between two ways of regarding death, which appear to be in hopeless contradiction with each other. First, there is the familiar and instinctive recoil from it as embodying the supreme and irrevocable disaster ... How often it smites, without discrimination, as if it had no law! It makes its horrible breach in our gladness with careless and inhuman disregard of us. We get no consideration from it. Often and often it stumbles in like an evil mischance, like a feckless misfortune. Its shadow falls across our natural sunlight, and we are swept off into some black abyss ... So we cry in our angry protest, in our bitter anguish, as the ancient trouble reasserts its ancient tyranny over us today. It is man's [sic] natural recoil ...

But, then, there is another aspect altogether which death can wear for us. It is that which first comes down to us, perhaps, as we look down upon the quiet face, so cold and white, of one who has been very near and dear to us ... And what the face says to us in its sweet silence to us as a last message from the one whom we loved is: *Death is nothing at all. It does not count. I have only slipped away into the next room. Nothing has happened. Everything remains exactly as it was. I am I, and you are you, and the old life that we lived so fondly together is untouched, unchanged ...* ' So the face speaks. Surely while we speak there is a smile flitting over it; a smile as of gentle fun at the trick played us by seeming death. It is not death; nobody is dead. Have we all felt like that now and again standing by the bed? ... Alas! it will pass from us. The long, horrible silence that follows when we become aware of what we have lost out of our daily intercourse by the withdrawal of the immediate presence will cut its way into our souls ... How black, how relentless, this total lack of tangible evidence for the certainty that we believe in! Once again the old terror will come down upon us. What is it that happens over there? What are the dead about? Where are they? How picture it? How speak of it? It is all blind, dismal, unutterable darkness. We grope in vain. We strain our eyes in vain.

The contrasted experiences are equally real, equally valid ... We are in a condition of process, of growth, of which our state on earth is but the preliminary condition. And this must mean that in one sense we know all that lies before us; and in another sense that we know nothing of it. 'Beloved, we are God's children now; what we will be has not yet been revealed' [NRSV]. Think that well over. We are now the children [literally 'sons'] of God. That we can know for certain. That is a direct and absolute experience ... 'Our life is hid with Christ in God.' ... It is no novel world, then, into which we shall enter when we pass away, but our own familiar world in which we shall have had our conversation and fellowship. Therefore, from this point of view, death is but an accident. Nothing is broken in our vital continuity. What we shall be there will be the inevitable continuation and development of what we are now and here.

And yet, and yet, 'what we will be has not yet been revealed' [NRSV]. Ah! How dreadfully true that is! ... We can see nothing ahead. No hint reaches us to interpret it. How can we picture it? ... We gaze and gaze, and the abyss is blind and black. Death shuts fast the door. Beyond the darkness hides its impenetrable secret. Not a sound comes back! Not a cry reaches us! Dumb! Dumb as the night, that terrifying silence! ... It is a fearful thing ... to be changed we know not how, to remain in our alarming identity through the change, to be ourselves for ever and ever under unimaginable conditions which no experience enables us to anticipate or forestall. Dreadful, the darkness, the silence of the unknown adventure. We know nothing of what will befall. Only we know that all which is already ours, by living experience, by intimate attachment, will be gone. The warmth of the present companionship, the comfort of familiar habits, the loving intimacy of deep and dear associations, the tender presence of this fond earth, the joy, the love, the hands that touch, the voices that charm, the hearts that beat. Ah! woe, woe! They must be surrendered. We go out stripped of all that has made us intelligible to ourselves, and it doth not yet appear what we shall be. Death, then, must retain its terror, even though it is but a stage in our growth, the terror of the unknown, the terror of loss, the terror of finality to what have been hitherto the movements of our very life.

We long for death to be nothing at all, but the reality is that we fear death. Yet the good news is that those who, like Mary, have put their trust in the Lord Jesus need not be afraid: death is but the gateway into God's eternal kingdom. As John wrote, and this time I quote using the GNB translation, 'My dear friends, we are now God's children, but it is not yet clear what we shall become. But we know that when Christ appears, we shall be like him, because we shall see him as he really is' (1 John 3:2).

So is death nothing at all? The late Christopher Idle, who was vicar of Sevenoaks, found himself in a quandary when people asked him to include the Henry Scott Holland passage in a funeral service, for wrenched out of their context, the words are misleading. He therefore decided to write a piece of prose which he could offer to the bereaved as an alternative. Let me read it to you.

Death is sometimes our enemy, sometimes our friend. As an enemy, it may shatter our lives, cut short our time, diminish our families and circle of friends. We do not often invite it to come, nor choose the time of its arrival. In this world we do have enemies, the Scriptures says death is the last.

Yet for the Christian, even death has lost its sting; Christ has made it a friend in spite of itself. Its victory is empty; its triumph will soon pass; it cannot have the last word. But it may still become our helper; not only a milestone but a signpost. It may lead us back to God if we have wandered away, or towards him if we have often been distant.

Death is a time for listening. Listening to friends, reading their words, listening to memories, hearing their music, listening to God in the quiet of my heart.

Death is a time for speaking. Telling the joys, memories past, telling of hopes, partly fulfilled; telling of growing and travelling, learning and finding, laughter and tears, a time for talk and a time for stories.

Death is a time for silence. When the words fail, sitting alone or quiet with my friends, watching or waiting, thinking and looking, the silence of prayer.

Death is a time for loving. Love never fails, love to the end; love all who love me and those who do not; love to heal wounds, love to accept, love to build bridges, love to forgive and know I'm forgiven. Love that is from God; God who is love; God who has first loved me.

To return to Mary. Mary knew that she was dying, but she was able to face up to the challenge death posed, for she was a woman of faith – many years ago in her youth she had committed her life to Jesus. As a result, Mary knew that death was not the end, but the beginning of a new and fuller life. She did not want to die, but she was not afraid to die. It is her faith, and of course the Lord Jesus himself, which makes all the difference to our service this afternoon. Yes, we shall miss Mary, but our loss is her gain. Mary has 'slipped away', not into the next room, but into the presence of God himself. At this very moment she sees God as he is! In the words of Julian of Norwich, the medieval English anchorite, for her, 'All shall be well, and all shall be well, and all manner of things shall be well.' One day, she and David, and indeed all God's people, will be reunited in that kingdom where there will be no more death, no more grief, crying or pain, for God will have made all things new (Rev. 21:4–5).

14

Revelation 7:9–17

We shall share in the life of heaven

⁹After this I looked, and there was a great multitude that no one could count, from every nation, from all tribes and peoples and languages, standing before the throne and before the Lamb, robed in white, with palm branches in their hands. ¹⁰They cried out in a loud voice, saying,

> 'Salvation belongs to our God who is seated on the throne,
>   and to the Lamb!'

¹¹And all the angels stood around the throne and around the elders and the four living creatures, and they fell on their faces before the throne and worshipped God, ¹²singing,

> 'Amen! Blessing and glory and wisdom
> and thanksgiving and honour
> and power and might
> be to our God for ever and ever! Amen.'

¹³Then one of the elders addressed me, saying, 'Who are these, robed in white, and where have they come from?' ¹⁴I said to him, 'Sir, you are the one that knows.' Then he said to me, 'These are they who have come out of the great ordeal; they have washed their robes and made them white in the blood of the Lamb.

> ¹⁵For this reason they are before the throne of God,
>   and worship him day and night within his temple,

and the one who is seated on the throne will shelter
   them.
[16]They will hunger no more, and thirst no more;
   the sun will not strike them,
   nor any scorching heat;
[17]for the Lamb at the centre of the throne will be their
   shepherd,
   and he will guide them to springs of the water of life,
and God will wipe away every tear from their eyes.'

Glory! Glory! Hallelujah!

'After this I looked' – and as he looked, John saw the 'church triumphant' 'standing before the throne and before the Lamb' (7:9).
What a wonderful encouragement this vision must have been to
John's contemporaries. 'Through Jesus the Lamb, slain and exalted,
all his followers can and will survive the greatest of ordeals.'[1]

Throughout the book of Revelation 'the throne' of God dominates.
Caesar's throne is as nothing compared to God's throne. John's
message is that the God who is enthroned in heaven is the God who
is working out his purposes here below. In the words of the heavenly
chorus, 'Hallelujah! For our Lord God Almighty reigns' (19:6) God,
however, does not sit on his throne alone. Sharing the throne of God
is 'the Lamb' (7:9–10; see also 5:6). The Lamb (*arnion*) is John's
principal and distinctive title for Jesus. Apart from John 21:15 (where
it is plural), it is only found in Revelation, where it occurs no fewer
than twenty-nine times (5:6, 8, 12, 13; 6:1, 16; 7:9, 10, 14, 17 and so
on), and with the exception of 13:11, where it is used of the Antichrist, who is the anti-type of Jesus, always refers to the exalted Jesus.

However, in Revelation 7, John's initial focus is not so much the
throne as the vast crowd standing before the throne. It is 'a great
multitude that no one could count' (7:9). God's promise to Abraham
that his people would be as many as the stars in heaven (Gen. 15:5)
and as the grains of sand by the sea (Gen. 32:12) has been well and
truly fulfilled. This huge crowd comes 'from every nation, from all
tribes, peoples and languages' (7:9; see also 5:9; 11:9; 13:7; 14:6 for the

same four-fold division). The people of God have transcended their Jewish roots. Every possible background is represented: 'National, social, political and cultural'.[2]

The people are 'robed in white' (7:9). The significance of these white robes is unpacked a little later in the vision, where, one of the elders declares, 'they have washed their robes and made them white in the blood of the Lamb' (7:14). To our way of thinking, this is a nonsense: blood stains rather than cleans! However, we are dealing here with symbolism. The symbolism of dirty clothes for an unclean life occurs frequently in the Old Testament (such as Isa. 64:6; Zech. 3:3), as does the corresponding idea of clean clothes for a pure life (see Zech. 3:4). The blood of the Lamb, which washes clean, is a symbol of the sacrificial death of Jesus on the cross, which cleanses us from sin (see Heb. 9:24; 1 John 1:7). It was through the outpouring of his life at Calvary that Jesus, the Lamb of God, took away the sin of the world (see John 1:29; 19:34). There may also be an allusion to Isaiah 1:18: 'Though your sins are like scarlet, they shall be like snow; though they are red like crimson, they shall be like wool' (see also Gen. 49:11). Here we have a reminder that God's people owe their place in heaven first and foremost to Jesus, the Lamb of God, and only secondarily to their faith, expressed in courage and endurance. As Eugene Boring, an American Disciples of Christ scholar, commented, 'Their own death is not an accomplishment of which they can boast. It is Christ's death . . . which has given them their victor's garment.'[3]

Those in the crowd were holding 'palm branches in their hands' (7:9). These palms are symbols of joy and victory (see John 12:13; also 1 Macc. 13:51; 2 Macc. 10:7). The waving of palms may be likened to the modern custom of waving scarves and banners at a football match!

They raised their voices to praise God and the Lamb. 'Salvation belongs to our God, who is seated on the throne, and to the Lamb' (7:10). As John Risbridger of Southampton's Above Bar Church noted, 'It is the song of salvation which provides the melody for the ultimate worship of heaven'[4] and which, in turn, should be the pattern of our worship too. 'They cried out in a loud voice' (7:10): John uses the present tense (*krazousin*) here, with the implicit suggestion that the crowd keep on shouting out. It is as if they cannot contain themselves with pride and delight at what God has done in Christ. As a crowd of jubilant football fans might go wild celebrating their team's success, so God's people continually celebrate his salvation with understandable excitement.

But what precisely are they celebrating? The word 'salvation' can be understood in several ways. With reference to the cleansing power of the blood of Christ, salvation may be understood as salvation from sin and from the dire consequences of sin. However, the use of the term salvation in 12:10 and 19:1 may suggest that the primary reference is to the Hebrew concept of salvation as salvation from enemies – that is, 'victory' over enemies (see, for example, 1 Sam. 14:6, 45; Ps. 118:14–15, 21) – as God in Christ has saved his people by gaining victory over the powers of evil. Alternatively, with reference to the political ideology of the time, which claimed Caesar to be the source of total well-being, salvation may be understood in terms of the true well-being that is only to be found in God and the Lamb, as the true source of all well-being. Clearly all three concepts are closely inter-related. We have much reason to celebrate.

Notice, too, the possessive pronoun: 'our God'. The crowd around the throne confess that God is their God, for they have responded in faith to 'the God who has taken us for his own and through Christ has redeemed us'.[5]

'All the angels stood around the throne' (7:11). In the words of Stephen Smalley, 'the air is thick with angels in Revelation', where they either fly (7:2; 10:1; 14:6; 20:1) or stand (as here, 7:1; 10:5; 19:17).[6] However, they never sit down. This may suggest an awareness of the Jewish tradition that angels had no knees and, as a result, were unable to sit! They also join their voices in praise to God. They echo the praise of the redeemed ('Amen!') and, in turn, ascribe their own worship to God: 'Blessing and glory and wisdom and thanksgiving and honour and power and might be to our God for ever and ever' (7:12). At first sight it appears that John has heaped together a random collection of words of praise, with the intention of their having an effect through their sheer quantity. Yet there is significance in each of the terms, for each expresses a different response to the divine. 'Blessing' (NRSV) or 'praise' (NIV) (*eulogia*) represents the loving adoration for God's grace beyond measure (see Eph. 1:3–10); 'glory' (*doxa*, from which is derived our English word 'doxology') represents the awesome acknowledgement of God's inestimable worth (Luke 2:24); 'wisdom' (*sophia*) is the joyful boast that God's wisdom is wiser than any human wisdom (1 Cor. 1:18–31); 'thanksgiving' (*eucharistia*) surely includes thanksgiving for the broken body and poured-out blood of Jesus (1 Cor. 11:23–25); 'honour' (*time*) is the reverential respect due to the King of the Universe, the 'Pantocrator'; 'power' (*dunamis*, from which is derived our English word 'dynamite'!) is the confession that God is able to do 'abundantly more than all we can ask or imagine' (Eph. 3:20); and 'strength' (*ischus*) is the celebration of the might of God, who raised Jesus from the dead and made him 'head over all things for the church' (Eph. 1:20). Although this outpouring of praise is attributed to the angels, this 'hymn' is also a fitting medium of praise for humans. We, too, can add our 'Amen'!

The focus of the vision now switches back to the crowd dressed in white. 'These are they who have come out of the great ordeal' (7:14). The use of the definite article probably indicates that the reference is primarily to the final series of 'trials' which will immediately precede the End (3:10: see also Dan. 12:1; Mark 13:19). However, with hindsight, it is perhaps not without significance that John uses a present participle (*erchomenoi*): trials and ordeals are an ongoing experience of God's people (see John 16:33; Acts 14:22). Interestingly, the noun 'ordeal' (*thlipsis*), which the NIV and ESV translate as 'tribulation', can refer to the process of 'grinding' or 'milling', which is when corn is ground between two heavy 'pressurizing' stones. Time and again the people of God have found themselves 'between a rock and a hard place', crushed between the demands of their faith and the 'pressures' of this world. In the words of the old spiritual, 'You cannot wear the crown if you do not bear the cross!'

John reminds his readers that for those who keep the faith a wonderful future is in store. Drawing upon a number of Old Testament passages, he develops a picture of life beyond the resurrection.

In the first place, 'they are before the throne of God' (7:15). As they live their life in the presence of God, 'they worship him day and night in his temple' (7:15; see also 22:3). The underlying Greek verb (*latreusin*), translated by the NRSV, ESV and REB as referring to worship, in other versions (GNB, NIV, RNJB) is translated as 'they served'. According to Arndt and Gingrich's Greek Lexicon, it was used 'of the carrying out of religious duties, especially of a cultic nature, by human beings'.[7] It is the word used of Anna, who never left the temple, but 'worshipped' (NRSV) there with fasting and prayer (Luke 2:37). Worship is the business of heaven.

Second, they are enveloped by the presence of God and by his accompanying glory, for, 'the one who sits on the throne will shelter them' (7:5). John perhaps recalls the prophecy of Isaiah 4:5–6: 'Then the Lord will create over the whole site of Mount Zion . . . a cloud by day and smoke and the shining of a flaming fire by night. Indeed, over all the glory there will be a canopy. It will serve as a pavilion, a shade by day from the heat, and a refuge and a shelter from the storm and the rain.'

Third, God's presence will both protect his people from all harm and meet their deepest needs: 'They will hunger no more, and will thirst no more; the sun will not strike them, nor any scorching heat, for the Lamb at the centre of the throne will be their shepherd, and he will lead them to springs of the water of life' (7:16–17). John not only anticipates Revelation 21 – 22 but also draws upon Isaiah 49:10 with its description of the exiles returning home from Babylon. There is also an undoubted reference to Psalm 23, where the Lord 'my shepherd . . . leads me beside still waters' (Ps. 23:1, 2). Through these images John conveys a picture of safety and security. He also points to the ultimate satisfaction of our deepest longing for spiritual wholeness: our thirst for God will be quenched (see Ps. 42:1–2; also Matt. 5:6; John 4:14; 6:35; 7:37), for we shall live in his very presence.

Fourth, all past hurts and causes of hurts will disappear: 'God will wipe away every tear from their eyes' (7:17). John anticipates Revelation 21:4 and alludes to Isaiah's vision of the day when God 'will wipe away the tears from all faces' (Isa. 25:8). The tears of grief and pain will belong to the past. Sorrow will be replaced by delight. What a wonderful future indeed!

Sermon: What is heaven like?

Reg died in his late seventies. He was blessed with a sense of humour, so, somewhat unusually for me, I began his funeral sermon with a joke. He was also keen on football, so I threw in a couple of football analogies. I like to think the sermon appealed to some of the many men in the congregation (and, hopefully, some of the women who liked football too!)

Reg enjoyed a good joke. So, on this day when we come together to thank God for his life, it is perhaps appropriate that I begin my sermon with a joke.

A taxi driver reaches the pearly gates. St Peter looks him up in his Big Book and tells him to pick up a gold staff and a silk robe and proceed into heaven.

Next in line is a minister. St Peter looks him up in his Big Book, furrows his brow and says, 'OK, we'll let you in, but take that cloth robe and wooden staff.'

The minister is shocked and replies, 'But I am a man of the cloth! You gave that taxi driver a gold staff and a silk robe. Surely I rate higher than a cabbie!'

St Peter responds, 'This is heaven and, up here, we're interested in results. When you preached, people slept. When the cabbie drove his taxi, people prayed.'[8]

Heaven is a butt for many jokes. Yet, for Reg, the hope of heaven sustained him when life was tough. The fact is that, however dark life may be, when we look to heaven, we will always have cause to praise and thank God. Today, I want to answer an often posed question on the basis of a vision John had and which is recorded in the book of Revelation. What is heaven like?

In the first place, heaven is a place which is home to the world's greatest family. John in his vision saw 'a great multitude that no one could count' (7:9). Reg liked football, but not even the biggest of stadia could accommodate this number. It was so large that John literally said, 'No one could do the maths.' Believe it or not, various estimates of the population of heaven have been made. According to one estimate, there have been over 5,500 million Christian deaths between the resurrection of Jesus and the present day. This kind of calculation needs to be taken with a pinch of salt. The wideness of God's mercy is such, there is little doubt that, at the end of time, we are going to be in for all kinds of surprises. The one known fact is that the company of heaven will be so large, it will be beyond computation. At a time when church congregations in the UK are generally declining, the media tends to write off the church. However, although there may be under five million Christians in the UK, worldwide there are some 2.4 billion – one in three people on this planet is Christian. But, as John reminds us, we are part of a great family which spans not only all six continents but also time itself.

In the second place, heaven, says John, is a place where God is on 'the throne' (7:9). Reg was about my age. I guess that, as children, we both used to sing the chorus:

God is still on the throne and he will remember his own;
Though trials may press us and burdens distress us
He never will leave us alone.
God is still on the throne, and he will remember his own.
His promise is true, he will not forget you, God is still on
the throne.

John was writing to the members of seven small struggling churches, who were being persecuted for their faith. This is the context in which John says God is on his throne. Above the tinpot throne of Caesar is the throne of the Lord God Almighty. That's a message we all need to hear. When things go wrong, we are sometimes tempted to wonder where God is. The truth is that God is on his throne; God is working his purposes out. Indeed, the sight of the crucified and risen Lord Jesus sharing the throne of God (7:9) is a reminder that Good Fridays are followed by Easter Day! It was in this faith that Reg lived and died.

Heaven is the place where the troubles of life are over. When John wrote of 'those who have come out of the great ordeal' (7:14), he had in mind Christians who had been put to death by the sword, who perhaps had been thrown to the lions in the Coliseum. However, there other forms of trouble too. Life can be tough in all sorts of ways. Loved ones will die, hopes will be disappointed, redundancy will take place or, in the case of Reg, cancer will strike. But the day is coming when the troubles of life will be over, and when 'God will wipe away every tear' from our eyes (7:17). Heaven, thank God, is a trouble-free zone!

Finally, we see from John's vision that heaven is reserved for those who 'have washed their clothes and made them white in the blood of the Lamb' (7:14). It's an odd image: blood stains, it does not clean. Here, however, we have a theological rather than a visual picture. John is speaking of Jesus, who died that we might be forgiven and who rose that we might enjoy a life that goes beyond the grave. It was when Reg was in his early teens that he put his faith in Jesus, who loved him and gave his life for him. He was baptized and became an active member of the church. Today, we celebrate that he is now part of the 'church triumphant' – he has joined that huge crowd around the throne. There he is, on the terraces, as it were, singing not some football ditty but the praises of Jesus. What a comforting thought that is.

15

Revelation 21:1–7

God will make all things new

[1]Then I saw a new heaven and a new earth; for the first heaven and the first earth had passed away, and the sea was no more. [2]And I saw the holy city, the new Jerusalem, coming down out of heaven from God, prepared as a bride adorned for her husband. [3]And I heard a loud voice from the throne saying,

> 'See, the home of God is among mortals.
> He will dwell with them;
> they will be his peoples,
> and God himself will be with them;
> [4]he will wipe every tear from their eyes.
> Death will be no more;
> mourning and crying and pain will be no more,
> for the first things have passed away.'

[5]And the one who was seated on the throne said, 'See, I am making all things new.' Also he said, 'Write this, for these words are trustworthy and true.'[6] Then he said to me, 'It is done! I am the Alpha and the Omega, the beginning and the end. To the thirsty I will give water as a gift from the spring of the water of life. [7]Those who conquer will inherit these things, and I will be their God and they will be my children.'

The city of God

One day, Saint Augustine, the Early Church Father who was Bishop of Hippo in North Africa, took a break from his writing about God and took a walk along the beach. He came across a boy scooping sea water into his hands and then pouring the water into a hole he had hollowed out in the sand. Puzzled, Augustine watched as the lad repeated his action again and again and again. Eventually his curiosity got the better of him.

'What are you doing?'

'Oh, I am emptying the ocean into my hole,' said the boy.

'But', replied Augustine, 'the ocean is too large for your hole.'

'And so, too, is God too large for your book!' retorted the boy.

John's visions in the book of Revelation are all about God. God is not just one item in the New Jerusalem; rather, it is God who creates the New Jerusalem. It is God who wipes away the tears. It is God who makes 'everything new' (21:5, NIV). 'God does not merely bring the End, God is the End,' said Eugene Boring.[1]

In God's new world everything will be radically 'new'. There will be 'a new heaven and a new earth' (21:1) and a 'new Jerusalem' (21:2). God will make 'all things new' (21:5). The 'newness' of this new world that is coming is indicated by the very adjective John employs (*kainos*), for it denotes not just that everything will be 'brand new', but something 'unknown, strange, and remarkable'.[2] Life in the kingdom of God will be radically different and radically better. So when the 'first things have passed away' (21:4), so, too, do the 'sea', 'death', 'mourning', 'crying' and 'pain' (21:1, 4).

The starting point for John's description of 'a new heaven and a new earth' (21:1 is found in Isaiah 65, where the prophet looks to the day in Jerusalem's history when children do not die, when old people live in dignity, when those who build houses live in them and when those who plant vineyards eat their fruit. The vision begins with God saying, 'I am about to create new heavens and a new earth; the former things shall not be remembered or come to mind. But be glad and rejoice for ever in what am creating, for I am about to create Jerusalem as a joy and its people as a delight' (Isaiah 65:17–18). However, whereas Isaiah 65 has in view a transformation of the present order, John envisages the creation of a completely new world, in which the distinction between heaven and earth is abolished: heaven comes down to earth and such a key distinctive geographical feature as the sea disappears. Yet the difference must not be pressed: we are dealing with a vision, where the overall impression rather than the detail is what counts.

In this new earth 'the sea is no more' (21:1) – 'it was no longer there' (NIV). To an islander accustomed to an island home, the lack of a seaside might appear to be a positive disadvantage! But not for John. For John, in exile on the island of Patmos, the sea symbolized separation from friends and loved ones. The sea kept John prisoner. The disappearance of the sea therefore represented the coming of freedom and the end of oppression. In this world, we all suffer limitations of one kind or another; with the coming of the new heaven and new earth, we shall be free at last.

However, there is another and more important thought present. The sea for John and his readers was 'a seething cauldron of evil'.[3] The roots of this metaphor are found in the Ancient Near Eastern mythologies. In Babylonian mythology, for instance, the sea represented the element of chaos which God had to overcome before he created the earth. God's triumph over Tiamat (Leviathan), the sea monster, was represented as a triumph over the sea (see Psalm 74:13–14; Isaiah 51:10). The sea in Jewish thought therefore became the symbol of all that was evil. According to one famous Jewish teacher, Rabbi Rashi, hell could be likened to the sea (Shab. 104a). Here in the book of Revelation, the sea is the place where the dragon goes when he is cast down from heaven (12:8); similarly, it is from the sea that the Antichrist beast rises (13:1). The absence of the sea in the new world that is coming therefore represents the abolition of evil. The devil has been thrown into the 'lake of fire and sulphur' (20:10), as also death and Hades (20:14) and all those guilty of sin in its many multifaceted forms (21:8). God's new city is 'holy' (21:2). 'Nothing unclean will ever enter it' (21:27). This is a wonderfully encouraging thought: one day sin and evil will be no more.

This holy city is named 'the new Jerusalem' (21:2). Ever since Jerusalem was destroyed by the Babylonians in 597 BC, Jews had dreamed of a rebuilt city. These dreams continued even after the physical rebuilding of Jerusalem at the end of the sixth century and surfaced even more vigorously after the destruction of the Temple in AD 70.

In the New Testament, the idea of a heavenly Jerusalem is found in Galatians 4:26 and Hebrews 12:22 (see also Phil. 3:20; Heb. 11:10; 13:14). In the letter of the risen Christ to Philadelphia, those who remain faithful are to be inscribed with 'the name of the city of my God, the new Jerusalem, that comes down from my God out of heaven' (3:12).

John sees the new Jerusalem 'coming down out of heaven from God' (21:2; also 21:10). What to us might appear as an element of a science-fiction film is a theological statement. The descent of the new Jerusalem 'out of heaven from God' is a pointer to the fact that this new world is of God's making and is not the product of human effort (see Ps. 46, 48; Isa. 2:1–4). 'I am making all things new', declares the one who is seated on the throne (21:5). The kingdom of God is not something we achieve; it is something which God alone brings about. The kingdom of this world becomes 'the kingdom of our Lord and of his Messiah' on the day when God takes up his rule and reigns (11:15–18).

The new Jerusalem is pictured 'as a bride' (21:2). This image of the people of God has its roots in the Old Testament (see Isa. 54:8; 61:10) and is taken up by Jesus (see John 3:29, 30; also Matt. 9:15; 25:1–13) and developed by Paul (2 Cor. 11:2; Eph. 5:29–30). John has already described the coming of God's reign as being the moment of the wedding of the Lamb, for which 'his bride has made herself ready' (19:7; see also 21:9; 22:17). The picture of a bride coming to meet her husband conveys the thought of joy and festivity, of union and of fulfilment.

Like any bride on her wedding day, she is 'adorned for her husband' (21:2), 'beautifully dressed' (NIV). By contrast with the church today, which seems 'like a ragged Cinderella, hideous among the ashes', she is beautiful.[4] The disfigurements of the church today 'with its countless divisions, chronic unbelief, tepid convictions and pervasive worldliness are no more'.[5]

The new Jerusalem becomes God's new home. A voice from the throne declares, 'See the home of God is among mortals. He will dwell with them as their God; they will be his peoples and God himself will be with them God' (21:3). The new Jerusalem is characterized by the presence of God. In the words with which Ezekiel closes his great vision of the restored Jerusalem, 'The Lord is there' (Ezek. 48:35). John alludes to the promise given to the people of God as they wandered in the wilderness: 'I will place my dwelling in your midst, and I shall not abhor you. And I will walk among you and will be your God, and you shall be my people' (Lev. 26:11–12; see also Jer. 31:33; Ezek. 37:27; Zech. 8:8). 'God's dwelling place is now among the people' (NIV).

John modifies that Old Testament prophecy in one important respect. This, however, is not clear in most English translations (for example, ESV, GNB, NEB, NIV, REB, RNJB), which speak of 'his people' in the singular (21:3): the best Greek texts read 'peoples' in the plural (which it is in the NRSV). The new Jerusalem will be made up of an exceedingly diverse multiracial population, with representatives 'from every nation, from all tribes and peoples and languages' (7:9). It is 'a radically inclusive city'.[6]

The voice from heaven continues, 'He will wipe every tear from their eyes. Death will be no more; mourning and crying and pain will be no more' (21:4). The Old Testament is not quoted literally, but there is a clear reference to Isaiah 25:8, 35:10 and 65:19. In the new world, death and suffering will have no place, for they belong to the old order, dominated by sin and evil. Interestingly, the new order of things is depicted primarily in terms of what it replaces. In describing the indescribable, it is easier to speak of what will not be rather than what will be, for 'no eye has seen, nor ear heard, nor the human heart conceived what God has prepared for those who love him' (1 Cor. 2:9; Isa. 64:3).

God declares, 'I am the Alpha and the Omega, the beginning and the end' (21:6). He is the beginning of history and the end of history, and Lord of all that is between. Gordon Fee added, 'The eternal God embraces all reality; there is absolutely nothing outside his jurisdiction.'[7]

God then issues an invitation: 'To the thirsty I will give water as a gift from the spring of the water of life' (21:6). In Middle East, with its desert wastes, water is a symbol of ultimate satisfaction. Had John been writing from Atlanta, Georgia, he might have drawn upon the imagery of a certain cola drink, with ice. As it is, 'the water of life' is 'the real thing'!

Sermon: The new Jerusalem

Grace was from east London and died at the age of ninety-seven. By the time I came to know her, she was the matriarch of a large family, many of whom had no Christian faith at all. I decided that an evangelistic funeral sermon was very much in order. However, Grace made things difficult for me since she had asked for 'Jerusalem' to be sung at her funeral.

Grace came to faith in her late teens and, throughout the next seventy or so years, sought to follow the Lord Jesus. He was at the centre of her life. I know that her wish for today is not for me to talk of Grace, but to talk of Grace's Saviour. However, I have to confess that she has made things a little difficult for me, because she requested that at her funeral we sing 'Jerusalem'. Although I acceded to her request, I feel uncomfortable.

'Why? What's wrong with "Jerusalem"?' you might say. 'It's set to a wonderfully uplifting tune' – and I agree. It is enormously popular. Adopted by the suffrage movement in 1917, it now is associated with the Women's Institute. In recent years it has become England's most popular patriotic song. It was chosen by Danny Boyle for the opening ceremony of the London 2012 Olympic Games. What's wrong with it?

My difficulty is the words. The feet of Jesus never trod on 'England's green and pleasant land'. Blake's hymn is based on a legend which told of Joseph of Arimathea taking Jesus as a young man on a boat trip to England. Last Easter, a cynic posted a blog in which he said:

There is no hard-documented evidence that Jesus visited England; to many it is just a fanciful fable. Much like any other aspect of religion, whether you believe in it or not, it is all about faith as without faith there can never be enough proof whilst with it, no proof is necessary. Happy Easter everyone!

To my mind, singing this 'hymn' at a Christian funeral service puts a big question mark over the whole Christian faith. It could imply that there is as much substance to God raising Jesus from the dead as to Jesus walking around in England's green and present land!

Well, enough of my reservations about William Blake's 'Jerusalem'. Some of us will just have to agree to disagree. Instead, today, I want to speak about the new Jerusalem we find in Revelation, the last book of the Bible.

John had a vision. He saw a 'holy city, the new Jerusalem, coming down out of heaven' (21:2). Wow. Can you imagine it? It reads like a piece of science fiction. There in this heavenly Jerusalem, wrote John, God will 'dwell' with his people: 'God himself will be with them' (21:3). What is more, 'He will wipe away every tear from their eyes. Death will be no more; mourning and crying and pain will be no more' (21:4). It is great stuff! But is it any more true than William Blake's 'Jerusalem'? The answer is yes.

John, of course, was using metaphor to describe the world to come. Heaven is beyond description. Heaven is way beyond our experience and understanding. As the apostle Paul once said, 'What no one ever saw or heard, what no one ever thought could happen, is the very thing God prepared for those who love him' (1 Cor. 2:9, GNB). But the fact that John was employing metaphor does not mean that he was spinning a fairy tale. Truth underlies his vision. I believe that there are a number of things we can say about the life to come.

First, there is a new world coming, in which God will make 'all things new' (21:5). It will be 'a new heaven and a new earth' (21:1). It will be a 'new Jerusalem'. The word John uses means 'radically new' – everything will be not just different but better. As a friend of mine once wrote, 'Heaven is not simply a polished, enhanced and sanitized version of earth, a different tune played on the old familiar instruments. It will be new!'[8] Or, in the words of an old song, 'Heaven is a wonderful place, full of glory and grace.' This is the world in which Grace today finds herself. I believe that Grace is more alive today than she has ever been.

In this new world, all the pain and suffering of this life will be at an end – 'mourning and crying and pain will be no more' (21:4).

What an amazing experience that will be. But instead of questioning it, let's thank God. It means that Grace is now free from all that terrible pain she experienced towards the end of her life – indeed, she is free from all the heartache and all the limitations she ever knew. What a relief!

Heaven is a 'holy city, a new Jerusalem' (21:2). Today, the last thing most people want to do is to live in a city – cities are unattractive places, associated with pollution and overcrowding, with the breakdown of law and order. But the new Jerusalem will be altogether different: it will be a 'holy city' (21:2). In other words, heaven will be a place where we are together with others; it will be a place of community, for that is what a city is. There we shall meet up with loved ones who have died entrusting their lives to Jesus, but also with so many more. Just imagine, Grace is talking nineteen to the dozen not just to her beloved husband Henry but also to so many more.

Heaven is a place where God is: 'He will dwell with them as their God' (21:3). And precisely because God is there, John described heaven as a place where God's people are constantly singing the praises of God (7:10, 15). In the words of St Augustine, 'We shall do nothing other than ceaselessly repeat Amen and Alleluia with insatiable satisfaction.' Certainly, RIP (Rest in Peace) is not very apt when it comes to heaven! Martin Luther said, 'Heaven is not heaven because joy is there, but because the praise of God is there.' Fortunately, Grace liked music but, even more, she loved her Lord. I have no doubt that she will be very happy to be part of the great throng praising God!

Heaven is a place open to all. The good news is that heaven is as wide as the heart of God. In heaven there is always room for more. John said, 'To the thirsty I will give water as a gift from the spring of the water of life' (21:6). But God does not force his gift of love and life upon us; at the end of the day, the choice is ours. As Jesus himself said, there are two ways: a way that leads to life and a way that leads to death. How Grace would long to see her family and friends choose the way that leads to life.

How do we know that all this is true? How do we know that the Christian faith has any more claim to truth than William Blake's poem about Jerusalem? Because of Jesus. Our hope for the future is based on Jesus. For Jesus not only lived and died; he was also raised to life on the third day and, as a result, he promises life in the world to come to all who love him. In the words we had read to us from 1 Corinthians 15, 'The truth is that Christ has been raised from death, as the guarantee that those who sleep in death will also be raised' (15:22, GNB). No wonder Paul exclaimed, 'Thanks be to God who gives us the victory through our Lord Jesus Christ.' Yes, Jesus has defeated the powers of sin and death, and we too may share in that victory.

I know from my many conversations with Grace that it was in this faith that she lived, and in this faith she died. Today we mourn our loss. But let us remember that our loss is but her gain, for heaven is a wonderful place!

Part 5

HOPE IN THE
OLD TESTAMENT

16
Job 19:25–27

Past injustices will be put right

²⁵I know that my redeemer lives,
and at the last he will stand upon the earth,
²⁶and after my skin has been thus destroyed,
then in my flesh I shall see God,
²⁷whom I shall see on my side,
and my eyes shall behold and not another.

There is a redeemer who stands by his people

Modern English Bible versions indicate a wide variety of approaches to translating Job 19:25–27. For instance, in addition to the NRSV cited above, we have:

I know that my Redeemer lives
and at the last he shall stand upon the earth.
And after my skin has thus been destroyed,
yet in my flesh I shall see God,
Whom I shall see for myself,
and my eyes shall behold and not another.
My heart faints within me.
(ESV)

But I know there is someone in heaven
who will come to my defence.
Even after my skin is eaten by disease,

while still in this body [or 'although not in this body']
    I will see God.
I will see him with my own eyes,
and he will not be a stranger.
(GNB)

I know that my redeemer lives,
and that in the end he will stand on the earth.
And after my sin has been destroyed,
yet in my flesh I will see God;
I myself will see him
with my open eyes – I and no other.
(NIV)

I know that my vindicator lives
and that he will rise last to speak in court;
I shall discern my witness standing at my side
and see my defending counsel, even God himself,
whom I shall see with my own eyes,
I myself and no other.
(REB)

I know that I have a living Redeemer
and that he will rise up at the last, on the dust of the earth.
After my skin has been thus stripped from me
from my flesh I shall look on God.
He whom I shall see will take my part:
my eyes will be gazing on no stranger.
(RNJB)

Many commentators believe that there is no reference to life beyond the grave. For example, Australian Baptist Paul Williamson, who teaches at Sydney's Moore College, wrote:

Job probably expresses confidence of vindication in this life (cf. 42:5). Thus understood, he maintains that his redeemer/

deliverer (*go'el*) – arguably God himself or the mediator mentioned in 16:19 – will eventually arrive and stand (i.e. testify) on Job's behalf at the ash heap (NIV's 'upon the earth' = literally 'on the dust'); that is, Job's anticipated grave. However, Job's *go'el* will do so prior to Job's death (although Job's skin by that stage may all be scraped off, Job will still be alive ['in his flesh'], and thus this, and Job's 'seeing God' (i.e. implying restoration of divine favour), is not anticipated as a post-mortem experience.[1]

Similarly, N. T. Wright, who described the regular Old Testament belief about the fate of the dead as a 'one-way street, on which those behind can follow but those ahead cannot turn back', wrote that it is difficult to suppose that Job 19 'suddenly holds out hope for a bodily life beyond the grave'.[2]

Other commentators are more ambivalent. John Goldingay, an Anglican now based at Fuller Seminary, California, wrote, 'Job expresses his hope in a tantalizingly oblique way . . . Maybe that in itself is a symbol of the way he is trying to express something that he can only partly find the right words to express.'[3] Similarly, John Job thought that 'the hope of resurrection is expressed – or something like it. But it is expressed as a hope against hope; as the logical consequence of faith in a God who must somehow, sometime, satisfy the claims of justice relating to one for whom death is imminent'. He went on, 'What we have here may perhaps be likened to a preliminary drawing-board sketch of a building which still lies from a human point of view almost entirely in the realm of fantasy.'[4] H. H. Rowley was of much the same view:

> To remove any trace of the thought of resurrection is as improper as to strengthen it. Two things seem clear. Job is assured that his Vindicator will arise to vindicate his innocence, and that he himself will see God . . . Though there is no full grasping of a belief in a worthwhile Afterlife with God, this passage is a notable landmark in the progress toward such a belief.[5]

By contrast, Gerald Janzen, who taught at Indianapolis's Christian Theological Seminary, contended that Job is referring to resurrection after death. For Job, resurrection is 'thoroughly relational, one may say covenantal . . . It is not simply life that Job hopes for . . . Job's hope reaches toward a restored vision of God, a God no longer estranged from him'.[6] Janzen based his argument on the following translation:

> As for me, I know that my redeemer lives,
> and the last one [a synonym for God as redeemer]
>   will arise on behalf of dust ['Job-gone-to dust']
> and after I awake, things will come around to this
>   [Job becomes once again an embodied living person
>   living in a renewed relationship with God]:
> From my flesh I shall see God,
> whom I myself shall see on my side
> and whom my eyes shall behold, and not estranged.[7]

So, in the light of this scholarly debate, are preachers justified in using Job 19:25–27 when preaching about the resurrection hope? I am convinced we are. Despite some of the uncertainties of translation, Job believed in a redeemer who will stand by us and will enable us to enjoy a renewed relationship with God in the life to come: three times, Job declares we will 'see' God. On the basis of this passage, we can declare that, in the world to come, the injustices of this life will be put right.

Sermon: I know that my redeemer lives

There are times when life just doesn't seem to be fair. Where is God when bad things happen to good people? It was for just such a situation that I prepared this funeral sermon.

'I know that my redeemer lives!' (Job 19:25). Whenever I hear or read these words of Job, I can't help but be reminded of Handel's glorious soprano solo: 'I know that my Redeemer liveth, and that he shall stand at the latter day upon the earth. And though worms destroy this body, yet in my flesh shall I see God.' Immediately, the chorus follows with the words of Paul: 'For now is Christ risen from the dead, the first fruits of them that sleep' (1 Cor. 15:21). It's wonderfully uplifting music. But the truth is that, when Job declared 'I know that my redeemer lives', he was desperate. Far from swinging from a chandelier, he was slumped on the floor. Nothing had gone right for him. He had lost everything – all his money, all his property, all his children, and now his health. To cap it all, none of his friends had any sympathy for him – they thought God was punishing him for some secret sin, while his wife complained of his bad breath!

At first, Job had been somewhat stoical about his losses: 'Naked I came from my mother's womb, and naked shall I return there; the Lord gave and the Lord has taken away; blessed be the name of the Lord' (Job 1:21). But there came a day when he had had enough. 'It's all your fault', he said to God. Or, in the words of Eugene Peterson's paraphrase, 'God tore me apart piece by piece – I'm ruined! Then he yanked out hope by the roots . . . He has launched a major campaign against me, using every weapon he can think of, coming at me from all sides at once. I'm nothing but a bag of bones, my life hangs by a thread' (Job 19:10–12, 17, *The Message*).

There are times when life isn't fair. In our family, for instance, I think of my cousin Johnny, who was doing well in the sixth form and had everything to live for but, at the age of seventeen, was sucked to death in a corn silo. Or I think of Caroline's Uncle Dick, a sailor in the merchant navy, who in his early thirties fell to his death, into a ship's hold, leaving a young wife with four small children to care for.

Why do bad things happen to good people? This was the question which Rabbi Harold Kushner sought to address after his son Aaron died at the age of fourteen. In his 1981 book *When Bad Things Happen to Good People*, he tried to answer the question, why, if the world was created and governed by a good and loving God, is there so much suffering and pain around? Frankly, he didn't get very far.

Why, God – *why*? This was the context in which Job railed against and shouted at God. Yet, in the midst of his pain, he could not give up believing. He held on to God with one hand, yet shook his fist at him with the other. In spite of his anger, he suddenly declares: 'I know that my redeemer lives, and at the last he will stand upon the earth, and after my skin has been thus destroyed, then in my flesh I shall see God, whom I shall see on my side' (Job 19:25–26).

The exact translation of this passage has been debated by scholars – some of the Hebrew is obscure. What seems to be clear is that Job believed God would come to his rescue: 'I know that my Redeemer lives.' The Hebrew word translated as 'redeemer' (*go'el*) was used of a family member with money and influence who would come to the aid of a relative who was in trouble. It's the word used of Boaz when he comes to the help of his distant cousin, Ruth. It's the word used of God delivering his people from slavery in Egypt (Exod. 6:6) or from exile in Babylon (Isa. 43:1, 14; 44:6, 24; 44:4; 48:17). It's also the word used of God delivering an individual from death (Ps. 103:.4) or rescuing one who is praying for help (Ps. 119:154).

'I know that my redeemer lives.' Despite all that had happened, Job was convinced God would rescue him from suffering and the mess that his life had become. How God would do that, he had no idea. But we know he will, for we live the other side of the cross and resurrection. We know that God has come to our rescue in the person of his Son, Jesus. To quote David Atkinson, a former Bishop of Thetford:

'I know that my Redeemer lives.' These words, read back through the window of the cross of Calvary, have often been a source of comfort to Christian people in a time of distress . . . Though the full Christian meaning which they hold for us today was merely a glimmer of first light before the dawn for Job, the God in whom he trusts is the God made known to us in Jesus as the Kinsman–Redeemer and Vindicator of those who trust in him. How marvellous that Job could have said so much, knowing so little! What a rebuke to some of us, who know so much more of God than Job ever did, that we trust him so little.[8]

'I know that my redeemer lives.' Despite his questions, Job knew that God would come to his aid. The good news is that God has come to our aid in Jesus, the Crucified Saviour and Risen Lord. As we mourn the loss of our loved one, we know that death is not the end. In the words of Job, 'after my skin has been destroyed . . . I shall see God' (19:26). In those words that in Handel's *Messiah* follow Job's affirmation of trust in God, 'For now is Christ risen from the dead, the first fruits of them that sleep' (1 Cor. 15:20) – or, as the GNB puts it, 'The truth is that Christ has been raised from death, as the guarantee that those who sleep in death will also be raised.'

'I know that my redeemer lives', said Job. 'I am convinced', said the apostle Paul, 'that neither death nor life . . . nor anything else in all creation, will be able to separate us from the love of God in Christ Jesus our Lord.' 'I know', said Job. 'I am convinced', said Paul. 'The whole of religion', said Martin Luther, 'lies in the personal pronoun.' In the midst of all our pain, God calls each one of us to believe and to discover the difference that Jesus can make in the midst of all our pain.

There is a legend of a man who was caught in quicksand and facing certain death. Confucius remarked, 'There is evidence that we should stay out of such places.' Buddha said, 'Let that be a lesson to the rest of the world.' Muhammed said, 'Alas! It is the will of Allah!' A Hindu said, 'Never mind, you will return to earth in another form.' But the risen Jesus said, 'Give me your hand and I will pull you out.'

17

Psalm 16

The path that leads to life

[1] Protect me, O God, for in you I take refuge.
[2] I say to the LORD, 'You are my Lord;
   I have no good apart from you.'
[3] As for the holy ones in the land, they are the noble,
   in whom is all my delight.

[4] Those who choose another god multiply their sorrows;
   their drink offerings of blood I will not pour out
   or take their names upon my lips.

[5] The LORD is my chosen portion and my cup;
   you hold my lot.
[6] The boundary lines have fallen for me in pleasant places;
   I have a goodly heritage.

[7] I bless the LORD who gives me counsel;
   in the night also my heart instructs me.
[8] I keep the LORD always before me;
   because he is at my right hand, I shall not be moved.

[9] Therefore my heart is glad, and my soul rejoices;
   my body also rests secure.
[10] For you do not give me up to Sheol,
   or let your faithful one see the Pit.

[11] You show me the path of life.
   In your presence there is fullness of joy;
   in your right hand are pleasures for evermore.

God is good

Psalm 16 is one of the happiest of psalms. From beginning to end, the psalmist celebrates the goodness of God. 'Its mood of sheer delight', wrote Canadian preacher Leonard Griffiths, 'climbs to such a crescendo of exuberant joy that you realize it could have been written only by a supremely happy man [or woman!]. You have the feeling that he must be the happiest man in the Bible.'[1]

Traditionally, that man is David. In my Bible, this psalm is headed 'A prayer of David'. For David, God was the secret to life. Listen to him: 'I say to the LORD, 'You are my Lord; I have no good apart from you' (16:2). In the words of the GNB, 'All the good things I have come from you.' John Goldingay commented, 'If you want to enjoy a full life in this world, you are wise to look to God who devised this bodily life for us.'[2]

However, David's eyes may not just have been fixed on life in this world, for towards the end of the psalm he says, 'You do not give me up to Sheol, or let your faithful one see the Pit' (16:10). 'Sheol' in the Old Testament is the place of the dead. It is literally a 'dead-end', a very grey kind of place. Some believe David was thanking God for protecting him and so saving him from a premature death.[3] However, David may well have been saying much more. He may have been speaking not of the past, but of the future. Thus the NIV translates this as, 'You will not abandon me to the realm of the dead'; similarly the GNB: 'You will not abandon me to the world of the dead.' Also the REB: 'You will not abandon me to Sheol'; the ESV and RNJB: 'You will not abandon my soul to Sheol.'

In a moment of inspiration, David expresses a hope in an after-life, where God will still be there for him. 'You do not give me up', he says; we might say, 'You do not give up on me.' David's hope was not based on any philosophical understanding of the afterlife but, rather, on his relationship with God.[4] As Michael Wilcock, a long-serving Anglican minister, argued:

The idea of an unbreakable covenant bond between the eternal God and moral humanity already had these mind-blowing implications, even if, quite understandably, they did not burst into full bloom until ... 'Christ Jesus destroyed death and brought life and immortality to light through the gospel' (2 Tim. 1:10).[5]

David ends, 'You show me the path of life. In your presence there is fulness of joy; in your right hand are pleasures for evermore' (16:11). Similarly, the NIV translates this as: 'You will fill me with joy in your presence, with eternal pleasures at your right hand' and the RNJB as: 'bliss for ever'. 'The path to life' leads into God's presence and into eternity ('for evermore'). As Derek Kidner, a former British Old Testament scholar, commented:

> The 'joy' (lit. joys) and 'pleasures' are presented as wholly satisfying (this is the force of 'fullness', from the same root as 'satisfied' in 17:15) and endlessly varied, for they are found in both what he is and what he gives – joys of his face (the meaning of 'presence') and of his 'right hand' [dispensing blessings and gifts].[6]

What a wonderful hope we have in Psalm 16, which 'for the Christian reader . . . provides a basis both for our confidence that God's blessings begin in this life as well as give us hope that our life in God's presence does not end with our death'.[7] In the words of an old children's song, 'God is good, yes He is'.

Sermon: Heaven is a wonderful place

Helen, who died at the age of seventy-five, had much to thank God for: she had a good marriage, a successful career and a fulfilling retirement. Above all, she was grateful to God for her faith, which had sustained her in this life, and for the hope that it offered for the next.

Today, I want to use Psalm 16 to talk of Helen, our friend and loved one for whom we give thanks. Like David, she, too, entrusted her life to God's safekeeping. Like David, she was still a teenager when she decided to make God Lord of her life, and what a difference that made. I dare to believe that she, too, could have said, 'You are my Lord, I have no good apart from you' (16:2).

She was a godly woman. Like David, she developed an on-going relationship with God. She rooted her life in the daily disciplines of prayer and of reading God's Word. With David she, too, sought to 'keep the Lord always before her' (16:8), and that made a difference. She, too, could have said, 'I am always aware of the Lord's presence; he is near, and nothing can shake me' (16:8, GNB).

She was a grateful woman – grateful for the way in which God had enriched her life. Looking back over the years, she could have echoed the words of David: 'The boundary lines have fallen for me in pleasant places' (16:6). David was here using a metaphor for the way in which God had shaped his life.[8] Helen, likewise, was aware of the way in which God had shaped and blessed her life. She had a happy marriage, a successful career and, in her retirement, found great fulfilment in serving as a volunteer in the local hospice. True, as with David, there were inevitably ups and downs in life but, overall, God was very good to her.

Today, however, we celebrate not just God's goodness to her in the past but also his goodness to her in the present. Listen to the penultimate verses of Psalm 16:

Therefore my heart is glad, and my soul rejoices,
    my body also rests secure.
For you do not give me up to Sheol,
    or let your faithful one see the Pit.
(16:9–10)

Significantly, both the apostle Paul and the apostle Peter used this psalm in their preaching on the resurrection. God did not give up on his Son, they declared (see Acts 2:25–28; 13:35). In the light of the resurrection of Jesus, we, in turn, can be confident that he will not give up on us. God does not give up on his friends. This was true of Helen and it will be true of us. When the day comes for us to die, he takes his friends by the hand and takes them to live with him for ever.

What an experience that will be! In the words of Psalm 16, 'You show me the path of life. In your presence there is fullness of joy; and in your right hand are pleasures for evermore' (16:11). Heaven, says David, is a place of endless joy (literally 'fulness of joys' – joy after joy). 'Joy', said C. S. Lewis, 'is the serious business of heaven.'[9] In the words of John Newton, who wrote 'Amazing Grace', the 'city of God' is where 'solid joys' are to be found.[10] It is also a place of endless pleasure – 'pleasures for evermore'. In the words of John Newton, heaven is all that we desire – and more!

Notice, too, how David links the endless joy and pleasure with the presence of God himself: it is God who is the source of joys and pleasures beyond description. We shall see God face to face. Literally, David says, 'in your face there is fullness of joy'. In the words of St Augustine, God 'shall be the end of all our desires, who will be seen without end, loved without cloy, and praised without weariness'.[11]

I know, from my many conversations wtih Grace, that it was in this faith that she lived, and it is in this faith that she died. Today we mourn our lost, but let us remember that our loss is her gain for, in the words of an old song I used to sing, 'Heaven is a wonderful place.'[12]

18
Psalm 23

The Good Shepherd will go with us

¹The LORD is my shepherd, I shall not want.
  ²He makes me lie down in green pastures;
he leads me beside still waters;
  ³he restores my soul.
He leads me in right paths
  for his name's sake.
⁴Even though I walk through the darkest valley,
  I fear no evil;
for you are with me;
  your rod and your staff –
  they comfort me.
⁵You prepare a table before me
  in the presence of my enemies;
you anoint my head with oil;
  my cup overflows.
⁶Surely goodness and mercy shall follow me
  all the days of my life,
and I shall dwell in the house of the LORD
  my whole life long.

God is with us in the darkest valley

Psalm 23 is the world's favourite psalm. Its expression of trust in God makes it a very suitable psalm for weddings – and for funerals. Yet David, of course, did not have either a wedding or a funeral in mind! So, before expounding this psalm, a word needs to be said about hermeneutics – the principles that lie behind the interpretation of Scripture. Are we right to read into a passage of Scripture meanings which were not present in the mind of the author? To be precise, are we right to use Psalm 23 in the context of a Christian funeral, and apply it to the difference God makes at the point of death? The truth is that, when David speaks of 'the darkest valley' (23:4), he is referring to the dark and difficult experiences of life, not death. In this regard, the translation adopted by the Authorized Version, 'the valley of the shadow of death', is misleading. So, too, when David concludes by saying, 'and I shall dwell in the house of the Lord my whole life long', he was not referring to the afterlife but, rather, to God's presence with him in this life.[1] Strictly speaking, the NIV and ESV are wrong to speak of dwelling in God's house 'for ever'. If we are to be true to the Hebrew text, which speaks of 'length of days', then the more subtle translations, such as 'through the years to come' (REB) or 'for the length of days unending' (RNJB), are perhaps better. To what extent can we justify reading Psalm 23 through the lens of the resurrection of Jesus?

C. S. Lewis addressed the issue of Christians finding 'a second or hidden meaning, an "allegorical", sense concerned with the central truths of Christianity' in their reading of the Psalms.[2] Living as we do this side of the cross and resurrection of Jesus, we see new depths of meaning the psalmist never intended, but nonetheless, in the light of the Gospels, reflect truth the psalmist never knew. In a way in which they could never have dreamed, men and women were 'moved by the Holy Spirit' to speak from God (2 Pet. 1:21).

This, I believe, is very much true of Psalm 23. There, David speaks about God who is with us through all the twists and turns of life's journey. In particular, he is with us as we walk through 'the darkest valley'. The good shepherd is there with us in all the dark experiences of life: depression, unemployment, serious illness – and, as an extension of his thinking, we can say that he is with us even in death. David's essential message is that, whatever evil may lurk around the corner, we need not fear – God will be there.[3]

Similarly, although David's closing affirmation had the life of this world in mind, it can also be applied to the life of eternity: 'Surely goodness and mercy shall follow me all the days of my life, and I shall dwell in the house of the LORD my whole life' (23:6). Indeed, the underlying Hebrew can refer to both the life of the psalmist and the life of the God. 'Why', asked Kenneth Bailey, 'should it not mean both "my days" and "God's days"?'[4] The latter is but the extension of the former. This is not a reading into ('eisegesis') of Scripture a truth which is not there, but a reading out ('exegesis') and application of a truth.

Sermon: With God there is nothing to fear

When I first knew John, he was already retired. He had fallen in love with a widow, whom he wanted to marry, so they began to attend our church. I married them and, some fifteen years, later took John's funeral when he died at the age of ninety-five.

John was a multifaceted character. It was my privilege to conduct his marriage to Rosemary here in this church. However, my task today is not to speak about John's character, but about John's faith. Brought up in the Lutheran church, John had a firm faith in the God who loved us and gave his Son for us all. He knew that God makes all the difference to living – and to dying.

Psalm 23 is the world's favourite psalm. Often chosen for weddings, it is also chosen for funerals. Indeed, I chose it for my own father's funeral.

'The LORD is my shepherd' (23:1). A shepherd, by definition, is one who cares for his sheep. The 'rod' of a shepherd (23:4) was a formidable weapon: some two-and-a-half feet in length, with a mace-like end into which pieces of heavy iron were often embedded, it was used to fend off threats to the sheep. The 'staff' (23:4), on the other hand, was about five feet and normally had a crook at the end to rescue a wandering sheep from danger.[5]

Although a shepherd was a familiar image for God's care of Israel,[6] 'its use in first person singular confession is unparalleled'.[7] The Lord is *my* shepherd. David sees himself as standing in a personal relationship with God. Yes, as a shepherd cares for each one of his sheep, so God loves and cares for each one of us.

He is there for us in good times and in tough times. So, in the familiar words of the Authorized Version, the psalmist says, 'Yea though I walk through the valley of the shadow of death, I will fear no evil: for thou art with me' (23:4). He is with us in all the dark experiences of life. In particular, he is with us in our dying, the darkest experience of life. God is with us. We are never alone, not even as we make our lonely way through death.

I am reminded of a story about a little boy starting his first term at junior school. He was asked, along with all the other children, to speak for a few moments on 'What I want to be when I grow up.' The little boy stood up and said, 'When I grow up, I'm going to be a lion tamer – I'll have lots of scary lions who will roar when I get into the cage.' Suddenly, overcome with the thought of what it might really be like to enter a cage of roaring lions, he added, 'But, of course, I'll have my mummy with me.'

The big question in life is this. Is there anybody there? Is there a 'mummy' in the universe? Does it matter to anyone what happens to me? Does my life matter? The psalmist declares 'Yes.' Life may be frightening, with its dark valleys, dangers and death, but it will be OK – we are not alone. God is there to help us if we will but look to him. 'The LORD is my shepherd.'

If you look closely at the structure of Psalm 23, you'll discover that God's name only appears twice: once at the beginning and once at the end. The psalm begins 'The LORD is my shepherd, I shall not want; (23:1); it ends 'And I shall dwell in the house of the LORD for ever' (23:6, NIV). That's the good news – from the beginning to the end, we are never alone.

'The LORD is my shepherd.' Whenever we see illustrations of Psalm 23, they usually show a wimp of a shepherd with an insipid smile, holding a little lamb in his arms. The reality is that, in the ancient world, shepherds were tough guys with a tough role. Not for them a nine to five job. They lived with their sheep twenty-four/seven. They were on duty all the time, caring, protecting and leading.

They knew their sheep well – they even knew each by name. What a wonderful picture of God's loving care for us.

The psalmist goes on to say, 'I shall not want', or, in the modern translation of the GNB, 'I have everything I need.' Or, rather, 'everything I *really* need'. Most of us would find we could do something with an additional £50,000, but money is nothing compared with the peace (23:3, 'he leads me beside still waters') and strength (23:3, 'he restores my soul' – that is, 'he gives me new strength', GNB) that God supplies.[8]

Notice, too, that God does not promise bad things will not happen to good people, but he does say that when bad things happen, we will never have to face them alone. As a result, the psalmist is able to say, 'Even though I go through deepest darkness, I will not be afraid, LORD, for you are with me' (23:4, GNB). The good news is that for those who put their trust in God, not even dying is to be feared. God is there to lead us home. In the words of the psalmist, 'and I shall dwell in the house of the LORD for ever' (23:6).[9]

For some, the thought of heaven turns them off. Karl Marx argued that religion was the opium of the people, shielding them from the realities of this life. Well, you can't accuse the Psalms of not being interested in this life – many of the psalms are this-worldly, pleading with God for justice, for an end to oppression, hunger and poverty. Nor can you accuse Christians in general of not being interested in this life – Christians do an enormous amount of good in this world. But – and it is a big but – there comes a day when this life comes to an end. What then? The good news is that the good shepherd will lead his sheep home.

Let me remind you of the words of Jesus with which we began our service: 'I am the resurrection and the life. Those who believe in me will live, even though they die' (John 11:25, GNB). How do we know this is not wishful thinking? Because Jesus the good shepherd, who laid down his life for his sheep, was raised on the third day. In a way which the psalmist could never have dreamed, the good shepherd leads his sheep home: 'Yea, though I walk through the valley of the shadow of death, I will fear no evil; for thou art with me' (23:4). There is nothing in this life or the next we need to fear. The good shepherd goes with us, even 'through the deepest darkness' (GNB).

This is the faith that sustained our friend and loved one. Today we rejoice that the good shepherd has led John to his heavenly home.

19

Psalm 121

God will keep us safe

¹I lift up my eyes to the hills –
   from where will my help come?
²My help comes from the LORD,
   who made heaven and earth.

³He will not let your foot be moved;
   he who keeps you will not slumber.
⁴He who keeps Israel
   will neither slumber nor sleep.

⁵The LORD is your keeper;
   the LORD is your shade at your right hand.
⁶The sun shall not strike you by day,
   nor the moon by night.

⁷The LORD will keep you from all evil;
   he will keep your life.
⁸The LORD will keep
   your going out and your coming in
   from this time on and for evermore.

Help for the journey of life

Psalm 121 is one of the 'Songs of Ascent' (Pss 120 – 134) originally sung by pilgrims on their way to Jerusalem. The psalm is 'an unqualified song of trust in the Lord's help'.[1] 'The LORD is your keeper' (121:5), declares the psalmist, not once, but six times over

(121:3, 4, 5, 7, 8). The emphasis is on the security that God offers his people: the word 'keep' is used in the sense of 'guarding' or 'protecting'. 'He watches over you' (NIV). 'There is', said Alec Motyer, 'a "keeping Lord" and we are a "kept" people. This is our faith, the faith in which we walk the pilgrim way.'[2] Or, in the words of the 1619 Heidelberg catechism, to believe in God the Father Almighty, the maker of heaven and earth, is to:

> trust in him so completely that I have no doubt that he will provide me with all things necessary for body and soul. Moreover, whatever evil he sends upon me in this troubled life he will turn to my good, for he is able to do it, being almighty God, and is determined to do it, being a faithful Father . . . We are to be patient in adversity, grateful in the midst of blessing, and to trust our faithful God and Father for the future.[3]

Over the years, I have preached on this psalm many times under the general heading of 'Help for the Journey of Life'. I have spoken on this psalm not just at regular Sunday services but also to theological students about to embark on Christian ministry and to couples celebrating a special wedding anniversary. I have often used this psalm at funerals, marking the end of a loved one's journey. Although there is no explicit reference to the world to come, nonetheless, the final phrase, 'for evermore', is suggestive. God's care 'runs on, not to the end of time but without end'. Or, in the words of former Canadian preacher Leonard Griffiths, 'This God has given us his word that he will see us through to the end of the journey. He will be with us when the night falls and we go into the darkness; he will be there to meet us when morning breaks and the shadows flee away.'[4]

Sermon: God is with us every step of the way

Alan and his wife Alison came to a renewed faith in their retirement years thanks to the witness of one of their neighbours. They became members of our church and it was my privilege to be there for Alan in his closing days. He died at the age of seventy-eight.

I remember visiting Alan in hospital when he had his triple bypass operation; at the time he was a very sick man. I read Psalm 121 to him and then prayed for him. It was his experience of God in his life at that time which resulted in a renewal of his faith, and soon both he and Alison were regular members of the congregation.

As Alan discovered, God does not live in some celestial tower, remote from the world he has made. He cares for his world; he cares for us; he cares for us amidst all the twists and turns of life's journey. It is that conviction which underlies Psalm 121, a psalm I read again to Alan in the last week of his life, a psalm which Alison has chosen for today's service of thanksgiving.

Psalm 121 is sometimes called 'the traveller's psalm'. It was a psalm sung by pilgrims as they made their annual journey to Jerusalem. It expresses their faith in God, but also reflects the unease they felt about travel. 'I lift up my eyes to the hills – from where will my help come?' (121:1). Or, in the words of the GNB, 'I look to the mountains; where will my help come from?' Mountains may be beautiful, but they can also be dangerous. Mountains are places where people lose their lives. The Authorized Version was wrong when it turned this verse into a statement: 'I will lift up mine eyes unto the hills, from whence cometh my help.' The hills are not the place from which help comes; rather, they are the place where help is needed. Here, the hills or mountains represent the perils of the journey, for it was in the ravines and gorges of the mountain ranges that wild beasts and robbers hid.

As the pilgrims looked to the mountain ranges they had to cross if they were to reach Jerusalem, they were filled with foreboding and wondered from where their help would come. It is in this situation that the psalmist declares, 'My help comes from the LORD, who made heaven and earth.'

God is depicted as the divine bodyguard. The Lord is your keeper (121:4); he is 'your Guardian God' (Eugene Peterson, *The Message*). He stays close to us at every step of the journey – 'He will not let your foot be moved' (121:3; 'he will not let you fall', GNB). God doesn't guard from a distance, waiting to receive a 999 call. He stands near at all times, ready to reach out his arm and steady us if we make the slightest of slips.

He guards us against all the dangers of the journey: 'The sun shall not strike you by day' (121:6a). In the Middle East people can go blind, even mad, with sunstroke; they can die of thirst by prolonged exposure to the sun's rays. Furthermore, 'the moon [shall not strike] by night' (121:6b). 'Whoever was hurt by the moon?', you might ask. The fact is that, in the past, lots of superstition was bound up with the moon. Mental illness was associated with the moon, hence our word 'lunacy'. We might say that God guards us against our fears, real and imaginary.

Yet what was true then remains true today. As we go through the ups and downs and twists and turns of life's journey, we travellers need to remember that God is there to help, if we will but let him. God doesn't force himself upon us, but he is there if we will but turn to him. God doesn't guarantee that difficulties will never occur, but he does promise that, when trouble arises, he will be right there.

Some people have argued that religion is a crutch for the weak and the neurotic – the 'no-hopers' and the 'no-copers'. 'The strong can do without God!', they say. That is a nonsense! Just as it would be stupid to try to climb Everest without a rope and a pickaxe and all the other paraphernalia of climbing, so it is stupid to try to do without God's help. God is not just for the weak, he is there for us all. The truth is that, in our own strength, all of us are weak. All of us need him if we are to rise to life's challenges.

When I was reading this psalm to Alan in hospital, I highlighted the line where the psalmist declares that the Lord 'will neither slumber nor sleep' (Ps. 121:5). God, I said, is the great insomniac.[5] God is always awake. He never has forty winks. He is there on duty in the night hours, as well as during the day, keeping guard over us.

That's all nice, comforting stuff, you may say, but is it true? Were the pilgrim people of God never attacked by robbers? The fact is that God does not allow us to live in some kind of protective bubble. As many of the other psalms demonstrate, the psalmist knew from his own experience that life can have its ups and downs. However, he says, whatever experiences life may bring, the Lord is there to protect us in the way that really matters.

The psalmist goes on, 'The LORD will keep you from all evil; he will keep your life' (121:7). 'He will keep' us not in the sense that we will not know suffering but, rather, he will protect us from the evils that suffering all too easily brings: the evils of bitterness and of cynicism; the evils of complaining and of despairing. He will protect our life in the sense that he will keep guard over our 'soul' (RNJB), our personality, 'the inner citadel of self which is the seat of human happiness and misery'.[6] Alan knew that protection in full measure.

The psalmist ends with the statement, 'The LORD will keep your going out and your coming in from this time on and for evermore' (121:8). I believe that this was particularly true for Alan in the last few difficult years of his life, as first his sight began to go, then his hearing. Even through all the difficulties associated with his cancer and multiple myeloma, God kept Alan positive. He was there for him right up to the end, and now has taken him into his eternal kingdom.

In all life's experiences, in its sorrows and its joys, in its failures and successes, and at its beginning and at its ending, God is there to give the help that really counts, if we will but open ourselves to him. So today we give thanks not just for the life of Alan but also for the God who sustained Alan in this life – and who continues to sustain him in the next.

20
Psalm 139:1–12

God is with us, even in the dark

¹O Lᴏʀᴅ, you have searched me and known me.
²You know when I sit down and when I rise up;
   you discern my thoughts from far away.
³You search out my path and my lying down,
   and are acquainted with all my ways.
⁴Even before a word is on my tongue,
   O Lᴏʀᴅ, you know it completely.
⁵You hem me in, behind and before,
   and lay your hand upon me.
⁶Such knowledge is too wonderful for me;
   it is so high that I cannot attain it.

⁷Where can I go from your spirit?
   Or where can I flee from your presence?
⁸If I ascend to heaven, you are there;
   if I make my bed in Sheol, you are there.
⁹If I take the wings of the morning
   and settle at the farthest limits of the sea,
¹⁰even there your hand shall lead me,
   and your right hand shall hold me fast.
¹¹If I say, 'Surely the darkness shall cover me,
   and the light around me become night',
¹²even the darkness is not dark to you;
   the night is as bright as the day,
   for darkness is as light to you.

God never gives up on us

Approximately a million people around the world kill themselves each year. In the UK there are over 6,000 deaths a year by suicide. Of these, men account for almost three-quarters. The collateral damage of a suicide is, of course, much greater, for every suicide leaves in its trail numerous other casualties or victims. According to the American Psychiatric Association, 'the level of stress resulting from the suicide of a loved one is ranked as catastrophic – equivalent to that of a concentration camp experience'.[1]

Augustine of Hippo said that suicide was worse than murder, for in killing another human being one was killing only the body, whereas in suicide one was killing both the body and the soul. A murderer might at least have an opportunity to repent and save his or her soul, but a person committing suicide had no opportunity to repent, and therefore lost his or her soul.[2] As a result of such teaching, people dying by suicide were regarded as the worst of sinners, totally outside the scope of God and his love. Suicides could not be buried in church graveyards. Instead, they were buried in unconsecrated ground. Their bodies were treated with little respect. For example, in 1823, a man who had died by suicide was buried at a crossroads in Chelsea with a stake pounded through his heart. Today, thank God, the climate is very different and people who end their life by suicide receive a good deal of sympathy and understanding. So what position should we, as modern Christians, take?

My position is as follows. Suicide is always wrong. Life comes to us as a gift from God. We are not free to return the gift whenever we feel like it. The ending of life is God's prerogative, not ours. For a person to seek to end his or her life is to take the place of God. Suicide, whatever the circumstances, can never be justified. I am conscious that in today's liberal and permissive society, to talk in this way is not popular.

We live in a society where everybody is deemed to have a right to do whatever they wish. But nobody has a right to take life, even their own. People may be free to commit suicide, but that does not make it right to do so. There may be mitigating circumstances, just as there may be when an abused wife kills her husband, but, whatever the circumstances, the taking of life is wrong.

Suicide does not end suffering: it creates yet more suffering. Suicide is a very selfish act, for it does untold damage to others. As one relative put it, 'He didn't just take his own life; he took part of ours too.' Or as another said, 'Suicide doesn't end pain. It only lays it on the broken shoulders of the survivors.'

Suicide is not an unforgivable sin. There is no unforgivable sin apart from the sin against the Holy Spirit (Mark 3:28–29), which, in effect, is a refusal to acknowledge that Jesus is God's Son. Few, if any, when they commit suicide, are seeking to defy God. Rather than shaking their fists in God's face, many are looking into their own faces and hating what they see. Suicide may be a sin, but it is no more serious than any other sin. What's more, when Jesus died, he not only died for the sins of us all, but for all our sins: 'The blood of Jesus his Son cleanses us from all sin' (1 John 1:7). True, the person committing suicide normally has not normally the opportunity to repent of sin, but many of us commit sins that we are all too blind to recognize for what they are. Furthermore, we all die with sins not named and repented of.[3]

Suicide, of itself, therefore cannot debar a Christian from God's heaven. Paul's words in Romans 8:38–39 remind us that 'neither death, nor life . . . nor anything else in all creation will be able to separate us from the love of God in Christ Jesus our Lord'. Christians whose loved one has committed suicide should not worry about his or her eternal fate. Jesus surely will welcome home such a loved one with special warmth and tenderness.

Suicide is not the answer to life's problems – the grace of God is. Such is the vulnerability of our minds and our bodies that even the strongest of Christians can become victims of suicidal despair. However, we need to remember that the grace of God is always sufficient, and that God's power is made perfect in weakness (2 Cor. 12:9). God has not promised us a trouble-free life, but he has promised that he will not test us further than we are able to bear, and that we are able to bear considerably more than we care to think.

No situation, however desperate it may appear to a person contemplating suicide, is hopeless. God is with us, and wherever God is, there is hope. Hope has been defined as the 'lived belief that with God no situation is the end of the story'.[4] True, we live in a world all too often characterized by pain and sorrow – 'We know that up to the present time all of creation groans with pain, like the pain of childbirth' (Rom. 8:22) – but, as the metaphor of childbirth reminds us, there is a new world coming, where there will be 'no more grief or crying or pain' (Rev. 21:4). In the meantime, we need to hold on to the fact that 'in all things God works for good with those who love him' (Rom. 8:28).

On the few occasions when I have had to take a funeral for a person who has committed suicide, I have preached on the opening verses of Psalm 139. Although Psalm 139 does not allude to suicide, it does speak about God being present with us even in the darkest experiences of life. Although the word 'love' is not present, nonetheless the implication is that we cannot escape God and his love. Even in the world of the dead ('Sheol'), 'your right hand shall hold me fast' (139:8, 10), declares the psalmist.

In the paraphrase of Kenneth Slack, a former General Secretary of the British Council of Churches:

> Go as high as you can, go as deep as you can, fly as far east as the sunrise, or westwards to the limit of the sea – and God is still there. There is no experience of life in which he does not confront you. He confronts you in the heavenly experiences, and the times that you call 'sheer hell', in the freshness of new experiences, that are like the dawn, and the time of life when the sun is setting in the west. In all of them God finds you, confronts you with his challenges and disturbances, and his strength and peace.[5]

This psalm formed the basis of Francis Thompson's famous poem 'The Hound of Heaven':

> I fled him, down the nights and down the days;
> I fled him, down the arches of the years;

I fled him, down the labyrinthine ways
Of my own mind; and in the midst of tears
I hid from him, and under running laughter.
Up vistaed hopes I sped;
And shot precipitated
Adown Titanic glooms of chasmèd fears,
From those strong feet that followed, followed after.

But with unhurrying chase
And unperturbèd pace,
Deliberate speed, majestic instancy,
They beat – and a Voice beat
More instant than the Feet –
'All things betray thee, who betrayest me'.[6]

This poem was rooted in Thompson's experience. He, too, had tried to escape from God, but had failed. After growing up in a Christian home, he had gone on to study first for the ministry and then to train as a doctor, but he had failed and had got hooked on drugs. He ended up sleeping on the streets. There, amidst the degradation, he was sought out and rescued by a publisher and his wife. Thompson came to realize that even though he had made his bed in the hell of misery and in the darkness of despair, he could not escape God and his love. He ended his poem:

Halts by me that footfall:
Is my gloom, after all,
Shade of His hand, outstretched caressingly?
'Ah, fondest, blindest, weakest,
I am He Whom thou seekest!
Thou dravest love from thee, who dravest Me.'

God is with us in all the ups and downs of life. He never gives up on us. No wonder Erskine of Linlathen, a great Scottish theologian and mystic, said, 'This is the psalm I should wish to have before me on my death-bed.'[7]

Sermon: Even in the darkness, God is there

Richard was a twenty-one-year-old student who had jumped in front of a train. His death came as total shock to everybody. There had been no warning signs. I had not known the young man and had only met his parents the week before at a church quiz night. The parents were not people of faith. However, in talking to them, I discovered that their son had started to attend church services while at university.

'A service of thanksgiving for the life of Richard' – that's what we've called today's funeral service, and rightly so, for in this service we do not just want to express our grief but also to express our thanks for the life of a good friend and a precious son.[8]

Sadly, I never knew Richard, so it has been instructive to listen to the family's tribute. Clearly, Richard was a much-loved young man. When I visited the family, his mother spoke of him as being kind and thoughtful, loving and giving, conscientious in his work, endowed with the gift of humour, but also with a strong sense of justice. Let me encourage you this morning to remember Richard, to bring to mind all those happy memories of Richard, and to thank God for them. From a Christian perspective, God is the giver of every good and perfect gift (Jas 1:17).

It is precisely because Richard was a likeable young man that his untimely death is so tragic. We can only guess at the pain and the darkness which must have filled his mind and heart. In our bewilderment, let us remind ourselves today that there is one who does understand, and that is God himself. As David wrote in Psalm 139, the Lord knows each one of us; he knows us intimately: 'You know when I sit down and when I rise up, you discern my thoughts from far away . . . You are acquainted with all my ways' (139:2, 4). God understands us through and through.

Let us remind ourselves, too, that this God who understands was there for Richard not just in the good times, but also in the bad times. Richard may not have been aware of God at the time, but even in his darkness God was there. 'Where can I go from your spirit? Or where can I flee from your presence? If I ascend to heaven, you are there; if I make my bed in Sheol [the land of the dead], you are there . . . If I say, "Surely the darkness shall cover me, and the light around me become night", even the darkness is not dark to you' (139:10–11). The good news is that there is no place where God is not. Furthermore, God is not just ever-present – he is also ever-loving. Even in Richard's darkness God was there, surrounding him with his love.

Richard never came to our church, but I am told that when he was at university in Cheltenham, he began to go to church regularly. Why he began to go, I don't know. Perhaps, in part, it was because he wanted to find friends; perhaps it was also because he wanted to find God.

One thing is certain: when Richard went to church, he will have heard about God and his love for him. He will have heard of how God sent his Son to die on a cross for him. He may well have heard of the parable Jesus told about the good shepherd who went out in search of the one lost sheep – the good shepherd who also cares even for the Richards of this world, who lose their way in life.

Some people worry about the fate of those who take their own lives and wonder whether God would even forgive such a person. Sadly, in the past, the church has been responsible for giving rise to such worries. Today, thank God, we think very differently. We now realize that suicide is not an unforgivable sin. Few, if any, people, when they end their lives by suicide, are seeking to defy God. They are not shaking their fists in God's face: no, many are looking into their own faces and hating what they see.

I do not believe that God would have us worry about the eternal fate of those who have ended their life by suicide. I believe that Jesus will welcome home people like Richard with special warmth and tenderness.

Today, let us comfort ourselves with the thought that there is 'nothing' which 'can separate from us the love of God' (Rom. 8:38) – nothing in this life, nor in the next, 'will ever be able to separate us from the love of God which is ours through Christ Jesus our Lord' (Rom. 8:39). And in this conviction let us commend Richard to God's safekeeping.

Part 6

HOPE FOR ALL?

God loves us all

Shall not the Judge of all the earth do what is just?
(Gen. 18:25)

Up until this point, all the sermons reproduced in this book were preached at funerals where the deceased were people of faith. However, many of the funerals I conducted as minister of a Baptist church were for people who appeared to have had little if any faith, but whose family felt that a Christian funeral would be appropriate. Often, there had been a tenuous link with a Baptist church at some stage in their lives: for instance, they had gone to a Baptist Sunday School, been part of a Boy's Brigade company that had been linked with a Baptist church or been married in a Baptist church. In such a context, when it came to the service, a difference in approach was called for. I could not, for instance, assure the mourners that their loved one was 'with Christ', but neither was I in a position to say that they were not 'with Christ' – only God knows that!

Every funeral needs to reflect that God loves us all. In the words of John 3:16, 'God so loved the world [the 'cosmos'] that he gave his only Son, so that everyone who believes in him may not perish but have eternal life.' Sadly, not all will experience the life that God offers. No one spoke more about the realities of heaven and hell than Jesus himself. Jesus said in the Sermon on the Mount that there are two ways: one which leads to hell and one which leads to life (Matt. 7:13, 14). Significantly, the very imagery of a 'narrow' road and a 'broad' road suggests that those who find the way to life will be a minority.[1] Paul was equally clear that the world is divided between 'those who are perishing' and those 'who are being saved' (1 Cor. 1:18; see also 2 Cor. 2:15). The Bible does not teach that all will be saved. The doctrine of a final judgement is rooted in Scripture.

Indeed, without judgement, there would be no morality in this world. In the words of Tom Wright:

> I wish it were otherwise but one cannot for ever whistle 'There's a wideness in God's mercy' in the darkness of Hiroshima, of Auschwitz, of the murder of children, and the careless greed that enslaves millions with debts not their own.[2]

The argument that God's love must win and that all will be saved in the end is based on a false understanding of love. Love, by definition, must allow its object freedom to choose to respond or not to love in return. In this regard, we need to pay attention to the question C. S. Lewis asked of those who object to the idea of hell:

> What are you asking God to do? To wipe out their past sins and, at all costs, to give them a fresh start, smoothing every difficulty and offering every miraculous help? But he has done so, on Calvary. To forgive them? They will not be forgiven. To leave them alone? Alas, I am afraid that this is what he does.[3]

But the Bible also teaches that God does not wish to exclude anybody from his heaven. 'God our Saviour', said Paul, 'desires everyone to be saved and to come to the knowledge of the truth' (1 Tim. 2:4). The gospel is universal in intention: as Paul wrote, 'in Christ God was reconciling the world to himself' (2 Cor. 5:19). However, as Paul's 'appeal' makes clear, we need to respond to God's love (2 Cor. 5:20).

As Abraham discovered in his bargaining with God, 'the Judge of all the earth' not only 'has to act justly' (Gen. 18:25, GNB) but is also far more merciful than Abraham could ever have imagined (Gen. 18:28–32). 'Yahweh', wrote Bill T. Arnold, 'introduced a new way of looking at grace and forgiveness.'[4] I have little doubt that we shall be surprised at the extent of God's mercy. We shall discover, for instance, that where people have never heard of Jesus, or never really understood what Jesus has done for them, or who have rejected Jesus because perhaps of the unloving or hypocritical actions of his followers, God will judge them according to the light which they have received (Acts 17:27; Rom. 2:12–16). In the words of F. W. Faber's great hymn:

> There's a wideness in God's mercy
> like the wideness of the sea;
> there's a kindness in his justice
> which is more than liberty.
> For the love of God is broader
> than the measure of man's mind,
> and the heart of the Eternal
> is most wonderfully kind.[5]

God makes all the difference

The LORD is my shepherd . . .
He leads me beside still waters;
   he restores my soul.
(Ps. 23:1–2)

How then, within the context of a funeral for a non-churchgoer, do we communicate the good news of God's love for us all? In the first place, we communicate God's love by the sensitive way in which we conduct the whole service. Indeed, I would maintain that, in this context, the prayers along with the Scripture readings are just as important as the sermon.

Second, we communicate God's love by the sensitive way in which we preach the sermon. This is not the time for a hard-hitting gospel sermon. I am appalled at some of the advice offered on the Internet on 'preaching at the funeral of an unbeliever'. For instance, one American pastor wrote:

> While I would not preach about Hell in all of its dreadfulness *per se* at a funeral, the funeral of an unbeliever is a God-given opportunity to teach men about the consequences of the fall, death and judgment in general . . . Preach the precious truths about the incarnation, the active obedience of Jesus, the passive

obedience of Jesus, the atoning death of Jesus, the wrath pro-
pitiation of Jesus, the resurrection of Jesus and the return of
Jesus . . . Exhorting men and women to put their trust in Jesus
is of paramount significance when preaching the funeral of an
unbeliever. We do not ever simply want to preach about Christ
in generalities without calling men [sic] to trust in Him.[6]

This kind of preaching is totally inappropriate on such an occasion
and will almost certainly evoke a negative response. By contrast, if
we focus on the difference that God makes, a positive response might
naturally be evoked. This is not 'diluting' the gospel, as some would
maintain – it is part of the gospel!

So how does this work out in practice? First of all, the Scriptures
need to speak of the difference God makes. When conducting the
funeral of a non-churchgoer I read from the Good News Bible (in
my judgement the most intelligible version for most non-churchgoers)
selections from Psalm 23, John 14 and 1 Corinthians 15.

- David reminds us that God can be likened to a shepherd who
  cares for each one of us sheep:

  > The LORD is my shepherd; I have everything I need. He lets
  > me rest in fields of green grass and leads me to quiet pools
  > of fresh water. He gives me new strength. He guides me in
  > the right paths, as he has promised. Even if I go through the
  > deepest darkness, I will not be afraid, LORD, for you are with
  > me. Your shepherd's rod and staff protect me . . . I know that
  > your goodness and love will be with me all my life; and your
  > house will be my home as long as I live.
  > (Ps. 23:1–4, 6)

- Jesus calls us to place our hope in him:

  > Do not be worried and upset. Believe in God and believe
  > also in me. There are many rooms in my Father's house,
  > and I am going to prepare a place for you . . . I am the way;

I am the truth; I am the life; no one goes to the Father except by me.
(John 14:1–2, 6)

- The apostle Paul works out the implications of the resurrection of Jesus for us:

  The truth is that Christ has been raised from death, as the guarantee that those who sleep in death will also be raised . . . This is how it will be when the dead are raised to life. When the body is buried it is mortal; when raised it will be immortal. When buried it is ugly and weak; when raised it will be beautiful and strong. When buried it is a physical body; when raised it will be a spiritual body . . . When what is mortal has been clothed with what is immortal, and when what will die has been clothed with what cannot die, then the scripture will come true: 'Death is destroyed; victory is complete. Where, O Death, is your victory? Where, O Death, is your power to hurt? Death gets its power to hurt from sin, and sin gets its power from the law. But thanks be to God who gives us the victory through our Lord Jesus Christ.'
  (1 Cor 15:20, 42–43, 54–57)

Second, the prayers need to reflect the difference that God makes. My practice is for the prayers following the sermon to praise God for the comfort of the gospel, thank God for the life of the loved one, and ask God's help for those who mourn. The basic shape is as follows (clearly, appropriate personalization is necessary).

- Father, we praise you for the comfort of the gospel. For Jesus has broken the power of death; he has brought life and immortality to light. We thank you for all that you have done for us in him. We praise you for his cross where our sins are forgiven – for his resurrection, on which our hope of life is anchored. We bless you that, through faith in him, the sting of death has been drawn.

- Father, we come, too, to thank you for the life of our friend and loved one, now gone from among us. We thank you for all the good and happy memories we have of her. We bless you for every quality in her character and every grace in her temperament. We thank you for all that she was to us – as a mother and grandmother, as a neighbour and as a friend. For all that she represented to us, we thank you.
- We pray for all those who mourn her going. We pray for [name] and all the wider family. Father, comfort them in their sorrow. May they know your love, feel your care. Give them – indeed give us all – faith to look beyond our present trouble to Jesus, the one who died and rose again and lives for evermore.

In particular, the sermon needs to speak of the difference that God makes. Over the years I have developed a standard 'template' for a sermon where the deceased was not a churchgoer. Needless to say, the template had always to be filled out and personalized.

Sermon: God offers comfort and strength to us all

Thanks be to God who gives us the victory through our Lord Jesus Christ.
(1 Cor. 15:57)

Death finds us at our most religious. Many no longer mark the birth of a child with any religious ceremony; likewise, most people no longer bother to go to church to get married. But few people do without a minister or priest at the point of death. Why is this so? Why don't we dispense with all the religious paraphernalia and hold a secular or humanist ceremony instead? Let me give three good reasons for holding a Christian funeral service.

- Today, we come to thank God for the life of our loved one. Sadly, I never knew [name], but let me encourage you to allow some of your memories to surface and then be grateful to God for them. For God is 'the giver of every good and perfect gift' (Jas 1:17, AV). So, look back and be grateful to God for all that [name] was to you . . .

- Today, we come to receive the comfort that God alone can offer. Death is always a troubling event, however expected it may have been. Alas, for the person without faith, all one can do is maintain a stiff upper lip. Death is the end. It is literally 'curtains' as the coffin makes its final journey. But where there is faith there is hope. As the apostle Paul said, 'When the body is buried it is mortal; when raised it is immortal. When buried it is ugly and weak; when raised it will be beautiful and strong. When buried it is a physical body; when raised it will be a spiritual body' (1 Cor. 15:42–44, GNB). How do we know that this is not just wishful thinking? Because of what Jesus has done. Jesus has broken through death's defences. He has carved out a path through the valley of death and, through faith, we may follow in his steps. So here at the point of death comfort is to be found. Death need not have the last word.

- Today, we come to ask God for strength to cope. The God and Father of our Lord Jesus Christ does not live in some remote ivory tower. He did not set the world in motion and then withdraw from the scene. Rather, he is involved in the everyday processes of life. The psalmist said, 'He gives me new strength. He guides me in the right way' (Ps. 23:3, GNB). He goes with us even through the valley of death. God is with us at every point of our living and of our dying. My prayer for you all is that you will open yourselves to experience the strength that God alone can give.

Part 7

APPENDICES

Appendix 1

Losing a loved one: a personal reflection

Following the death of my father in February 2000, I wrote an article for our church magazine, which became a leaflet on bereavement entitled 'Losing a Loved One'.[1] Here, I reflected on my experience of loss and the difference that the Christian hope made to me.

Following a major stroke two weeks earlier, my father died aged eighty-three. His death was a learning experience for me. Although, as a Baptist minister, I have been alongside many people when a loved one has died, I myself had never experienced the loss of someone who was really close to me. I wrote the leaflet in the hope that what I learnt might in some way help you in your own experience of bereavement.

Death is a shock to the system

Time and again I have said in my funeral sermons that 'Death is always a troubling event, however expected it may be.' When my father died, I found out how true that statement was. Ever since the stroke, we knew that his time was limited. Yet, when the news of his death reached me, I was numb with shock. Death for our loved one may be a wonderful release, but for those of us who are left, the experience is always traumatic. Shock is only the beginning of the 'grief experience'. Feelings of guilt and anger often surface. It is even possible to begin to think that our loved one has not actually died.

The interval between the death and the funeral can seem an eternity

In our case, we had to wait ten days. Ten days by modern British standards is not long.[2] Indeed, over the last Christmas and New

Year period, many people had to wait much longer than that. Nonetheless, those ten days of 'limbo' seemed so very long. Somehow it is not until the funeral is over that people can begin to come to terms with the death which has taken place. And even then, that takes a while. It is generally reckoned that it can take over a year before one has truly come to terms with the loss of a loved one. For that reason, if at all possible, it is good for the bereaved to delay making any major decision for at least six months, if not a full year.

The tasks following a death are many

First, we had to get a certificate from the hospital, and then to go on to the registrar to get copies of the formal death certificate (banks, building societies and the like all need to see a copy before they will transfer funds). Afterwards, we met the undertaker to discuss our requirements. Fortunately, my father had made it clear that he wanted to be cremated. Later, the minister came to see us to discuss the arrangements for the church service – in our case, we had already chosen the hymns. In addition to seeing the many kind people who called by to express their sympathy, there were phone calls to be made to relatives, letters to be sent to friends. We also wanted to place a death announcement in the newspapers. All these and many other tasks took up the first five days.

Exhaustion sets in after the tasks have been completed

Once these initial tasks were over, I felt totally drained of energy – physically, emotionally and spiritually. I was glad that I was able to take a week's compassionate leave. In the week following the funeral, I deliberately paced myself and cancelled some of my non-urgent commitments for that week. As for my mother, who had had the stress of caring for my father over a number of months, she needed quite some time before she regained her old energy.

An expensive funeral is unnecessary

The hearse apart, we had no funeral cars. We had the cheapest of coffins and ordered only one floral arrangement on behalf of the family (we suggested that, instead of sending flowers, friends give money to one of my father's favourite charities). We were not being mean. My mother felt very strongly that there were better ways of honouring my father. I believe she was absolutely right. I discovered, for instance, that although I saw my father's coffin at the crematorium, I did not 'see' it in the sense that it did not occur to me to take a critical look at the coffin – my mind was elsewhere. Indeed, it was not until three days afterwards that I suddenly realized this had been so. In our case at least, a more expensive coffin would have been an irrelevance. However, as I discovered, even the cheapest of funerals is not cheap.

People can be unexpectedly kind

Even the local bank sent my mother flowers! She was inundated by messages of sympathy. To my surprise, I, too, received many letters and cards. In receiving them, I have discovered what a real silver lining they are at a time of deep sadness. I have been challenged to discover that some of the busiest of people went to a good deal of trouble in sharing their memories of my father. I shall make more effort in this regard in future.

A loving family is a great support

I hope this has been true for my mother. It has certainly been true as far as I am concerned. For me, it has been a humbling experience to discover, yet again, how much my wife and children care for me. At a time like this I am so grateful to God for them.

Finally, Jesus makes all the difference

Again, this is something I have often said as a preacher. But I have discovered this also to be very true in my own experience, and not least in these last few weeks. Of course, we were sad. I am not ashamed to say that I shed some tears, as indeed Jesus did when his friend Lazarus died. But, in the words of the apostle Paul, we did not grieve 'as those who have no hope', for 'We believe that Jesus died and rose again, and so we believe that God will take back with Jesus those who have died believing in him' (1 Thess. 4:13–14, GNB). For this reason, we concluded my father's death announcement in *The Times* with another quotation from the apostle Paul: 'Thanks be to God who gives us the victory through our Lord Jesus Christ!' (1 Cor. 15:57).

Jesus does indeed make all the difference, both to our living and to our dying.

Appendix 2

The funeral of a baby who died in the womb

This service, drawn up with the needs of a family from Uganda in mind, took the following shape.

Call to worship

I am convinced that neither death nor height, nor life, nor depth, nor anything else in all creation, will be able to separate us from the love of God in Jesus Christ our Lord.
(Rom. 8:38–39)

An assurance of God's love for us all

We gather here on what is for all of us a sad occasion. We were looking forward to a time of joy and happiness, and now there are tears and grief. We are left with a feeling of emptiness. All that has happened seems futile and pointless. Our minds are filled with questions to which there appear to be no answers: so many things we do not know; so many things we do not understand.

But there are some truths we do know. We know that the God who made us loves us; that he loves us always; that, through his Son Jesus Christ, he has promised never to leave us, nor forsake us. And we know also, as others before us have found, that his strength is available for us, especially at those times when we feel we have no strength of our own. My prayer for Paul and Fiona, as indeed my prayer for every person present here this evening, is that you will experience the strength which God in his love wishes to offer to us all.

Hymn

'Through All the Changing Scenes of Life'.

Prayer

O Lord our God, how good it is at a time like this to know that you are a God who loves us and cares for us, even as a Father loves and cares for his children. We thank you for the hymn we have just sung, and for its reminder that you are with us 'through all the changing scenes of life, in trouble and in joy'. Loving Father, Father of all mercies and God of all comfort, help us in this time of distress and grief to rest ourselves within the circle of your love. Grant us now the assurance of your living presence to cheer and to guide. Comfort us as we hear the promises contained in your Word; may we find in you the strength and peace we need.

Scriptures

Psalm 139:1–6, 13–17 (GNB): God knows and understands.

LORD, you have examined me and you know me.
You know everything I do;
    from far away you understand all my thoughts.
You see me, whether I am working or resting;
    you know all my actions.
Even before I speak,
    you already know what I will say.
You are all round me on every side;
    you protect me with your power.
Your knowledge of me is too deep.
    it is beyond understanding . . .

You created every part of me;
    you put me together in my mother's womb.
I praise you because you are to be feared;
    all you do is strange and wonderful.
    I know it with all my heart.
When my bones were being formed,
    carefully put together in my mother's womb,

when I was growing there in secret,
   you knew that I was there –
   you saw me before I was born.
The days allotted to me
   had all been recorded in your book,
   before any of them ever began.
O God, how difficult I find your thoughts;
   how many of them there are!

John 14:1–2, 6 (GNB): Jesus calls us to place our hope in him.

Do not be worried and upset. Believe in God, and believe also in me. There are many rooms in my Father's house, and I am going to prepare a place for you … I am the way; I am the truth; I am the life; no one goes to the Father except by me.

1 Cor. 15:20, 42–43, 54–57 (GNB): Jesus alone can give us life.

The truth is that Christ has been raised from death, as the guarantee that those who sleep in death will also be raised … This is how it will be when the dead are raised to life. When the body is buried it is mortal; when raised it will be immortal. When buried it is ugly and weak; when raised it will be beautiful and strong. When buried it is a physical body; when raised it will be a spiritual body … When what is mortal has been clothed with what is immortal, and when what will die has been clothed with what cannot die, then the scripture will come true: 'Death is destroyed; victory is complete.' Where, O Death, is your victory? Where, O Death, is your power to hurt? Death gets its power to hurt from sin, and sin gets its power from the law. But thanks be to God who gives us the victory through our Lord Jesus Christ.

Mark 10:13–16 (GNB): Jesus has a special love for children.

Some people brought children to Jesus for him to place his hands on them, but the disciples scolded the people. When

Jesus noticed this, he was angry and said to his disciples, 'Let the children come to me, and do not stop them, because the Kingdom of God belongs to such as these. I assure you that whoever does not receive the Kingdom of God like a child will never enter it.' Then he took the children in his arms, placed his hands on each of them, and blessed them.

Song

'Emirembe' ('Peace'), sung by the Watoto children's choir, based in Kampala. The lyrics speak of God being our peace in a storm when, in our brokenness, we call out to him.

Sermon

Prayers

Our Father God, we praise you for the comfort of the gospel. For Jesus, your Son, has broken the power of death – he has brought life and immortality to light. We thank you for all that you have done for us in him. We praise you for his cross where our sins are forgiven – for his resurrection, on which our hope of life is anchored.

Father God, you have loved us from the moment when you shaped and formed us in our mother's womb. Today, we give thanks for Philip Tendo Bakibinga. O Lord, you know him and you love him, for you created his innermost self. Help us as we now entrust him to you, knowing that he is safe in your care. As we do so, we think of those who have gone before him – and not least Paul's father, George William Bakibinga, and we bless you for the great company of those who you have brought through death to be with you for ever in glory.

We pray for all those for whom today is a day of great sorrow and loss. In particular, we pray for the family – for Paul and Fiona; for Paul's mother, Joyce; and for Fiona's parents,

Michael and Edith; and for all the wider family. Father, comfort them and indeed us all in our sorrow. Amid all our questions, help us to trust you. In our time of darkness, shine into our lives with the light of your presence. We pray, too, for Martin and for Paula – we thank you for all the joy that they bring in this time of sadness. Continue to bless them and may they, too, in due time, come to know the security which we find in your love for us all.

Song

'Blessed be Your Name', a song written by Matt Redman after his wife had suffered three miscarriages. It was also a song Paul and Fiona had at their wedding.

Benediction

The peace of God, which is beyond our utmost understanding and of far more worth than human reasoning, keep guard over your hearts and thoughts, through Christ Jesus our Lord (Phil. 4:7).

Postlude

'You Raise Me Up', Josh Groban.

When I am down and, oh my soul, so weary;
When troubles come and my heart burdened be;
Then, I am still and wait here in the silence,
Until you come and sit awhile with me.
You raise me up, so I can stand on mountains;
You raise me up, to walk on stormy seas;
I am strong, when I am on your shoulders;
You raise me up. To more than I can be.

Appendix 3

Reflections on the funeral
of a twenty-one-year-old suicide

Preaching is more than a sermon

Traditionally, when we think of preaching, we think of delivering a sermon, but there are occasions when it is only part of the process of declaring the good news of Jesus. In my experience, funerals involving non-churchgoers are often such occasions, when the 'liturgy' (the prayers, the reading of Scripture and the singing of hymns) also becomes a medium for proclamation.

The opening act of worship

As with the funeral of Philip, the baby who died in the womb, the call to worship took the form of an affirmation of the love of God, in which I read the wonderfully reassuring words of the apostle Paul: 'I am certain that nothing can separate us from his love: neither life nor death – there is nothing in all creation that will ever be able to separate us from the love of God which is ours through Christ Jesus our Lord' (Rom. 8:38–39).

After singing 'Praise My Soul the King of Heaven', a hymn chosen because it was likely to be known by older people from their school days, I led the congregation in a prayer asking for God's help at this time. Normally, prayers are directed towards God alone, but on this occasion I worded the prayer in such a way to declare God's love for us all.

O Lord our God, the Creator of the universe and the Sustainer of all life, but also the God and Father of our Lord Jesus Christ, and our God and Father too. This morning, we bless you for our hymn's reminder that, like a father, you tenderly care for us. Lord, may we experience that tender care today. How we thank you that, in Jesus, we have discovered that your love has no limits, and there is nothing in this life or in the world to come which can separate us from you. As we come to you in our pain, help us to remember that you, too, have known the pain of loving, for you are the father of a crucified son and know the anguish of a broken heart. As we come to you in our bewilderment, remind us that, although Richard is beyond our reach, he is not beyond your touch of care and love. As we come to you with our feelings of guilt, forgive us for those times when we failed Richard; help us to forgive him for the hurt he has inflicted upon us; and help us to forgive ourselves for any harm we may have caused him. So bless our service this morning. Help us as we now hear your promises contained in your Word; help us to believe them and, in believing, receive the comfort they offer.

From prayer, we moved on to Scripture. The very reading of Scripture is a declaration of the Word of God. However, it is my custom at funerals to preface the Scripture readings with a statement summarizing the thrust of each passage, so I prefaced Psalm 139:1–11 with the statement, 'The psalmist reminds us that God is with us at all times – he is with us in the good times, and also in the tough times.' We then moved on to John 14:1–2, 6: 'Jesus calls us to place our hope in him.' We concluded with 1 Corinthians 15:20, 42–43, 54–57: 'The apostle Paul works out the implications of the resurrection of Jesus for us.'

The tributes

I suggested that, while we listened to a track from one of Richard's favourite CDs, we showed pictures of him on our big screen. To my surprise, twenty-one photos of Richard were shown, one for each year of his all-too-brief life. It was an incredibly emotional, but cathartic, experience. The showing of the photos was then followed by three brief tributes from family members.

The sermon

My funeral sermons are always relatively short but, on this occasion, the sermon was briefer than normal. In the context of such tragedy, a sermon of any greater length just did not seem appropriate.

The prayers

The sermon was then followed by three brief prayers. The first prayer was a summary of the gospel. The second was a prayer of thanksgiving for Richard's life. The third was a prayer encouraging the congregation to look to Jesus. I would maintain that, therefore, the first and last prayers were a form of preaching.

Father, we praise you for the comfort of the gospel. For Jesus has broken the power of death – he has brought life and immortality to light. We thank you for all that you have done for us in him. We praise you for his cross, where our sins are forgiven – for his resurrection, on which our hope of life is anchored. We bless you that, through faith in him, the sting of death has been drawn.

Father, we come, too, to thank you for the life of Richard now gone from among us. We thank you for all the good and happy memories we have of him. His smile, his kindness and thoughtfulness, his loving and giving nature, his sense of humour, his passion for justice. We thank you for the way in which he enriched the lives of many. Yes, we thank you for all that he was to us – as a son, as a brother, as a grandson, as a nephew and as a friend.

We pray for all those who mourn his going. In particular, we pray for his parents, his brothers, his grandparents . . . let us pray, too, for the wider family, for the close friends . . . Let us remember also the train driver . . . Father, comfort them in their sorrow. May they know your love, feel your care. Give them – indeed give us all – faith to look beyond our present trouble to Jesus, the one who died and rose again and lives for evermore.

The concluding act of worship

We sang another well-known traditional hymn, 'Dear Lord and Father of Mankind', which in the context of a suicide speaks volumes. The service ended with a benediction based on words of the apostle Paul in Philippians 4:7: 'May the peace of God, which is beyond our utmost understanding and of far more worth than human reasoning, keep guard over your hearts and thoughts, through Christ Jesus our Lord.'

A final reflection

I see funerals as an opportunity to exercise pastoral care, as distinct from engaging in evangelism. Even within the context of a non-Christian funeral, I see my role as, first and foremost, that of ministering the grace of God to the mourners. Although I seek to present the gospel, I do not feel it right to present a direct gospel challenge. This would be an abuse of my position: I am there to bring God's comfort into the situation. Even then, I sometimes wonder how much the mourners take in – they are often too upset or too numb to hear.

But, of course, the funeral service itself is not the only opportunity to talk about Christian faith. Every funeral demands at least one home visit (and often two or three) before the service and ongoing care after the service. When I visit a family, I always leave a copy of *Losing a Loved One* (Christian Publicity Organisation, 2000), which I wrote after my own father's death. This spells out the difference Jesus makes to living and to dying, as well as offering practical advice.

Appendix 4

Practicalities following a death

The initial visit

Meetings with the bereaved vary immensely. Some families know their way around what to do at death, but others do not. Sometimes families have already been in touch with an undertaker; sometimes I have made the phone call. Sometimes families know what happens at a funeral; at other times, I have to explain the process step by step. My custom on the initial visit is simply to listen and then to highlight the issues which will need decisions, but leave the decision making to a further visit before the funeral.

To help me in the initial visit, I devised a bereavement checklist.

Name and dates

Name [NB: by which known]:
Date and place of birth:
Date of death:
Date of funeral:
[NB: service of commemoration on first Sunday evening after All Saints' Day]

Burial or cremation?

Church service required

Undertaker to provide list of mourners?
Committal or funeral service first?
If committal first, then refreshments at church?

Order of service

Chief mourners follow coffin or seated first?
Normal pattern:
Any favourite hymns? [A wedding hymn?]
Any favourite Scripture? [A marked Bible?]
Any special music or other requirements?
Printed order of service? [to be agreed with minister!]
Choice of organist?

Where committal at crematorium separate from service

Hymn?
Other music?
Organist? [Fees for organist]

Flowers

Family flowers only?
Flowers to be provided at church?
Donations in memory of loved one?

Church connections

Date and place of baptism?
Offices held in this or another church?

Family and friends

Date and place of marriage?
How long married?
Name of spouse?
Children?
Names of other immediate relatives/in-laws?
Names of friends/neighbours or of district nurse/carer that next of kin want to pray for?
Who will be there?
Who can't be there?

Biodata

Where did X grow up?
Occupation:
Interests and achievements:
Any 'interests' to be represented at the funeral [such as membership of a club]?
We first met . . .
When I think of X I think of . . .
I am grateful to X above all for . . .
What single word might sum up the life of X?

Contact person

Contact details
Relation to the deceased

Three key decisions relating to the funeral

When the loved one has not made known their wishes, then the bereaved find themselves faced with three key decisions to make regarding the funeral.

Burial or cremation?

This can be a hard decision to make. Some do not like the thought of their loved one being burnt – burial seems more natural and allows more easily for a permanent memorial. But burial is not only more expensive but it also involves the ongoing need to care for the grave. Most people today opt for cremation. Certainly, with the vagaries of the British weather, cremation can be much more convenient.

If cremation is the chosen option, the question of the disposal of the ashes then arises. Some people prefer to entrust this task to the undertaker, while others prefer to scatter the ashes themselves. Another possibility is to bury the urn containing the ashes, and to accompany the burial with a brief service of committal.

A church service?

In our increasingly secular society, many funerals simply take place in a crematorium chapel. Where the mourners are few in number, the crematorium chapel may be welcomed as being more intimate than some barn of a church. Equally, for Christians it is generally more natural to come to church to receive the comfort that God can give. Although God is not limited to particular buildings, nonetheless there is something to be said for having a service in a building where down through the years God has made himself known to his people, and perhaps also where our loved one has worshipped. One great advantage of a church service is that time need not be an issue: in some crematoria, twenty minutes is the maximum length for a service. A church is also usually much more accessible to older mourners than a crematorium.

The committal before the church service?

Traditionally, the committal has taken place after the church service. However, there is a lot to be said for the increasingly common custom of preceding the service with the committal. The fact is that the committal marks the darkest moment of the day. There is something extremely stark about the curtains being drawn or the coffin being lowered into the ground. How much better if, after the committal, we can all go back to church and receive there the comfort which God can give. Furthermore, after the service, it is then possible to serve light refreshments to everybody who has attended and, in this way, make it possible for the family to have a word with everybody.

One possibility, particularly where a large family is involved, is to have a private service of committal in the morning, then have a break for lunch, followed by a public service of thanksgiving in the afternoon. The service of committal is the place for the expression of grief and tears. A private lunch then gives an opportunity for family members to meet up with one another and to catch up on their news, before having to face the wider world at the public service of thanksgiving. After the service, there can then be a tea for everybody, where friends can meet up with the family and express their sympathy.

Rites of passage for the grieving

Grieving takes time

Grieving is part of the cost of loving and takes time. It is generally reckoned that the grieving process can take anywhere from two to five years and, in some cases, even longer. Clearly, the latter part of the grieving process will not be as acute as the first few months, but – thank God – time does heal. Although we never forget our loved one, the pain of parting does ease, as we learn to cope with our loss.

Grieving is a complex process and is different for each one of us. Nonetheless, the grief 'journey' normally takes the following pattern.

In the first two weeks or so after the death of a loved one, we experience a phase of numbness and shock, when everything seems unreal and difficult to take in, with the result that we may even deny the reality of what has happened.

This period of denial gives way to a phase of yearning, with an urge to recover what has been lost. At this stage, we no longer deny our loss, but seek to find our loved one as we visit familiar places or look through old photographs. It is not unusual for people to hallucinate and think that they have seen or heard their loved one.

Then comes the phase of disorganization, despair and a gradual coming to terms with the reality of our loss. We perhaps become unnaturally forgetful or feel we cannot cope. This phase is often marked by anger, depression or guilt.

Finally, we move into a phase of reorganization and resolution, when we begin to accept the loss of our loved one. Gradually, healing comes, tears stop flowing and we find that we can start to make plans for the future.

How does the church help its members in this journey of grief? Are there particular moments when we need to be there for the bereaved once the funeral has taken place? Most ministers will visit in the week or so after the funeral, but there are other times when a visit might be appreciated, too, such as on the anniversary of the death or on a birthday or wedding anniversary.

The fortieth day

Relatively recently, I have become aware of a rite of passage developed by the Eastern Orthodox Church that takes place on the fortieth day after the death of a loved one. On this day, the family invites friends to come with them to visit the grave and return home for a memorial meal. What is more, either at the graveside or at the meal table, there are special prayers in which the loved one is commended to God's care.

This memorial has its roots in the ascension of Jesus. Just as the ascension marked the end of the appearance of Jesus to his disciples, so in Eastern Orthodox tradition, the fortieth-day memorial service is an opportunity to say a final goodbye to a loved one, although there may be further memorials after six months, a year and three years. Although, as Western Christians, we may not share the popular Orthodox belief that, for forty days, the soul of the departed wanders on earth, as already noted, there is a period in the grieving process when people do frequently see loved ones who have died. The rituals associated with the fortieth-day service aim to help the bereaved to let go and move on. Interestingly, in the Oriental Orthodox Church, including the Ethiopian, there is also a memorial service on the fortieth day.

As I was reflecting on these memorial services, the thought came to me that this must involve a good deal of diary planning on the part of the minister or priest. But then I realized that, within the Orthodox culture, these memorials are primarily family occasions, not church ones, and it must be the families who take the initiative to invite their pastor to come and share in the memorial event.

Although, as Western Christians, we may not feel comfortable with some of the Orthodox rituals associated with the fortieth day, nonetheless, I think that the idea of a family coming together for a meal forty days after the death of a loved one has much to commend it. Indeed, in some ways, this is a better day for the sharing of memories than the funeral itself, for by that time the initial numbness of grief will have passed. The fact is that grieving takes time. A sharing of memories around a meal together with a prayer of thanksgiving for the loved one could well form a most helpful rite of passage to enable the family to move further on in their grief journey. If such a memorial meal were then repeated on the first anniversary, and then a year and forty days later, so much the better!

Celebrating All Saints' Day

All Saints' Day provides a wonderful opportunity to thank God for loved ones who have died in the past year, and in past years too. All Saints' Day is always the first day of November. Hallowe'en, as its very name suggests, is the day before All Saints' Day. The Anglican Lectionary, however, allows the celebration of All Saints on the Sunday nearest to it.[1]

This is a day to invite to church the relatives of all those whose funerals have been taken by the minister over the past year. It is good, too, to remind those within the church who have lost loved ones (but whose funerals have taken place elsewhere) that this is an opportunity for them also to remember parents and grandparents, brothers and sisters – anybody who has been special to them.

Within the context of a service drawn up with the needs of the bereaved in mind, there is an opportunity, through the Scriptures and the sermon, to remind people of the difference that Jesus makes. All this builds up to the highpoint of lighting candles in memory of loved ones. It can be an incredibly moving and cathartic experience. The worship becomes the key vehicle for experiencing God's grace. Here is a liturgy which evangelical Christians can feel comfortable using too.

Leader We find it hard to let go of our loved ones and leave them in God's keeping. Today, I light this candle to remind us that Jesus rose from the dead to bring us God's new life, and that he is the Light of the world. Today, let it be a sign of the new life and love of God. We invite everyone who wishes, whether your loved one died in recent years or many years ago, to come and take a candle and light it in memory of him or her, so demonstrating your faith that all who trust in the risen Christ are in God's safekeeping.

(Lighting of candles, accompanied by music with appropriate images projected on a screen.)

Leader (after the candles have been lit) We remember, Lord, the slenderness of the thread which separates life from death, and the suddenness with which it can be broken. Help us also to remember that, on both sides of that division, we are surrounded by your love. Persuade our hearts that, when our dear ones die, neither we nor they are parted from you. Let us find our peace in you; and in you be united with them in the glorious body of Christ, for you have conquered death and are alive – our saviour and theirs – for ever and ever.[2]

After a hymn, a benediction Let us trust God for the past – for the forgiveness of past sins and the healing of past hurts. Let us trust God for the present – for the meeting of daily needs and for guidance in daily living. Let us trust God for the future – for help with tomorrow's troubles and for the hope of eternal life. So may the blessing of God Almighty, Father, Son and Holy Spirit be upon us all.[3]

Notes

Preface

1 An exception is Nick Watson, *Preaching at Funerals: How to Embed the Gospel in Funeral Ministry* (Cambridge: Grove, 2019), but that is only a twenty-five-page booklet!

Part 1 Introduction
The gospel is a message of hope

1 Jürgen Moltmann, *Theology of Hope* (London: SCM Press, 1967), p. 32.

2 Quoted by Nicky Gumbel, *Questions of Life* (Eastbourne: Kingsway, 1999).

3 Payne Best, *The Venlo Incident* (London: Hutchinson, 1950), p. 200. See also Eberhard Bethge, *Dietrich Bonhoeffer: A Biography* (Minneapolis, MN: Fortress, 2000), p. 927.

4 *Common Worship: Pastoral Services* (London: Church House Publishing, 2000), p. 269.

5 Stanley Hauerwas, *Christian Existence Today: Essays on Church, World and Living in Between* (Durham, NC: Labyrinth, 1988), p. 211: 'Optimism – hope without truth – is not sufficient for dealing with the pretentious powers that determine a person's existence in the world.'

6 Paul Beasley-Murray, *The Message of the Resurrection* (Leicester: IVP, 2000).

7 Pope Francis, *My Door Is Always Open: A Conversation on Faith, Hope and the Church in a Time of Change* (London: A&C Black, 2014), p. 100.

8 Hesiod, *Works and Days*.

9 Friedrich Nietzsche, *Human, All Too Human* (1878) Section 71: Hope.

10 Book 5.103.1.

11 Robert Ingersoll, speech, Manhattan Liberal Club, 28 February, 1892.

12 Stephen Travis, 'Hope', in Sinclair Ferguson and David Wright (eds), *New Dictionary of Theology* (Leicester: IVP, 1988), p. 321. Unfortunately, in the second edition of the *New Dictionary of Theology: Historical and Systematic* (London: IVP, 2016), edited by Martin Davie, Tim Grass, Stephen Holmes, John McDowell and Y. A. Noble, Travis's article was replaced by a new article by David Rainey, which is more interested in historical theology than biblical theology, although there is still an acknowledgement that with the life, death and resurrection of Jesus, 'the future has now become present' (Travis, 'Hope', p. 427).

13 Moltmann, *Theology of Hope*, p. 20.

14 Sam Allberry, *Lifted: Experiencing the Resurrection Life* (Nottingham, IVP: 2010), p. 80.

15 A 1959 film based on the 1957 novel *On the Beach* by Nevil Shute.

16 Aristotle, *The Nicomachean Ethics*, 1115a8, 26.

17 See Dale C. Allison, *Night Comes: Death, Imagination, and the Last Things* (Grand Rapids, MI: Eerdmans, 2016), p. 10.

18 Josh Glancy, *Sunday Times Magazine*, 10 May 2020. As Grayson Perry commented in his 2018 art show Rites of Passage, 'The cause of death is birth.'

19 An online poll of 1,018 adults undertaken for Theos by ComRes: see *Theos News*, 18 May 2009.

20 'RIP' reflects the traditional Christian prayer at a funeral: 'May (s)he rest in peace and rise in glory.' Although 'peace' was the repeated greeting of the Risen Christ in the Gospels, the richness of this biblical word (perhaps best paraphrased as 'God's very best') does not tend to convey much to people today.

21 Douglas Davies and Alistair Shaw, *Re-Using Old Graves: A Survey of Popular Attitudes* (Crayford, London: Shaw & Sons, 1995), cited by Vernon White, *Life Beyond Death* (London: Darton, Longman & Todd, 2006), p. 74.

22 ComRes survey of 2,010 British adults for BBC local radio, conducted by telephone between 2 and 12 February 2017.

23 'Death has a sharper sting for the faithful', *The Times*, 31 October 2018, p. 13.

24 See Paul Beasley-Murray, *Make the Most of Retirement* (Abingdon: Bible Reading Fellowship, 2020), p. 125.

25 Ernest Becker, *The Denial of Death* (New York: Free Press, 1973).

26 H. P. Lovell Cocks, source unknown.

27 Bertrand Russell, *The Autobiography of Bertrand Russell* (London: George Allen & Unwin, 1978), p. 393.

28 C. S. Lewis, *Miracles* in *Selected Works of C. S. Lewis* (London: HarperCollins, 1999), p. 1,210. *Miracles* by C. S. Lewis © copyright C. S. Lewis Pte Ltd 1946, 1960. Reprinted with permission.

29 Paul Beasley-Murray, 'The coronavirus pandemic – a time for overcoming the fear of death', *Church Matters*, 23 April 2020.

30 Paul Beasley-Murray, 'Perspectives: reflections on twelve years' worth of funerals', *Quadrant*, May 2006.

31 See 'Lesson 15: Funerals are Multi-faceted', in Paul Beasley-Murray, *Fifty Lessons in Ministry: Reflection after Fifty Years of Ministry* (London: Darton, Longman & Todd, 2020): 'As a young minister I believed that tributes at a funeral were wrong. A Christian funeral was not a place for eulogies, but for preaching. My task was to speak about the grace of God, and not about the departed. I followed William Carey's instructions for his own funeral: "Speak not of Carey, speak of Carey's Saviour." I never encouraged tributes from friends and relatives. Instead, I would say a few words about their loved one, before getting on with "the real job" of speaking about Jesus. Eventually I changed my mind. I now believe there is a place for tributes. For many years I have had a "tribute slot" when one or two family members or friends have shared memories of the deceased. Why the change of mind? Perhaps because I now see a distinction between a eulogy and a tribute. Although technically a "eulogy" means only "a speaking well", all too often it involves an exercise in praise so unreal that it contravenes the Trades Description Act. In a Christian funeral there is no place for such a glorification of the departed – for "all have sinned and fall short of the glory of God" (Rom. 3.23). Along with our virtues we have our vices . . . Although in the introduction to my sermon at a funeral I normally say a few words about the deceased, I tend to keep my tribute short. As I discovered on one memorable occasion, it is

possible to get things wrong. It was a funeral of a lady, who I had only really known in the closing stages of her life. I thought she was a wonderful Christian lady and told the congregation so, only to discover at the funeral tea that there had been a mean and unkind streak to her character. I am now much more careful in what I say. As a Christian minister I cannot afford to engage in unreal eulogizing, for it then calls into question my own integrity, which in turn could give the congregation reason to be sceptical about my affirmations of the gospel.'

32 Paul Sheppy, *In Sure and Certain Hope: Liturgies, Prayers and Readings for Funerals and Memorials* (Norwich: Canterbury Press, 2003), p. 4.

33 Thomas G. Long, *Accompany Them with Singing: The Christian Funeral* (Louisville, KY: Westminster John Knox, 2009), p. 81.

34 Winn Collier, *A Burning in My Bones* (Milton Keynes: Authentic, 2021), p. 301.

35 Long, *Accompany Them with Singing*, p. 81.

36 Ibid., p. 187.

37 Ibid., p. 188.

38 *The Alternative Service Book 1980: Services Authorized for Use in the Church of England in Conjunction with The Book of Common Prayer* (London: Hodder & Stoughton, 1980), p. 313.

39 *Common Worship: Pastoral Services* (London: Church House Publishing, 2011), p. 263.

40 See, for instance, Ernest E. Payne and Stephen F. Winward, *Orders and Prayers for Church Worship*, 4th edn (London: Baptist Union of Great Britain & Ireland, 1967), p. 204: 'If desired an address may be given.'

41 Christopher Ellis and Myra Blyth, *Gathering for Worship: Patterns and Prayers for the Community of Disciples* (Norwich: Canterbury Press, 2005), p. 232.

42 Ibid., p. 228, who entitle the section on funerals with the words 'Confronting Death, Celebrating Resurrection'.

43 Jenny Hockey, *Making the Most of a Funeral* (London: Cruse Bereavement Care, 1992), quoted by David Saville, *The Funeral Service: A Guide* (London: Hodder & Stoughton, 1996), p. 76.

44 See Frank Pagden, *Laughter and Tears: Forty-Eight Addresses for Baptisms, Weddings and Funerals* (Crowborough: Monarch, 1995).

45 Much has been written about what Paul had in mind when he urged Timothy to 'rightly explain the word of truth' (2 Tim. 2:15). Literally, the underlying Greek word (*orthotomeo*) means to 'cut straight' and is only found elsewhere in Prov. 3:6 and 11:5, where, according to William Arndt and Wilbur Gingrich, *A Greek–English Lexicon to the NT and Other Early Christian Literature*, 4th edn (Cambridge: Cambridge University Press, 1952), 'it means "cut a path in a straight direction" or "cut a road across country (that is forested or otherwise difficult to pass through) in a straight direction", so that the traveller may go directly to his destination.' If this is the underlying meaning of the metaphor, then the emphasis is on the word of God reaching its destination. Preaching has to be faithful to 'the word of truth', but above all it needs to be clear to the listener.

46 Michael J. Quicke, *360-Degree Preaching: Hearing, Speaking and Living the Word* (Carlisle: Paternoster, 2003), p. 27.

47 Opinions do, however, vary on the length of a funeral sermon. For instance, according to Desmond Forristal, an Irish Roman Catholic priest, 'A few well-chosen sentences about the deceased, a word of condolence to the family, and a message of Christian hope from the readings, should not take more than five minutes', 'Parish Practicalities', in Eltin Griffin (ed.), *Pastoral Commentaries, Creative Ideas and Funeral Homilies* (Dublin: Columba Press, 1998), p. 33. By contrast, on Google, an American preacher stated that 'funeral sermons are typically not as long as a church sermon and are generally about 15–25 minutes in length'!

48 With the blessing of my church, I ended up defining my responsibilities as follows.
    1. Leading the church, not managing the church. I love to spark with fellow leaders and to cast the vision, but I need to be freed from running the church.
    2. Expounding God's Word on a Sunday, but not organizing the small group programme.
    3. Welcoming newcomers, but not overseeing their integration into church life. I love to visit newcomers, but then pass them on!

4. Pastoring God's people, but not engaging in routine pastoral care. I want to be alongside families as they go through the lifecycle of birth, marriage and death, but otherwise want to leave pastoral care to others.

5. Growing leaders, not attending meetings. I want the focus in the week to be on developing and supporting my members of staff in their ministry.

6. Reflecting on ministry issues, writing for and encouraging fellow ministers.

See further Paul Beasley-Murray, *Living Out the Call: Book 1: Living for God's Glory*, 2nd edn (FeedARead, 2016).

49 See Paul Beasley-Murray, *Living Out the Call: Book 3: Reaching out to God's World*, 2nd edn (FeedARead, 2016), pp. 53–60.

Part 2 Hope in the gospels
1 Mark 10:13–16

1 James Edwards, *The Gospel According to Luke* (Nottingham: IVP, 2015), p. 507.

2 The National Society for the Prevention of Cruelty of Children.

3 O. M. Bakke, *When Children Became People: The Birth of Childhood in Early Christianity* (Minneapolis, MN: Fortress, 2005), p. 16.

4 See Lawrence Stone, *The Past and the Present Revisited* (London: Routledge & Kegan Paul, 1987), pp. 321–323.

5 Rodney Clapp, *Families at the Crossroads: Beyond Traditional and Modern Options* (Leicester: IVP, 1993), p. 41.

6 Anne Richards, *Children in the Bible: A Fresh Approach* (London: SPCK, 2013), p. 116.

7 James Edwards, *The Gospel According to Mark* (Leicester: IVP, 2002), p. 307.

8 Richards, *Children in the Bible*, p. 125.

9 R. T. France, *The Gospel of Matthew* (Grand Rapids, MI: Eerdmans, 2007), p. 687.

10 David Saville, *The Funeral Service: A Guide* (London: Hodder & Stoughton, 1996), p. 111.

11 I find it of interest that in the Church of England's *Common Worship* (London: Church House, 2000), one of the introductory sentences

for the funeral of a child is Mark 10:14 and one of the suggested readings is Mark 10:13–16.

12 See Appendix 2: The funeral of a baby who died in the womb, p. 205.

2 Luke 20:27–40

1 N. T. Wright, *The Resurrection of the Son of God* (London: SPCK, 2003), p. 415.

2 Dawn Ottoni Wilhelm, *Preaching the Gospel of Mark: Proclaiming the Power of God* (Louisville, KY: Westminster John Knox, 2008), p. 211

3 Ben Witherington III, *The Gospel of Mark: A Socio-Rhetorical Commentary* (Grand Rapids, MI: Eerdmans, 2001), p. 329.

4 James Edwards, *The Gospel According to Luke* (Leicester: IVP, 2002), p. 580.

5 Frederick Dale Bruner, *The Churchbook: Matthew 13–28*, 2nd edn (Grand Rapids, MI: Eerdmans, 2004), p. 406.

6 Witherington, *The Gospel of Mark*, p. 328.

7 R. T. France, *The Gospel of Matthew* (Grand Rapids, MI: Eerdmans, 2007), p. 839.

8 Timothy Keller, *On Marriage* (London: Hodder & Stoughton, 2020), pp. 96, 97.

9 France, *The Gospel of Matthew*, p. 839.

10 Michael Green, *The Message of Matthew*, 2nd edn (Leicester: IVP, 2000), p. 235.

11 Ian Paul, 'Are We Sexed in Heaven? Bodily Form, Sex Identity and the Resurrection', in Thomas A. Noble, Sarah K. Whittle and Philip S. Johnston (eds), *Marriage, Family, Relationship: Biblical, Doctrinal and Contemporary Perspectives* (London: Apollos, 2017).

12 Wright, *The Resurrection of the Son of God*, p. 423.

13 France, *The Gospel of Matthew*, p. 841.

14 Similarly, Douglas R. A. Hare, *Matthew* (Louisville, KY: Westminster John Knox, 2009), p. 257: 'Those whom God chooses to relate in covenant love, he does not abandon.'

15 Edwards, *The Gospel According to Luke*, p. 581.

16 Witherington, *The Gospel of Mark*, p. 330.

17 A. Michael Ramsey, *The Resurrection of Christ: A Study of the Events and Its Meaning for the Christian Faith* (London: Fontana, 1961), p. 9.

18 Vernon White, *Life Beyond Death* (London: Darton, Longman & Todd, 2006), p. 74.

19 Paul wrote that, when Jesus returns, we shall be reunited with loved ones who have died in Christ. He described the Thessalonians as his 'crown of boasting before our Lord Jesus at his coming' (1 Thess. 2:19); similarly, within the context of Jesus' return, he described the Philippians as 'my joy and crown' (Phil. 4:1). Ben Witherington III commented: 'Paul envisions a grand celebration, perhaps like that at the end of the Olympic games, where the victors are given their wreaths and there is much rejoicing' (quoted by Walter Hansen, *The Letter to the Philippians*, Nottingham: Apollos, 2009, p. 280). Then, in 1 Thess. 4:13–18, there is Paul's description of the coming of the Lord: whatever else this passage means, it surely 'encourages' (4:18) Christians to believe that we will meet up with one another. To quote Witherington again, 'It will be the ultimate family reunion with the king' (*1 & 2 Thessalonians*, Grand Rapids, MI: Eerdmans, 2006, p. 141).

20 Eberhard Busch and John Bowden (trans.), *Karl Barth: His Life from Letters and Autobiographical Texts* (Eugene, OR: Wipf & Stock, 2005), p. 395.

21 John Bunyan, *The Pilgrim's Progress* (first published Part I 1678, Part II 1884; my edition London: Collins, 1953), p. 171.

22 Justin Thacker, 'Heaven', in Stephen Holmes and Russell Rook (eds), *What are We Waiting For? Christian Hope and Contemporary Culture* (Milton Keynes: Paternoster, 2008), p. 119.

3 John 3:16; 10:10

1 George Raymond Beasley-Murray, *The Gospel of Life: Theology in the Fourth Gospel* (Peabody, MA: Hendrickson, 1991), p. 2.

2 Colin G. Kruse, *John* (London: IVP, first published 2003; reprinted 2008), p. 114.

3 Don A. Carson, *The Gospel According to John* (Leicester: IVP, 1991), p. 385.

4 Craig R. Koester, *The Word of Life: A Theology of John's Gospel* (Grand Rapids, MI: Eerdmans, 2008), p. 45.

5 See also Raymond E. Brown, *The Gospel According to John: I–XIII* (New York: Doubleday, 1966), p. 507. He went on to say, 'The difference between divine life and natural life is primarily qualitative . . . But we do not imply that there is no connotation of "everlasting" in John's understanding of this life. If death cannot destroy it, obviously it has no definite terminus' (see 6:58).

6 Arthur Fay Sueltz, *Deeper into John's Gospel* (New York: Harper & Row, 1979), pp. 53, 54.

7 Dale C. Allison, *Night Comes: Death, Imagination, and the Last Things* (Grand Rapids, MI: Eerdmans, 2016), pp. 122, 123.

8 Ibid., p. 123.

4 John 11:1–44

1 Craig L. Blomberg, *The Historical Reliability of John's Gospel* (Leicester: Apollos, 2001), p. 164.

2 Margaret Magdalen, *The Hidden Face of Jesus: Reflections on the Emotional Life of Jesus* (London: Darton, Longman & Todd, 1994), p. 138.

3 Blomberg, *The Historical Reliability of John's Gospel*, p. 164.

4 Magdalen, *The Hidden Face of Jesus*, p. 135.

5 Richard Llewellyn, *How Green Was My Valley* (London: Michael Joseph, 1939; London: Penguin Classics, 2001).

6 George Raymond Beasley-Murray, *John*, WBC 36, 2nd edn (Nashville, TN: Thomas Nelson, 1999), p. 192.

7 Ibid., *John*, p. 193.

8 Gordon Bridger, *The Man from Outside* (Leicester: IVP 1978), p. 121.

9 William Barclay, *And He Had Compassion* (Edinburgh: St Andrew Press, 1975, revised edition), p. 205.

10 Donald Coggan, *The Prayers of the New Testament* (London: Hodder & Stoughton, 1967), p. 58. Coggan added, 'It is a scene of action. But in the midst of it is a pool of quiet – "Father, I thank Thee . . ." And in that quiet there comes to Him the strong assurance that the Father is there, and that He is listening. All will

be well. The victory will be won. In that assurance, He faces death and brings life.'

11 See Beasley-Murray, *John*, p. 199: 'He who wrote the Gospel of the Word made flesh viewed history as of first importance; he would never have related a story of Jesus, still less created one, that he did not have reason to believe took place.'

12 Ibid., p. 190.

13 Marianne Meye Thompson, 'The Raising of Lazarus in John 11', in Richard Bauckham and Carl Mosser (eds), *The Gospel of John and Christian Theology* (Grand Rapids, MI: Eerdmans, 2008), p. 240.

14 C. S. Lewis, *A Grief Observed* (London: Faber & Faber, 1961; this edition 1966), p. 21. *A Grief Observed* by C. S. Lewis © copyright C. S. Lewis Pte Ltd 1961. Reprinted with permission.

15 Carl Jung, *Memories, Dreams, Reflections* (first published in English 1962; new edition London: Fontana, 1995), edited by Aniela Jaffe.

16 John Diamond, *C: Because Cowards Get Cancer Too* (London: Vermilion, 1998).

17 Roy Castle (1932–1994) was a mainstay on British television in the 1970s and 1980s, particularly well known for his very popular children's show *Record Breakers*. He was also an extremely talented musician, actor and singer. His lung cancer diagnosis in 1992 led to his early death in 1994. Castle had never smoked, and his death raised awareness of the dangers of passive smoking and played a pivotal role in the banning of smoking in enclosed spaces. The Roy Castle Lung Cancer Foundation continues his work.

18 See also Fiona Castle, *No Flowers, No Fuss . . . Just Lots of Joy* (Eastbourne: Kingsway, 1996).

19 This is reminiscent of a question posed by John Ruskin in a letter to his friend Susie Beever: 'Why should we wear black for the guests of God?'

20 Francis Bridger, *23 Days: A Story of Love, Death and God* (London: Darton, Longman & Todd, 2004), p. 32.

21 Ibid., p. 119.

22 On the order of service for Elinor's funeral were words by Minnie Louise Haskins used by King George VI in a radio broadcast to the

nation at Christmas 1939: 'And I said to the man who stood at the gate of the year: "Give me a light that I may tread safely into the unknown." And he replied: "Go out into the darkness and put your hand into the Hand of God. That shall be to you better than light and safer than a known way." So I went forth, and finding the Hand of God, trod gladly into the night. And He led me towards the hills and the breaking of day in the lone East.' To these words she appended the following stanza:

> So heart be still:
> What need our little life
> Our human life to know,
> If God hath comprehension?
> In all the dizzy strife
> Of things both high and low,
> God hideth His intention.

5 John 14:1–6

1 Gerard Sloyan, *John* (Louisville, KY: Westminster John Knox, 2009), p. 178.

2 William H. Willimon, *Who Will Be Saved?* (Nashville, TN: Abingdon, 2008), p. 99.

3 George Raymon Beasley-Murray, *John*, WBC 36, 3nd edn (Nashville, TN: Nelson, 1999) p. 249.

4 N. T. Wright, *The Resurrection of the Son of God* (London: SPCK, 2003), p. 446.

5 See Rodney A. Whitacre, *John* (Nottingham: IVP, 2008), p. 349.

6 Wright, *The Resurrection of the Son of God*, p. 446.

7 Beasley-Murray, *John*, p. 250.

8 Craig L. Blomberg, *The Historical Reliability of John's Gospel* (Leicester: Apollos, 2001), p. 198.

9 Tom Wright, *John for Everyone, Part 2: Chapters 11 – 21* (London: SPCK, 2002).

10 Craig R. Koester, *The Word of Life: A Theology of John's Gospel* (Grand Rapids, MI: Eerdmans, 2008), p. 210.

11 Whitacre, *John*, p. 349.

12 Willimon, *Who Will Be Saved?*, p. 99.

Part 3 Hope in the letters of Paul
6 Romans 8:31–39

1 Some have suggested that Rom. 8:31–39 is an actual 'hymn'. However, as Arland J. Hultgren rightly noted, 'It is better to say that the passage contains liturgical, hymnic, and confessional elements which have been brought together by the apostle to exult in the love of God expressed in Christ and to form a fitting conclusion to the chapters that have gone before', in *Paul's Letter to the Romans: A Commentary* (Grand Rapids, MI: Eerdmans, 2011), p. 335.

2 See Paul Beasley-Murray, 'The Lordship of Christ over the World in the Corpus Paulinum' (PhD, Manchester University, 1970), pp. 209–214.

3 C. E. B. Cranfield, *Romans Vol 1: I–VIII* (Edinburgh: T & T Clark, 1975), p. 436.

4 James Dunn, *Romans 1–8* (Dallas, TX: Word, 1988), p. 499.

5 Ibid., p. 500.

6 Cranfield, *Romans*, p. 436.

7 See, for instance, Gen. 12:7; 13:14–17; 22:17–18; 25:3–5.

8 Cranfield, *Romans*, p. 435. However, Dunn, *Romans*, p. 502, thought there could be an allusion to our sharing in Christ's lordship over the world ('all things' = 'the creation').

9 Paul J. Achtemaier, *Romans* (Atlanta, GA: John Knox Press, 1985), p. 149.

10 That Christ is in mind is shown by the parallelism between 'Through him who loved us' (8:37) and 'who shall separate us from the love of Christ' (8:35).

11 Cranfield, *Romans*, p. 440.

12 Dunn, *Romans*, p. 512.

13 Cranfield, *Romans*, p. 441.

14 See also Rom. 14:14; 15:14; 2 Tim. 1:5, 12.

15 I believe that Martin Luther personified death as 'the great adulterer', but more commonly it is envisaged as a 'thief': 'he was taken from us'. In medieval thought, death was viewed as the grim reaper.

16 Dunn, *Romans*, p. 513.

17 Aristotle, in his *Nicomachean Ethics*.

18 Blaise Pascal, *Pensées*, 1670.

19 Graham Greene, *Brighton Rock* (London: Heinemann, 1938).

7 1 Corinthians 15:3–5, 20, 24–28, 54–57

1 Roy E. Ciampa and Brian S. Rosner, *The First Letter to the Corinthians* (Nottingham: Apollos, 2010), p. 768.

2 Anthony C. Thiselton, *1 Corinthians: A Shorter Exegetical and Pastoral Commentary* (Grand Rapids, MI: Eerdmans, 2006), p. 270.

3 Ibid., p. 273

4 The underlying Greek verb (*katargeo*) translated as 'destroyed' can have the meaning to annihilate (such as in 2 Thess. 2:8; 1 Cor. 6:13), but its primary meaning is to 'render ineffective'. If the latter meaning be adopted, death may still continue to exist, but no longer as an effective enemy to God. Rather, it is an instrument in his hand which may be used against those whom he sees fit to punish (see Rom. 6:21–23; 1 Cor. 1:18–31; 2 Cor. 2:16; 4:3, 4; Phil. 1:28).

5 Gordon Fee, *The First Epistle to the Corinthians*, 2nd edn (Grand Rapids, MI: Eerdmans, 2014), p. 841.

6 Ibid., p. 841.

7 Ibid., p. 890.

8 Barry Albin Dyer, *Don't Drop the Coffin* (London: Hodder & Stoughton, 2002).

8 1 Corinthians 15:35–48

1 Roy E. Ciampa and Brian S. Rosner, *The First Letter to the Corinthians* (Nottingham: Apollos, 2010), p. 801.

2 Anthony C. Thiselton, *1 Corinthians: A Shorter Exegetical and Pastoral Commentary* (Grand Rapids, MI: Eerdmans, 2006), p. 280.

3 Ibid., p. 280.

4 Ibid., 281.

5 Ibid., p. 282.

6 Ibid., p. 282.

7 Ibid., p. 282.

8 Ciampa and Rosner, *The First Letter to the Corinthians*, p. 817.

9 N. T. Wright, *The Resurrection of the Son of God* (London: SPCK, 2003), p. 352.

10 Thiselton *1 Corinthians*, p. 283.

11 Ibid., p. 282.

9 1 Thessalonians 4:13–18

1 John Wyatt, *Dying Well* (London: IVP, 2018), p. 122; also 'The Art of Dying Well', in Kristi Mair and Luke Crawley (eds), *Healthy Faith and the Coronavirus* (London: IVP, 2020), p. 74.

2 Source unknown.

3 N. T. Wright, *The Resurrection of the Son of God* (London: SPCK, 2003), p. 217.

4 G. K. Beale, *1–2 Thessalonians* (Leicester: IVP, 2003), p. 141.

5 Ben Witherington III, *1 and 2 Thessalonians: A Socio-Rhetorical Commentary* (Grand Rapids, MI: Eerdmans, 2006), p. 133, notes: 'The aorist participle here, *koimethentas*, favours this interpretation since it refers to the moment, not the condition, of death – they died in the Lord.'

6 Gene L. Green, *The Letters to the Thessalonians* (Leicester: Apollos, 2002), p. 221.

7 Ibid., p. 223

8 Witherington, *1 and 2 Thessalonians*, p. 141.

9 Wright, *The Resurrection of the Son of God*, p. 215, draws a parallel between 4:16–17 and 1 Cor. 15:51–52 and suggested that this is 'functionally equivalent, in Paul's mind, to being "changed" so that one's body is no longer corruptible, but now of the same type as the Lord's own risen body'.

10 See further Paul Beasley-Murray, 'Paul as Pastor' in G. F. Hawthorne and R. P. Martin (eds), *Dictionary of Paul and his Letters* (Leicester: IVP, 1993), pp. 654–658.

11 See Colin Murray Parkes, *The Price of Love: The Selected Works of Colin Murray Parkes* (Abingdon: Routledge, 2015), p. 1: 'The pain of grief is just as much a part of life as the joy of love; it is, perhaps, the price we pay for love, the cost of commitment. To ignore this fact, or to pretend that it is not so, is to put on emotional blinkers which leave us unprepared for the losses that will inevitably occur in our lives and unprepared to help others with the losses in theirs.'

10 2 Timothy 4:6–8

1 Ben Witherington III, *Letters and Homilies for Hellenized Christians Vol. 1: A Socio-Rhetorical Commentary on Titus, 1 – 2 Timothy and 1 – 3 John* (Nottingham: Apollos, 2006), p. 366.

2 Ibid., p. 368.

3 Ibid., p. 369, refers to the French scholar Charles Spicq, who noted that it was a common practice to pour out a drink offering to the gods before loosing the ropes from the mooring for the boat to depart. Both these metaphors are present here.

4 Robert W. Yarborough, *The Letters to Timothy and Titus* (London: Apollos, 2018), p. 443.

5 Thomas C. Oden, *First and Second Timothy and Titus* (Louisville, KY: John Knox, 1989), p. 172.

6 David Frampton, 'Caring for those struggling with terminal illness', *Ministry Today* 68 (Summer 2006), pp. 16–18. A similar observation was made by medical professor John Wyatt in *Dying Well* (London: IVP, 2018), pp. 63–64.

7 For instance, J. N. D. Kelly, *The Pastoral Epistles: I and II Timothy, Titus* (London: Adam & Charles Black, 1963), p. 208, wrote, 'As in 1 Tim. 6.12 the picture is not of warfare, but of an athletic contest, probably a wrestling match.' Oden, *First and Second Timothy and Titus*, p. 172, likewise thought Paul had in mind an 'athletic struggle – running, wrestling or boxing'. Gordon Fee, *1 and 2 Timothy, Titus* (Peabody, MA: Hendrickson, 1988), p. 289, and Witherington, *Letters and Homilies for Hellenized Christians*, p. 369, were of the opinion that Paul had in mind 'a running race'. By contrast, Yarborough, *The Letters to Timothy and Titus*, p. 444, believed Paul was referring to a 'fight'.

8 Oden, *First and Second Timothy and Titus*, p. 172. However, Fee, *1 and 2 Timothy, Titus*, p. 289, interpreted the term 'good' (*kalon*) differently: 'The word *kalon* . . . does not imply that Paul's running was "good" but that he, as he had also urged Timothy (1 Tim. 6.12), has been running in the noblest, grandest run of them all – the ministry of the gospel.'

9 See, for instance, Yarborough, *The Letters to Timothy and Titus*, p. 445.

10 Oden, *First and Second Timothy and Titus*, p. 173.

11 Witherington, *Letters and Homilies for Hellenized Christians*, p. 370.

Part 4 Hope in the rest of the New Testament
11 Hebrews 6:17–19

1 David G. Peterson, *Hebrews* (London: IVP, 2020), p. 106.

2 Ibid., p. 180.

3 Rob Merchant, *Broken by Fear, Anchored in Hope* (London: SPCK, 2020), p. 81.

4 Ben Witherington III, *Letters and Homilies for Jewish Christians: A Socio-Rhetorical Commentary on Hebrews, James and Jude* (Nottingham: Apollos, 2007), p. 225.

5 Witherington, *Letters and Homilies for Jewish Christians*, p. 226.

6 Ask the Editors, 'What is the origin of the anchor as a Christian symbol, and why do we no longer use it?', *Christianity Today*, 8 August 2008 (available online at: <www.christianitytoday.com/history/2008/august/what-is-origin-of-anchor-as-christian-symbol-and-why-do-we.html?utm_medium=widgetsocial>, accessed 10 July 2021).

12 1 Peter 1:3–8

1 Joel B. Green, *1 Peter* (Grand Rapids, MI: Eerdmans, 2007), p. 24.

2 This expression appears in the New Testament only in doxological contexts: Rom. 15:6; 2 Cor. 1:3; Eph. 1:3; Col. 1:3; here in 1 Pet. 1:3.

3 Green, *1 Peter*, p. 26.

4 Lewis R. Donelson, *I and II Peter and Jude* (Louisville, KY: Westminster John Knox, 2010), p. 31.

5 Wayne Grudem, *1 Peter* (Leicester: IVP, 1988), p. 55, suggests that Peter thereby 'indicates that it grows and increases in strength year by year'.

6 The underlying Greek (*lupethentes*) indicates that the suffering has been marked by grief.

7 J. N. D. Kelly, *The Epistles of Peter and of Jude* (London: Adam & Charles Black, 1969), p. 57.

8 Donelson, *I and II Peter and Jude*, p. 35.

9 N. T. Wright, *The Resurrection of the Son of God* (London: SPCK, 2003), p. 466.

10 Andrew Brown, 'Christianity Considered as True', *The Guardian*, 6 October 2012 (available online at: <www.theguardian.com/commentisfree/andrewbrown/2012/oct/06/christianity-considered-as-true>, accessed 7 July 2021).

11 Scott MacDougall, 'Christian Logic: Life after Death', *Huffington Post* 14 October 2012 (available online at: <www.huffpost.com/entry/christian-illogic-life-after-death_b_1955641>, accessed 7 July 2021).

13 1 John 2:28 – 3:3

1 N. T. Wright, *The Resurrection of the Son of God* (London: SPCK, 2003), p. 464.

2 Martyn Lloyd-Jones, *Life in Christ: Children of God. Studies in 1 John, Volume 1* (Leicester: Crossway, 1993), p. 231.

3 I. Howard Marshall, *The Epistles of John* (Grand Rapids, MI: Eerdmans, 1978), p. 165.

4 Stephen S. Smalley *1, 2, 3 John* (Waco, TX: Word, 1984), p. 129.

5 See 1 John 1:2; 2:25; 5:11, 18.

6 The nearest we get to that expression is in Heb. 9:28: 'Christ . . . will appear a second time, not to deal with sin, but to save those who are eagerly waiting for him.'

7 *Common Worship: Services and Prayers for the Church of England* (London: Church House, 2000), p. 189.

8 Derek Tidball, *The Message of Holiness* (Nottingham: IVP, 2010), pp. 281, 282.

9 Marshall, *The Epistles of John*, p. 165

10 Ibid., p. 165.

11 Raymond E. Brown, *The Epistles of John* (New York: Doubleday, 1982), p. 395.

12 Alister E. McGrath, *A Brief History of Heaven* (Oxford: Blackwell, 2003), p. 181.

13 Quoted in ibid., p. 182.

14 Ibid., p. 183.

15 John Donne, Sermon 15 February 1631.

16 Colin G. Kruse, *The Letters of John* (Leicester: Apollos, 2000), p. 116.

17 Smalley, *1, 2, 3 John*, p. 130.
18 Brown, *The Epistles of John*, p. 381.
19 Tom Wright, *Simply Christian* (London: SPCK, 2006), p. 189.
20 Kruse, *The Letters of John*, p. 116.

14 Revelation 7:9–17

1 Stephen Smalley, *The Revelation to John: A Commentary on the Greek Text of the Apocalypse* (London: SPCK, 2005), p. 190.
2 Ibid., p. 190.
3 M. Eugene Boring, *Revelation* (Louisville, KY: Westminster John Knox, 1989), p. 131.
4 John Risbridger, *The Message of Worship* (Nottingham: IVP, 2015), p. 93.
5 Gordon D. Fee, *Revelation* (Eugene, OR: Wipf & Stock, 2007), p. 112.
6 Smalley, *The Revelation to John*, p. 193.
7 William F. Arndt and F. Wilbur Gingrich, *A Greek–English Lexicon of the New Testament and Other Early Christian Literature*, 4th edn (Cambridge: Cambridge University Press, 1952), p. 468.
8 Adapted from joke 1160 found online at: <www.unijokes.com>.

15 Revelation 22:1–7

1 M. Eugene Boring, *Revelation* (Louisville, KY: Westminster John Knox, 1989), p. 215.
2 William F. Arndt and F. Wilbur Gingrich, *A Greek–English Lexicon of the New Testament and Other Early Christian Literature*, 4th edn (Cambridge: Cambridge University Press, 1952), p. 305.
3 Kenneth H. Maahs, *Of Angels, Beasts and Plagues* (Valley Forge, PA: Judson, 1999), p. 270.
4 Michael Griffiths, *Cinderella with Amnesia* (Leicester: IVP, 1975), p. 7.
5 Bruce Milne, *The Message of Heaven and Hell* (Leicester: IVP, 2002), p. 311.
6 Boring, *Revelation*, p. 221.
7 Gordon D. Fee, *Revelation* (Eugene, OR: Wipf & Stock, 2007), p. 294.
8 Milne, *The Message of Heaven and Hell*, p. 310.

Part 5 Hope in the Old Testament

16 Job 19:25–27

1 Paul Williamson, *Death and the Afterlife: Biblical Perspectives on Ultimate Questions* (London: Apollos, 2017), p. 80.

2 N. T. Wright, *The Resurrection of the Son of God* (London: SPCK, 2003), pp. 96–98.

3 John Goldingay, *Job for Everyone* (London: SPCK, 2013), p. 98.

4 John Job, *Where Is My Father?: Studies in the Book of Job* (London: Epworth, 1977), p. 36.

5 H. H. Rowley, *Job* (London: Nelson, 1970), p. 174.

6 Gerald Janzen, *Job* (Louisville, KY: Westminster John Knox, 1985), pp. 144–145.

7 Ibid., pp. 140–145.

8 David Atkinson, *The Message of Job* (Leicester: IVP, 1991), pp. 94, 95.

17 Psalm 16

1 Leonard Griffiths, *God in Man's Experience*, 2nd edn (London: Hodder & Stoughton, 1970), p. 16. Strictly speaking, Griffiths should have said that the mood of sheer delight climbs 'in' such a crescendo of delight, for in musical terms a crescendo describes the journey and not the point of arrival.

2 John Goldingay, *Psalms for Everyone: Psalms 1 – 72* (London: SPCK, 2013), p. 50.

3 For instance, Arnold Anderson, *Psalms: Vol 1* (London: Marshall, Morgan & Scott, 1971), p. 145: 'It is just possible that the psalmist may have hoped that, in some way or other, his fellowship with God would not come to an end. But since such a view would have been a novelty, one would have expected a more explicit description of this daring faith.' Goldingay, *Psalms for Everyone*, p. 50: 'It's referring to the wonder of this life that God has given us to enjoy.'

4 N. T. Wright, *The Resurrection of the Son of God* (London: SPCK, 2003), p. 104, pointed out that God is the basis of the psalmist's hope: It is YHWH himself, the one the psalmist embraces as his sovereign one (v2), his portion and cup (v5),

the one who gives him counsel in the secret places of his heart.'

5 Michael Wilcock, *Psalms 1 – 72* (Leicester: IVP, 2001), p. 58.

6 Derek Kidner, *Psalms 1 – 72* (Leicester: IVP, 1983; reprinted 2008), p. 103.

7 Tremper Longman III, *Psalms* (Nottingham: IVP, 2014), p. 106.

8 As James L. Mays, *Psalms* (Louisville, KY: John Knox, 1994), p. 87, pointed out, David was 'using the vocabulary and concepts that are employed in the book of Joshua to describe Israel's occupation of the promised land as the outcome of God's salvation of Israel. Tribes, clans and individuals were given a portion as their heritage that was laid off by lines determined by casting the sacred lot.'

9 C. S. Lewis, *Letters to Malcolm: Chiefly on Prayer* (London: Geoffrey Bles, 1964), p. 93.

10 From the penultimate line of the last stanza of John Newton's hymn 'Glorious Things of Thee Are Spoken'.

11 Augustine, *City of God*, Book XII.

12 O. A. Lambert.

18 Psalm 23

1 See, for instance, Tremper Longman III, *Psalms* (Nottingham: IVP, 2014), p. 137.

2 C. S. Lewis, *Reflections on the Psalms* (London: Fontana, 1967), p. 84. *Reflections on the Psalms* by C. S. Lewis © copyright C. S. Lewis Pte Ltd 1958. Reprinted with permission.

3 Walter Brueggemann, *The Meaning of the Psalms* (Minneapolis, MN: Augsburg, 1994), p. 156: 'It is God's companionship that transforms every situation. it does not mean that there are no deathly valleys, no enemies. But they are not capable of hurt, and so the powerful loyalty and solidarity of Yahweh *comfort*, precisely in situations of threat.'

4 Kenneth E. Bailey, *The Good Shepherd: A 1000-Year Journey from Psalm 23 to the New Testament* (London: SPCK, 2015), p. 62.

5 Ibid., pp. 50, 52.

6 See, for instance, Pss 89:1; 95:7; 100:3.

7 James L. Mays, *Psalms* (Louisville, KY: John Knox, 1994), p. 24.

8 See Brueggemann, *The Meaning of the Psalms*, p. 155: 'The "I" statements are filled with gratitude, yielding, trust and thanksgiving. The "I" here knows that in every case, life is fully cared for and resolved by this thou who responds to and anticipates ever need. Life with Yahweh is a life of well-being and satisfaction.'

9 There, in the kingdom of God, a banquet is prepared. God our companion turns out to be our host: 'You prepare a table before me in the presence of my enemies; you anoint my head with oil; my cup overflows' (23:5). In the world to come, God will publicly bless those who put their trust in him, while their enemies have to look on. Some Christians have struggled with this idea and have suggested that the table will be a table of reconciliation, where our enemies have become friends. But this thought is not present in the psalm: rather, David almost certainly is saying that God will vindicate his people. The fact is that, for many, following Jesus leads not just to misunderstanding but also to rejection, persecution and to suffering of one kind or another: God will reward their faithfulness and place his friends in a place of honour.

19 Psalm 121

1 James L. Mays, *Psalms* (Louisville, KY: John Knox), p. 390.

2 Alec Motyer, *Journey: Psalms for Pilgrim People* (Nottingham: IVP, 2009), p. 32.

3 Heidelberg Catechism, Questions 26 and 28, quoted by Mays, *Psalms*, pp. 391, 392.

4 Leonard Griffiths, *God in Man's Experience: The Activity of God in the Psalms*, 2nd edn (London: Hodder & Stoughton, 1970), p. 150.

5 On reflection, 'insomniac' is perhaps not the right word. Insomnia is a condition where sleep is wanted, but is unobtainable. God's sleeplessness is a way of saying that God does not run out of energy. He is the Great Watchman!

6 Griffiths, *God in Man's Experience*, p. 148.

20 Psalm 139:1–12

1 See Albert Y. Hsu, *Grieving a Suicide* (London: IVP, revised 2017), pp. 9–10. See also Michael Parsons, *Suicide and the Church:*

A Pastoral Theology (Cambridge: Grove, 2010) and, more generally, Kari Dyregrov, Einar Plyhn and Gudrun Dieserud, *After the Suicide: Helping the Bereaved to Find a Path from Grief to Recovery* (London: Jessica Kingsley, 2012; first published in Norway, 2010).

2 Augustine, *City of God*, Book I.

3 See Hsu, *Grieving a Suicide*, p. 114: 'Virtually all deaths occur without wholly cleansed consciences. If someone dies from a sudden heart attack, chances are that person died without asking for forgiveness for any number of sins.'

4 Martin Wroe, *The Church–English Dictionary* (Eastbourne: Kingsway, 1991).

5 Kenneth Slack, *New Light on Old Songs: Studies in the Psalms in the Light of New Translations* (London: SCM Press, 1995).

6 Francis Thompson, *The Hound of Heaven* (London: Burns & Oates, 1893). A more contemporary setting of the psalm is Bernadette Farrell's hymn 'O God, You Search Me and Know Me', in which the fourth verse reads:

> Although your Spirit is upon me,
> still I search for shelter from your light.
> There is nowhere on earth I can escape you;
> Even the darkness is radiant in your sight.

7 Quoted by Leonard Griffiths, *God in Man's Experience: The Activity of God in the Psams*, 2nd edn (London: Hodder & Stoughton, 1970), p. 176.

8 In the context of a funeral where somebody has ended his or her life by suicide, the liturgy (the readings and the prayers) has a vital role to play. See Appendix 3: Reflections on the death of a twenty-one-year-old suicide, p. 211.

Part 6 Hope for all?

God loves us all

1 See also Luke 13:23–24, where Jesus replies to the question 'Lord, will only a few be saved?'

2 Tom Wright, *Surprised by Hope* (London: SPCK, 2007), p. 193.

3 C. S. Lewis, *The Problem of Pain* in *C. S. Lewis: Selected Books* (London: HarperCollins, 1999), p. 538. *The Problem of Pain* by

C. S. Lewis © copyright C. S. Lewis Pte Ltd 1940. Reprinted with permission.

4 Bill T. Arnold, *Genesis* (Cambridge: Cambridge University Press, 2009), p. 183.

5 Fredrick William Faber (1814–1863). The original had thirteen verses, of which the first verse, which is often omitted, begins 'Souls of men! Why will ye scatter/Like a crowd of frightened sheep?' In the words of A. E. Gregory, the hymn shows 'yearning sympathy for the erring', in *The Hymn Book of the Modern Church* (1905; republished Oxford: Blackwell, 2016), p. 195.

6 Nick Batzig, 'Preaching the Funeral of an Unbeliever', 18 January 2017 (available online at: <www.placefortruth.org/blog/preaching-the-funeral-of-an-unbeliever>, accessed 7 July 2021).

Appendices

Appendix 1

1 Paul Beasley-Murray, *Losing a Loved One* (Worthing: Christian Publicity Organisation, 2000).

2 Since writing this leaflet I need perhaps to acknowledge that, in other contexts, funerals tend to take place within a matter of just two or three days.

Appendix 4

1 An excellent resource is the booklet '"All Souls" Services of Remembrance: Our Mission to the Bereaved', Worship 223 (Cambridge: Grove, 2015) by John Leach. I particularly appreciated his underlining the difference between a funeral, where the focus is on the 'departed', and a service of remembrance, where, instead, the focus is on those still living with the loss of a loved one and travelling the road of bereavement. My one quibble is his use of the term 'All Souls' services, since All Souls, traditionally, has Roman Catholic associations with the church penitent in purgatory, whereas All Saints' Day is the occasion when we rejoice in the church triumphant in heaven. See also N. T. Wright, *For All the Saints?: Remembering the Christian Departed* (London: SPCK, 2003).

2 A prayer written by Dick Williams, *Prayers for Today's Church* (London: CPAS, 1972), p. 273.
3 An adaptation of a benediction in John Drescher (ed.), *Invocations and Benedictions for Revised Common Lectionary* (Nashville, TN: Abingdon, 1998), p. 130.

Index of authors and subjects

Index of authors and subjects

Index of Scripture references

Index of Scripture references